HARVARD STUDIES IN BUSINESS HISTORY

1. JOHN JACOB ASTOR, *Business Man, by Kenneth Wiggins Porter*

2. JAY COOKE, *Private Banker, by Henrietta M. Larson*

3. THE JACKSONS AND THE LEES: *Two Generations of Massachusetts Merchants, 1765–1844, by Kenneth Wiggins Porter*

4. THE MASSACHUSETTS–FIRST NATIONAL BANK OF BOSTON, *1784–1934, by N. S. B. Gras*

5. THE HISTORY OF AN ADVERTISING AGENCY: *N. W. Ayer & Son at Work, 1869–1949, Revised Edition, by Ralph M. Hower*

6. MARKETING LIFE INSURANCE: *Its History in America, by J. Owen Stalson*

7. HISTORY OF MACY'S OF NEW YORK, *1858–1919: Chapters in the Evolution of the Department Store, by Ralph M. Hower*

8. THE WHITESMITHS OF TAUNTON: *A History of Reed & Barton, 1824–1943, by George Sweet Gibb*

9. DEVELOPMENT OF TWO BANK GROUPS IN THE CENTRAL NORTHWEST: *A Study in Bank Policy and Organization, by Charles Sterling Popple*

10. THE HOUSE OF HANCOCK: *Business in Boston, 1724–1775, by W. T. Baxter*

11. TIMING A CENTURY: *History of the Waltham Watch Company, by C. W. Moore*

12. GUIDE TO BUSINESS HISTORY: *Materials for the Study of American Business History and Suggestions for Their Use, by Henrietta M. Larson*

13. PEPPERELL'S PROGRESS: *History of a Cotton Textile Company, 1844–1945, by Evelyn H. Knowlton*

14. THE HOUSE OF BARING IN AMERICAN TRADE AND FINANCE: *English Merchant Bankers at Work, 1763–1861, by Ralph W. Hidy*

15. THE WHITIN MACHINE WORKS SINCE 1831: *A Textile Machinery Company in an Industrial Village, by Thomas R. Navin*

16. THE SACO-LOWELL SHOPS: *Textile Machinery Building in New England, 1813–1949, by George Sweet Gibb*

17. BROADLOOMS AND BUSINESSMEN: *A History of the Bigelow-Sanford Carpet Company: 1825–1953, by John S. Ewing and Nancy P. Norton*

18. NATHAN TROTTER: *Philadelphia Merchant, 1787–1853, by Elva Tooker*

19. A HISTORY OF THE MASSACHUSETTS HOSPITAL LIFE INSURANCE COMPANY, *by Gerald T. White*

HARVARD STUDIES IN BUSINESS HISTORY

XIX

Edited by

HENRIETTA M. LARSON
Associate Professor of Business History

and

THOMAS R. NAVIN
Assistant Professor of Business History
Graduate School of Business Administration
George F. Baker Foundation
Harvard University

NATHANIEL BOWDITCH

The First Executive Officer of the Trustee Company
Having the Title of Actuary

A HISTORY OF THE MASSACHUSETTS HOSPITAL LIFE INSURANCE COMPANY

By Gerald T. White
ASSOCIATE PROFESSOR OF HISTORY
SAN FRANCISCO STATE COLLEGE

HARVARD UNIVERSITY PRESS
Cambridge, Massachusetts
1955

Distributed in Great Britain by
Geoffrey Cumberlege, Oxford University Press, London

Library of Congress Catalog Card Number 55–9442
Printed in the United States of America

TO MY MOTHER AND FATHER

CONTENTS

TABLES

Tables

EDITORS' INTRODUCTION

This volume is presented as a case study in the history of investment institutions and investment management in the United States. The Massachusetts Hospital Life Insurance Company was established to insure lives, but almost from the beginning it undertook to manage the investment of deposits in trust.

In this latter field it was a pioneer. Its creative innovating in the trust field was soon imitated in the establishment of other trust companies. These younger companies were conducted, however, as vigorous competitors for trust deposits, whereas the Hospital Life restricted its business largely to such persons as were especially in need of the service it could give. Its semicharitable orientation had a strong influence on the institution's history.

As one of the largest financial institutions in Boston in the nineteenth century, the Massachusetts Hospital Life was an important supplier of funds for industrial growth in New England. In this work it gained a reputation which probably helped to establish trust companies as important factors in the mobilization of individual savings for industrial needs.

This volume is something of a pioneer in itself. It is an exposition of the origin and functioning of one institution, the first study of its kind in the investment trust field. It is, moreover, the story of a group of men of a particular business and social background who had a common purpose in supporting the Massachusetts Hospital Life. Because of the importance of individuals and the group, the author treats the subject in that personal way which was the very life of this company.

The history of this company raises a question of broad significance to the student of the history of business. Why did this company cease growing after many vigorous and productive decades? In the absence of studies of the experience of other companies in this and related fields, the author does not venture any positive answer. The material he presents, however, raises issues and suggests answers that might well be explored by scholars going further in the study of the history of investment institutions.

Those who hold that business institutions, like animate beings, go through certain stages of growth and decline will be interested in the efforts to restore the vigor of the Massachusetts Hospital Life after a period of decline. Only the future will tell if the efforts to save the company by modernizing its charter and its operations will really work. The historian observes that in modernized form the company still follows some of its old policies, particularly giving due recognition to the principle of the prudent investment of funds and stressing the importance of responsible management.

The publication of this volume was made financially possible by gifts from the Massachusetts Hospital Life Insurance Company, the Business Historical Society, and the Graduate School of Business Administration of Harvard University.

HENRIETTA M. LARSON
THOMAS R. NAVIN

AUTHOR'S PREFACE

The Massachusetts Hospital Life Insurance Company came into being early in the nineteenth century when many financial institutions were far less specialized as to type than in our day. As the name indicates, it was conceived primarily as a life insurance company, but most readers will be more interested in noting its pioneering relationship to the modern trust company and the modern investment company. The company is also of special interest because of its community, Boston, and its officers, "proper Bostonians," who have always directed the company and who have come to stand in American history for a conservative pattern of financial behavior quite in contrast with that of America generally. In writing primarily from the records of the company, I have sought to permit the reader to develop a feel for the men who organized it and the generations of leaders who guided it thereafter; to arrive at an understanding of their goals, policies, and problems; and to note the importance of their institution both to the community it has so long served and to other similar financial institutions for which, early in its history, it was an example.

In attempting a history of the Massachusetts Hospital Life, I have had the full co-operation of its officers and directors. Its records have been made available to me without restraint. Fortunately, these records have been most complete during the first forty-five years of its history, the period during which the company is of greatest interest to business historians because of its relative size and of its impact upon the development of other financial institutions. Much of the executive correspondence of this period has been saved in bound letter books, and a good deal of incoming correspondence has also been preserved, to about 1850. Corporate and accounting records exist without gap for the whole sweep of the company's history, and reliance has been placed mainly upon them after the body of executive correspondence ends in the later 1870's. That the narrative is less intensive after 1878 is due primarily, however, not to shortage of materials, but to the fact that the company thereafter was not so significant among financial institutions as in its earlier years. In addition to permitting free access to its records, the company has contributed to the book through a financial grant to help meet the costs of publication, but it has sought to influence the content of the book in no way.

My debt in using the records of the Massachusetts Hospital Life is particularly great to D. George Sullivan, formerly its vice-president and an ardent proponent of business history, and to Paul T. Litchfield, the present vice-president and secretary of the company. Both of these men were most helpful in answering my numerous queries, in locating elusive research materials, and in reading the entire manuscript critically. I am also grateful to the late president, Edward H. Osgood, for the kindly interest he took in the project, and to his successor, Henry R. Guild, for his helpful reading of the manuscript.

I have profited from the cordial co-operation of strategically placed persons in institutions whose own history helps illumine that of the Massachusetts Hospital Life. These include: Cora Holbrook, archivist of the Massachusetts General Hospital; Mrs. Bernice D. Parks, assistant treasurer of the Provident Institution for Savings in the Town of Boston; S. L. de Vausney, vice-president and secretary of the Bank of New York & Fifth Avenue Bank; H. H. Kelly, vice-president and secretary of the Rhode Island Hospital Trust Company; Fletcher C. Chamberlin, secretary of the New England Trust Company; and Horace W. Cole, secretary of the Boston Safe Deposit & Trust Company.

My indebtedness is greatest of all to the current joint editors of the Business History Series, Professors Henrietta M. Larson and Thomas R. Navin of the Graduate School of Business Administration of Harvard University. They have given me unfailing support in the prosecution of this project, and their criticisms and suggestions have been of the greatest value in improving the manuscript. I can hardly express too strongly my appreciation of their friendly interest and zealous endeavor in behalf of this book. Hilma B. Holton of the staff of the business history department in the Graduate School of Business Administration has also made a valued contribution in assisting with the editing of the manuscript and in preparing the index.

It is a pleasure to record my gratitude to the Business Historical Society, whose Fellow I was during the academic year 1951–52 when this research was undertaken. I have also a keen appreciation of favors received from Harvard's Graduate School of Business Administration, both institution and staff, including a grant to facilitate publication.

On this Coast, I wish to express my gratitude to the administration of San Francisco State College for granting me leave for so stimulating a year at Harvard University and in the Boston community; to Lester M. Stewart, assistant trust officer of the Wells Fargo Bank & Union Trust Company, for his careful reading of the manuscript; and to my wife, who has helped so cheerfully with so many of the chores of authorship.

GERALD T. WHITE

[illegible] my gratitude to the [illegible] Society [illegible] the [illegible] this [illegible] [illegible]

[illegible] the [illegible] [illegible]

A HISTORY OF THE MASSACHUSETTS HOSPITAL LIFE INSURANCE COMPANY

I

SIGNIFICANCE OF THE MASSACHUSETTS HOSPITAL LIFE INSURANCE COMPANY

The Massachusetts Hospital Life Insurance Company was one of several important financial institutions chartered when New England mercantile capitalism was at its zenith during the half century following American independence. It was in this period also, in 1784, that the Massachusetts Bank was established, the first commercial bank to be chartered in New England and the second in the United States.[1] Hardly less well-known is the Suffolk Bank, which was chartered in 1818. A commercial bank, the seventh to be established in Boston, the Suffolk is famous for the system it devised for maintaining the bank notes of New England at a parity with specie in the years prior to the Civil War.[2] The Provident Institution for Savings in the Town of Boston, chartered in 1816, was the first mutual savings bank incorporated in the United States and the second to begin operations.[3] The Massachusetts Hospital Life Insurance Company, chartered in 1818, was the second life insurance company to be established in the United States,[4] but its greater importance lies in foreshadowing the modern trust company and the modern investment company. These latter areas of activity its name fails to reveal.

All four of these financial institutions had European antecedents. They were a part of that great forward movement in the development of institutions associated with the needs of merchants for ever greater sources of capital to carry on their larger ventures, as they moved between the thirteenth and nineteenth centuries to make the world economically one. Over time a series of financial institutions had emerged controlling and investing capital belonging to others: commercial banks, fire and marine insurance companies, life insurance companies, and, by the turn of the nineteenth century, savings banks. These held a middleman's position in making capital available to trade and industry.[5] As institutions, they usually had greater resources than most individuals in their localities. The scale and constancy of their lending usually permitted their officers a greater experience and skill at investment than was possible for individuals acting alone. Diversification in their loans and investments minimized risk to a degree rarely possible for individuals acting as middlemen in finance or for individuals investing their own capital directly.

To these earlier types of financial institutions, three important additions were made in the nineteenth century: the trust company, the investment banking firm, and the investment company. The American economy, no longer so immature in comparison with Europe, was important in the development of all three. In two of these, the Massachusetts Hospital Life Insurance Company played a pioneering role. Though chartered as a life insurance company, its great achievement came through its acceptance of money in trust. Because of the terms of contract under which it accepted funds, it has been recognized as the earliest forerunner both of the modern trust company and of the modern investment company.[6]

Though the Massachusetts Bank, the Suffolk Bank and, in somewhat less degree, the Provident Institution for Savings are well-known to the student of economic and business history, the Massachusetts Hospital Life is known in a shadowy sense, if at all. This is a commentary on its long, quiet past. Those who managed it and whose interests it primarily served – the first families of Boston – knew the company well, but after its early years of meteoric success the rest of society knew it hardly at all.[7] For more than a century after 1830 it did not advertise, nor was it aggressive in seeking funds. Historians have merely glimpsed it and have by no means recognized fully its importance to the past economic development of Massachusetts or its impact upon the creation and operation of other financial institutions, especially in the trust field.[8]

The main impetus in chartering the Massachusetts Hospital Life was the desire of most of its founders to supply additional funds for the operation of Boston's newly organized first hospital and great civic institution, the Massachusetts General Hospital. According to the company's charter, one-third of the net profits from its life insurance business was to be paid annually to the Hospital. By the time the Massachusetts Hospital Life began operation in 1823, the enormously significant power to accept deposits in trust had been brought into its scope with greater clarity by an amendment to the charter. Shortly after, by another amendment, all aspects of the company's activities, including its trust business, were placed within the limits of the profit-sharing provision. By the middle 1840's the company's always minor life insurance business began to fall away rapidly before the onslaught of the new mutual life insurance companies. But its trust business continued to grow and to provide a very helpful supplemental income to the Hospital, especially during the early years.

In offering to accept money or securities in trust, the company had moved into a field which historically had been occupied by private parties rather than by a specialized financial institution. Most frequently the need for trusteeship had arisen when a person of means had become too old and infirm to manage his property successfully, or when after his death, property had been willed to a widow, sisters, or minor children who lacked the necessary competence to care for it. Trustees had been generally relatives or close friends of the man placing his property in trust. If an institution was involved, that institution was usually the Church.[9]

The growth of mercantile capitalism in New England in the seventeenth, eighteenth, and early nineteenth centuries resulted in large aggregates of capital accumulating in the hands of the leading merchants.[10] Private trusteeship, then imperfectly defined by law, was the prime means of trusteeship when the need arose. The Massachusetts Hospital Life stepped into the field offering an institutional equivalent, though within specified limits: it would accept, in trust, money or securities with respect to which the income recipient and the ultimate recipient of the principal were clearly designated.

The company's trust business grew rapidly, and by 1830 it was by far the largest financial institution in New England. Its early and striking success was an important stimulus to the establishment of similar life insurance and trust companies elsewhere in the nation. If successful in the long run, these companies, like the Massachusetts Hospital Life, found the basis for their success in the trust field. Possibly the Hospital Life was also influential, by its mere presence, in improving the standards of private trusteeship in New England.

For more than a century, the Massachusetts Hospital Life changed little in the services it offered its public. This was probably due in greatest measure to the company's original goal. Founded in part to assist the Massachusetts General Hospital, for at least a half-century the Hospital Life continued to be viewed primarily as a charity by many of its leaders. The company early established the policy that no stockholder except the Massachusetts General Hospital (which held 10 per cent) could hold more than 1 per cent of its stock. This obvious link to the Hospital, combined with the early and great success achieved by the founders, probably explains much of the company's subsequent lack of aggressiveness in seeking new opportunities to serve individuals and corporations. Although the company did not increase the field of its service, during the later nineteenth century many of its officers and directors helped found competing institutions in Boston which offered the full range of modern trust company services.

From the beginning, the Massachusetts Hospital Life showed a marked resemblance not alone to a modern trust company but also to a modern investment company. In its investments the company commingled all its resources, from whatever source, in a single fund. The depositors, by the terms of contract, shared proportionately in the gains or losses on the investments of the total fund, subject to an annual fee, which was originally ½ of 1 per cent on the principal of each depositor. At the will of the individual depositor, interest [i.e., dividends] was payable quarterly, semiannually, or annually, or was permitted to accumulate as new capital.

As late as the beginning of the last quarter of the nineteenth century, only one financial institution in Boston (the New England Mutual Life Insurance Company) could match the Massachusetts Hospital Life in resources. By 1900 the Hospital Life still ranked among Boston's five largest financial institutions. Consequently, it may be said that the Massachusetts Hospital Life was one of the leading sources of investment capital in nineteenth-century New England.

Historians can feel an interest in the Massachusetts Hospital Life not only because of the type of institution it was, but also because its full records present one of the few good pictures of the investment pattern of a major financial institution during most of the nineteenth century. These records reveal that, except during the Civil War years and immediately thereafter, mortgages were the main means of investment for the company's funds. Initially, the company was quite important in supplying some of the credit needs of the farmers of western Massachusetts through mortgages, but at least by the 1840's it was tending to concentrate its mortgages almost exclusively in Boston and the immediate vicinity. In the pattern of the old mercantile banking institutions, the company also made numerous collateral loans to its own officers, stockholders, members of their families and friends. As the industrial revolution was increasingly felt in New England and the company's investment authority was liberalized by law, the company's investments grew to include New England manufacturing and railroad companies. The company became probably the most important single source of intermediate term credit for the Massachusetts textile industry during the nineteenth century. In no instance did the company seek to establish control over a borrowing company; in every instance, and with striking success, it tried to make certain that its loans and investments were safe.

The Massachusetts Hospital Life is also of interest for another reason: the nature of the people who were associated with its origin and who have continued to be associated with it throughout its history. These men were mostly members of Boston's first families. In its first century fully one-third of the 240 officers and directors of the company came from 18 of Boston's great families.

On its Committee of Finance were business and financial leaders of the Boston community whose personal investments must have reflected those of Boston capital generally. Many of these men were private trustees, developing that "prudent man" skill at investment which has caused Boston trustees to be viewed so favorably by careful investors everywhere. This reputation is one great basis for the location today in Boston of so disproportionate a percentage, in both number and assets, of the open-end diversified investment companies. As of the end of the year 1950, companies with $2,530,000,000 in total assets, or 48 per cent of the total assets of all open-end funds, had their headquarters in Boston.[11]

During the first years of the company, the members of the Committee of Finance were mainly mercantile capitalists whose fortunes derived primarily from trade. Much of their capital at that time, however, was being shifted from commerce to industry, especially textiles. Their successors on the committee were among New England's leading industrial capitalists and were predominantly textile manufacturers.

Late in the nineteenth century the members of the Committee of Finance were most notable for their positions of control in a large number of Boston commercial banks, savings banks, and trust companies. But, unlike their predecessors, their interests were much wider, ranging far outside New England into western railroads and national industrial corporations. They represented Boston capital in a great period of expansion, seeking outlets beyond New England in the development of the nation.

Early in the twentieth century, members of the Committee of Finance continued to serve as directors of a series of Boston commercial banks, savings banks, and trust companies, but they are no longer so impressive for their membership on boards of companies engaged in great national enterprises or on boards of major companies operating outside New England. We may infer, then, that Boston capital was no longer of such magnitude to be relatively so significant in the larger enterprises of the twentieth century. Although Boston capitalists continued to invest large sums in companies located and operating outside New England, their positions of control seem to be restricted more to New England companies.

Today, as investment companies, so many of which are located in New England, grow ever more rapidly, one may ask whether New England's position as a source of capital is moving back toward that which it once held in the later nineteenth century. At present, however, a sizable proportion of New England's capital is being recruited by its investment companies and life insurance companies from outside New England and is being managed by professional investors. In the case of investment companies the professional administrators are usually widely respected trustees. At least the Investment Committee of the Massachusetts Hospital Life today, if not so striking for the capital position of its individual members, is impressive for the number of important directorships and trusteeships held by its members.

II

FOUNDING OF THE MASSACHUSETTS HOSPITAL LIFE

The Massachusetts Hospital Life Insurance Company was a by-product of the movement to bring into being and adequately finance the Massachusetts General Hospital. The founding of the Hospital had been sparked by the chaplain of the Boston Alms House, Reverend John Bartlett, and by doctors from two of Boston's most important families, James Jackson and John C. Warren. As a result of their efforts to provide Boston with its first hospital and a center for medical training, the Massachusetts General Hospital had been incorporated on February 25, 1811.

Throughout its history the Massachusetts General Hospital has been distinguished for its care of the sick, for its training of doctors, and for its research. From its earliest years it has been closely linked to the Harvard Medical School, offering many Harvard students clinical instruction and various post-degree educational opportunities. The Hospital is especially famed as the site in 1846 of the first public demonstration of the effectiveness of ether as an anesthetic in major surgery, and for the epoch-making research on the vermiform appendix by Dr. Ronald H. Fitz later in the century.[1]

The names of its 56 incorporators read like a list from a blue book of the public and business figures of that day. But despite such impressive leadership and a gift by the legislature of the Province House Estate as the site for the building contingent upon the Hospital's raising $100,000 during the next five years, the Hospital experienced great difficulty in getting under way. The drive for the $100,000 proved less effective than its sponsors had hoped because of the depressed conditions of commerce during and after the War of 1812. Subsequently the legislature extended the time period to seven years. At the request of the trustees of the Hospital, the legislature on February 24, 1814, also sought to help by granting the Hospital a monopoly of the sale of annuities in the Commonwealth.[2]

Shortly after receiving the new power, the trustees wrote Samuel Williams, a Bostonian then in London, for any information he could gather "respecting the mode of managing annuity associations." [3] Though annuities were little known in this country, the trustees did know that for centuries European governments and Church bodies had resorted to them in raising funds. The English government, for example, had used this technique on several occasions in the seventeenth and early eighteenth centuries.[4] During the eighteenth century, moreover, a number of private companies and mutual associations, particularly in England, had begun to sell annuities for the care of the aged.[5]

The fund-raising campaign came almost to a halt in 1814 and 1815. No further action was taken on the annuity question until the spring of 1816 when the trustees instructed a fellow member, Colonel Joseph May, to seek the advice of Dr. Nathaniel Bowditch.[6] The Colonel and the Doctor were experienced insurance men. May had been secretary of the Boston Marine Insurance Society for many years. Bowditch was then president of the Essex Fire & Marine Insurance Company of Salem. He was also New England's most distinguished mathematician. Another exploratory meeting was held on February 16, 1817, when Trustees John Lowell, Josiah Quincy, Ebenezer Francis, and Tristram Barnard met with Nathaniel Bowditch, Francis C. Lowell, and Peter C. Brooks. The last was probably the outstanding figure in marine insurance in New England. Francis C. Lowell, a brother of the trustee, was a leading pioneer in New England's textile industry.

The new committee recommended that the matter of annuities be dropped by the Hospital at that time.[7] It may have been their feeling that the business of annuities alone provided too weak a base for successful operation. On the other hand, life insurance may have seemed more attractive. By the late eighteenth century life insurance was by far the larger part of the business of those English companies selling both insurance and annuities. At any rate, early in 1818 the trustees again appointed John Lowell, Josiah Quincy, and Ebenezer Francis to consider the subject of annuities and, if expedient, to apply to the legislature for a grant of power to include insurance on lives.[8]

The committee found another group headed by David Hinckley,

an important Boston merchant, also seeking the insurance power. After a brief discussion, the two groups merged. The Hinckley group was solely motivated by private profit, but it did agree to co-operate in seeking a charter for a company which would share profits with the Hospital.[9] Thus the standard goal of business activity – profits – was clearly added to the charitable impulse so obviously present in the minds of those desiring to help the Hospital.

As a result of their joint efforts, the legislature speedily chartered the Massachusetts Hospital Life Insurance Company on February 24, 1818. By the terms of the legislative act, the new company was obligated to pay annually to the Hospital one-third of the net profits from its life insurance business. This obligation was to endure as long as the company held a monopoly in issuing life insurance or until the legislature chartered some other insurance company without requiring the same profit-sharing provision for the Hospital.[10]

The statute also outlined the general framework for the company. It specified the amount of capitalization ($500,000), and the number of shares (5,000 at $100 par), and established the procedure for the initial stock subscription. It provided for a governing board of 13 directors, a majority of whom were to be citizens of Massachusetts, and specified voting rights and the time of the stockholders' annual meetings. It defined the nature of the company's business, "to make insurance on lives, . . . and to contract for reversionary payments, and generally to make all kinds of contracts, in which the casualties of life and interest of money are principally involved." It limited its investment of capital and premiums to "the funded debt of the United States, or of this Commonwealth, or in the stock of the bank of the United States, or of any of the banks incorporated within this Commonwealth, or in the purchase of ground rents, or mortgages on real estate. . . ." Once each year the directors of the company were required to make a "full, fair and explicit statement" of their "real estate, funds and investments of every kind" to the Secretary of the Commonwealth. Both branches of the legislature were authorized to examine the records and activities of the company.[11]

All this notwithstanding, no successful attempt was made to activate the company until the early months of 1823. That life insurance was a completely novel enterprise in New England may have been one factor in the delay, but more basic was the loose language of the charter. Although some pledges for stock had been made prior to 1823, other prospective stockholders were unwilling to share one-third of the net profits with the Hospital. They believed the potential returns too low for a speculative venture of this sort. From the point of view of the Hospital, the charter also seemed deficient, for according to its terms the Hospital shared only from the profits arising from insurance on lives. The company also had the right to issue annuities and endowment policies, in the profits of which, it could be argued, the Hospital had no right to share.

Still eager for funds, it was the Hospital which finally took the steps necessary to bring the company to life. Early in January, 1823, the trustees of the Hospital appointed a committee headed by Ebenezer Francis to investigate and report on the powers of the Hospital with reference to annuities and life insurance.[12] After hearing the report of its committee, on January 10, 1823, the trustees sought to allay the fears of prospective stockholders in the Massachusetts Hospital Life Insurance Company. They set forth a self-limiting interpretation of the profit-sharing provision in that company's charter. The trustees resolved that profit-sharing should take place only after the stockholders had been paid simple interest (6 per cent) on their investment. They also declared, however, that the profit-sharing provision as thus interpreted must apply to profits from all aspects of the company's business.[13]

With the position of the Hospital clear, Ebenezer Francis and William Prescott, trustees of the Hospital and two of the nine incorporators of the company, issued a call for a meeting of the company stockholders. On January 10, 1823, they placed an advertisement in three Boston newspapers calling for a meeting to be held at noon, January 21, 1823, in a hall over the Suffolk Bank at the corner of Kilby and State streets.[14] Attending the first meeting, in addition to Francis and Prescott, were two others: John Phillips, an incorporator of the company and the first mayor of the city of Boston, and Ebenezer Appleton, attorney for David Hinckley, who had retired from his mercantile business. Perhaps the scant turnout was one reason for locating a second meeting in the counting room of Ebenezer Francis, also at 1 Kilby Street, on January 28. Attendance at this meeting was hardly more impressive. In addition to Francis, Prescott, and Ebenezer Appleton, there appeared Josiah Quincy, lawyer and former Congressman, who was soon to succeed John Phillips as mayor, and T. K. Jones, attorney for Thomas M. Jones. Both Quincy and Thomas M. Jones, who was then in London, were among the company's incorporators. In these two meetings it was voted to accept the charter of incorporation and to organize the company.[15]

Of this little group, Ebenezer Francis and William Prescott played the most critical roles. Both men were important figures in the Boston community. Both were sons of heroes of the Revolution. Colonel Francis of Beverly, the father of Ebenezer, had been killed in a battle at Hubbardton, New York, in 1778, while Colonel William Prescott had gained immortality in the battle of Bunker Hill.

Ebenezer Francis had made his way upward from orphan boy to merchant and financier. He had married Elizabeth, a daughter of Israel Thorndike of Beverly, one of the great merchants of the day. As Francis prospered in trade, he branched over into finance.[16] In 1809 he was elected a director of the Boston Bank, third of the banks to be chartered in Boston. Nine years later he became a founder and the first president of the Suffolk Bank. He became in time a heavy investor in Boston real estate and a substantial investor in New England's growing textile industry. For a time he was president of the Cocheco Manufacturing Company of Dover, New Hampshire, one of the earliest of the New England cotton textile companies. Francis also was an energetic supporter of the Massachusetts General Hospital and of Harvard College. Becoming a trustee of the Hospital in 1817, he had much to do with its planning and construction. He served as member of its Committee of Finance, treasurer, and board chairman and, in 1836, as president. From 1827 to 1830 he served as treasurer of Harvard College, reorganizing and strengthening the financial position of the College at a time when its records were badly confused and its financial situation difficult. In one contemporary account, Francis was rated with Peter C. Brooks as one of the two wealthiest citizens of Massachusetts in the first half of the nineteenth century.[17]

William Prescott was a foremost Boston lawyer. He had held various public offices, including membership in both houses of the Massachusetts legislature and on the Governor's Council, judge of the Court of Common Pleas in Boston, and first president of the

Boston Common Council. Prescott served the Hospital in its purchase of land for construction of its first building and had been both an overseer and member of the Corporation of Harvard College. He was also the father of the historian, William Hickling Prescott. Daniel Webster was to say to Prescott at his death that "at the moment of his retirement from the bar of Massachusetts [1828], he stood at its head for legal learning and attainment." [18] It is indicative of the continuity of Boston families in positions of prominence, and also in the Massachusetts Hospital Life Insurance Company, that the present chairman of its Board of Directors, Samuel H. Wolcott, is a great-grandson of William Prescott.

Two other individuals also important in getting the company under way were John Lowell, lawyer and celebrated Federalist pamphleteer, and Josiah Quincy. Both men were active in a wide variety of civic and philanthropic causes, including the Massachusetts General Hospital. Lowell, in fact, had been chairman of the Committee of Trustees which in 1814 had gained from the legislature the right to grant annuities. Both men, and especially Lowell, had been among the most energetic of a group of philanthropically minded gentlemen in establishing the Provident Institution for Savings.[19] The experience gained in this latter activity seems to have influenced certain of the patterns of organization and operation of the new insurance company.

These four men were the prime movers in meeting the problems which had to be solved in launching the company. At the meeting of January 28 Ebenezer Francis and Josiah Quincy were appointed to draw up a list of desirable persons for stockholders.[20] The list they presented shortly thereafter included 20 prospects for 2,400 shares.[21] In addition, the trustees of the Hospital had authorized a subscription by the Hospital of 500 shares.[22] Of the prospects, four individuals – Ebenezer Francis, William Phillips (former lieutenant governor of Massachusetts, president of the Massachusetts Bank and of an astonishing number of civic and philanthropic enterprises, including the Massachusetts General Hospital), Samuel Parkman, merchant, and Peter C. Brooks – were considered likely candidates for 200 shares each, but the latter two accepted only half of this number. There were 16 candidates for 100 shares each.* Almost

* These men were: William Prescott, Josiah Quincy, and John Lowell, lawyers;

without exception these men were supporters of the Hospital either through substantial contributions or active participation in the management of its affairs.

On February 6 Prescott, Lowell, and Francis were appointed to distribute the remaining 2,400 shares. Since so much of the stock had already been sold to so few holders, in only one instance were more than 50 shares sold to an individual. Nathaniel Bowditch was allowed 65. These 2,400 shares were allotted among 56 shareholders.* Two of the new stockholders, John C. Warren, 50 shares, and James Jackson, 30 shares, were the doctors who had led the campaign for the establishment of the Massachusetts General Hospital.[23] Nearly all were residents of the Boston community, but a few were from the north shore of Massachusetts Bay – Salem especially, but also Beverly, Marblehead, and Newburyport.

Concurrent with the stock subscription campaign, another committee was at work drawing up regulations governing the transfer of Massachusetts Hospital Life stock after its issue. The committee sought to eliminate the possibility that some of the stock might later be acquired by individuals interested in speculation. The founders were particularly anxious that the confidence of the community, so necessary to a fiduciary institution, never be jeopardized.

The committee's report was adopted on February 3. Holders who desired to sell their shares were obliged to offer them to the directors at the original cost to the holder plus accrued dividends. If on resale by the directors, the selling price was more than 6 per cent above that paid the former holder, he was to be paid the excess above 6 per cent. If the directors failed to buy the shares within 30 days, the holder was free to sell elsewhere. Similar provisions governed the transfer of stock following the death of a stockholder. The only dif-

---

Gardiner Greene, president of the branch of the Bank of the United States in Boston; John Phillips, mayor of Boston; and Joseph Head, T. H. Perkins, Joseph Coolidge, David Sears, William Pratt, John Parker, Israel Thorndike, Thomas M. Jones, Theodore Lyman, James Perkins, and William Gray, all merchants or of mercantile families. Only William Gray refused to participate.

* Many rivals in prominence to the larger stockholders were among this group: e.g., Thomas Wren Ward, George Cabot, Amos Lawrence, William Sturgis, John Bryant, Thomas Motley, Thomas Wigglesworth, Harrison Gray Otis, Nathan Appleton, Charles Jackson, Joseph May, Daniel Parker, Henry Codman, Patrick Tracy Jackson, William Appleton, Samuel P. Gardner, George Ticknor, John C. Gray, Benjamin Guild, and Nathaniel Silsbee.

ference was that the directors were required to offer to purchase the stock at the appraised value plus accrued dividends or to free the stock from their control. The possibility of discrimination ranging up to 6 per cent between the original purchase price paid to a living shareholder and the appraised value paid to his estate was undoubtedly intended to encourage original holders to keep their stock. Shares acquired by the company were to be sold by the directors "to such persons, not Directors, as shall appear to them, from their situation and character, most likely to promote confidence in the stability of the Institution."

There is no indication from where these provisions were derived, for bank stock generally at the time and stock of most insurance companies were sold on the Boston Stock Exchange. The provisions suggest, however, the high value placed by the Massachusetts Hospital Life founders "on the confidence of the public in the permanence, value and stability of its Capital, and the prudence and discretion of those who have the management of its affairs. . . ." [24] During the first 15 years of the company, stock was relinquished in only 19 instances. In 16 of these death was the cause.[25]

These provisions continued with only slight change until the present. The most important changes occurred in 1845.[26] At that time a committee consisting of John Amory Lowell and William Sturgis recommended that the appraisal procedure be used for living stockholders desiring to sell as well as for estates. A second change prescribed 50 shares as the maximum holding for new purchasers or for individuals at the time holding 50 shares or less. Its effect was to insure a greater spread of Massachusetts Hospital Life ownership, thus giving the company a broader base in the community. But the modest capital investment of each stockholder probably lessened the possibility of the company's developing an aggressive spirit.

Bylaws were adopted at an organizational meeting, held on February 11, which was attended by 27 of the stockholders.[27] John Lowell presented a series of proposals which were adopted by the stockholders. The bylaws provided for a Board of Directors of 13 members, one of whom was to be president, to be elected at the annual stated meeting of the stockholders on the third Monday in January. The board was to have general management of the affairs of the company and to appoint and control the executive officers. The fact that the office of secretary alone was specified in these bylaws seems to suggest the still tentative organization of the company in 1845.

The stockholders also accepted a proposal for a Board of Control, which had not been mentioned in the charter. This board of 28 members was comprised of 15 vice-presidents in addition to the 13 directors. Like the directors, the vice-presidents were subject to annual election by the stockholders. The Board of Control was to meet twice a year on the second Mondays of January and July to examine the affairs of the company, including its records and accounts and the minutes of the Board of Directors. The Board of Control had ultimate authority in amending the bylaws or other rules and regulations and in fixing a maximum size for the business of the company. Beginning in 1825, it was also given the duty of making an annual internal audit of the company.[28] A five-member Committee of Examination, including three vice-presidents, was constituted annually from the Board of Control. This committee examined the books of the company and made it "their special duty to require the exhibition of all Notes, Bonds and Mortgages, Certificates of stocks taken as collateral security, and the evidence of all other property – and to examine them carefully . . . so as . . . to enable them to report as to their agreement or nonagreement with the statements made" by the executive officers of the company. Members of the committee were chosen by rotation, and no individual was permitted to serve two successive years.

The Board of Control thus permitted the company to achieve at least two desirable goals. The company was able to go before the community with a considerably larger body of distinguished officers than a Board of Directors alone would permit, yet it placed a lesser burden upon the vice-presidents because of the infrequent meetings. Consequently, men could be persuaded to serve as vice-president who would have been less likely to have accepted the more exacting role of director. The Board of Control also performed a useful function in its audit activity, especially at a time when outside accountants were unknown. After the employment of outside accountants began in the middle 1880's, the Board of Control had no substantial function apart from the advertising value of the names of its vice-presidents, but it was kept as an integral part of the company's administration until the spring of 1949.[29]

Despite a difference in name, the pattern of the Board of Control seems a direct appropriation from the Provident Institution for Savings.[30] John Lowell had also been chairman of the committee which had drawn its bylaws. The Board of Trustees of the latter institution included 12 vice-presidents and 24 trustees. At least a dozen of these were also original stockholders of the Massachusetts Hospital Life. Many individuals have served simultaneously as officers of both institutions. That so many prominent figures were willing to lend their names and give some of their time to these institutions suggests that they were viewed as civic rather than as strictly money-making enterprises.

Following the adoption of the Hospital Life bylaws, the first election of members of the Board of Control and the Board of Directors took place. William Phillips, probably New England's outstanding philanthropist, was elected president. Phillips had served as lieutenant governor of Massachusetts for 12 successive terms. He was also president of the Massachusetts Bank, New England's first commercial bank, of which his father had been a principal founder. His presidencies of civic, religious, and philanthropic organizations included, among others, the Phillips Academy at Andover, founded by his family, the American Education Society, Massachusetts General Hospital, Boston Dispensary, Provident Institution for Savings, American Bible Society, and the Society for Propagating the Gospel. Phillips was president of the Massachusetts Hospital Life until his death in 1827, when he was succeeded by William Prescott, who had formerly been a director. The other directors were Ebenezer Francis, John Lowell, Gardiner Greene, William Sturgis, Nathan Appleton, Amos Lawrence, Patrick Tracy Jackson, Thomas Motley, Theodore Lyman, Jr., Samuel Hubbard, and John C. Gray.[31] The directors represented a blend of some of Boston's finest talent in law, trade, industry, and finance.

The directors next faced the tasks of discovering how a life insurance company operates and of finding a man to manage it. A last action on February 11 was the appointment of a committee consisting of John Lowell and John C. Gray, lawyers, and Gardiner Greene, banker, "to collect and digest information on the subject of Life Insurance, annuities and the other objects connected with the act of incorporation. . . ." [32] Subsequently, at the directors' meeting on February 18, the committee recommended that Nathaniel Bowditch of Salem be asked to attend the next meeting of the board.[33] This he failed to do.

On March 3 another committee, consisting of William Prescott, William Sturgis, and Patrick Tracy Jackson, was appointed to select someone to "take the charge and superintendence of this Institution." This committee also turned to Dr. Bowditch. It offered him a salary of $2,500 if he would accept the chief executive office, that of actuary, in the new company. In addition, it offered a second salary of $2,000 if he would serve simultaneously as president of the Commercial Insurance Company, a newly organized fire and marine insurance company, in which several of the Hospital Life directors were interested. At first Bowditch refused, but when the committee, early in April, raised the actuary's salary to $3,000, he accepted. In the meantime he intended to do some preliminary planning, including a trip to Philadelphia to observe the operations of the only other American life insurance company, the Pennsylvania Company for Insurance on Lives and Granting Annuities.[34] This company had been incorporated in 1812.

During the course of the negotiations with the committee, Bowditch made a pointed observation. He did not think there was sufficient life insurance and annuity business in the Boston community to warrant a company of the size of the Massachusetts Hospital Life. For this reason he suggested that the company seek an extension of powers from the legislature to permit it to accept monies in trust.[35] The fact that Bowditch for some years had been a trustee of a fund for the support of the minister of the First Church of Salem and also of a large estate of a deceased Salem merchant may have sharpened his perception of the possibilities of this type of business.[36]

The idea of accepting deposits in trust could also have sprung readily from the experience of the Provident Institution for Savings. That institution had flourished beyond the expectation of its founders, causing its trustees in 1818 to attempt to fix a limit of $300,000 as the maximum for its deposits.[37] John Lowell had been chairman of committees in both 1818 and 1821 to investigate the reasons for the rapid growth of the savings bank and to determine in particular if the growth was due to deposits by others than the frugal poor, for whom the institution had been designed. The earlier committee had secured passage of a resolution forbidding deposits by any corporate body, including charitable organizations. Its successor in 1821 declared that: [38]

> It was not the intention of the founders of this Institution to act as Trustees, or as a Court of Chancery, and to receive and invest the property of all minors, widows, active and intelligent, young or old men, who had either capacity to manage their own affairs or friends to advise them; and any attempt at any future time to deposit money by any other persons than those above described [the frugal poor] must be received as a violation of the law creating this corporation and an act of injustice to the meritorious and proper objects of the law.

If the Provident Institution was not a proper place for the care of funds of the more dependent members in society – widows, orphans, minors, single women, and the aged – who were of some means or better and who needed security for their property, might not the Massachusetts Hospital Life be such an institution? This thought could have occurred to several of the founders of the Massachusetts Hospital Life, including John Lowell.

Whatever the cause, a committee was appointed on June 5, 1823, to ask the legislature to revise the charter of the company so as to permit it to receive "property in trust for minors and others on such terms and conditions as may be mutually agreed upon by the Corporation and the persons creating such trusts." [39] An amendment was obtained by the middle of June. It authorized the company to invest all monies derived from the sale of annuities, or held "in trust for and during the lives of any person or persons in notes secured by Mortgages of Real Estate, or by collateral assignment of any of the species of stocks mentioned" in the statute of incorporation.[40] This amendment is basically an expansion of the company's powers of investment. Consequently, it seems that the committee concluded that the language of the charter empowering the company "to make all kinds of contracts, in which the casualties of life and the interest of money are principally involved" was already broad enough to include trust powers. But the new statute did have the merit of specifically using the words "monies held . . . in trust. . . ." The right of the company to invest in notes backed by specified collateral was also significant, for it gave the company another and valuable way of investing its funds in addition to mortgages and outright ownership of the types of securities mentioned in the statute of incorporation.

From the very start of its operations, receiving monies in trust became the bulk of its business. It thus early provided an institutional mechanism, both large and unique for its day, for the investment of funds placed with it in trust from private sources. The subsequent history of life insurance suggests that had the new company been at all "sales-minded," it would have had little difficulty in gaining success solely in the life insurance field. The near total absence of selling effort characteristic of this period in life insurance history, however, also indicates that the company was undoubtedly wise in venturing into a trust business.

The arrival of Dr. Bowditch in Boston early in August, 1823, marks the beginning of operations for the Massachusetts Hospital Life Insurance Company. Early in that month an office was rented in the heart of Boston's financial district at 70 State Street, on the north side and a short distance west from Ebenezer Francis' counting room. This has been the approximate location of the company throughout its history. On August 18, 1823, the company opened for business. Simultaneously, a 50-page booklet of *Proposals* was published, calling the public's attention to the various services offered and their value to the community.

A number of other matters remained to be settled, however. In mid-August a first call was made to the stockholders for $20 on each share of stock for which they had pledged. Subsequent assessments for the remaining $80 were made in August and December, 1825.

At the August and September meetings of the directors the nature of the company's staff was definitely outlined. In mid-August, Moses L. Hale, secretary of the Commercial Insurance Company, was also appointed secretary of the Massachusetts Hospital Life. Since the company existed for the purpose of making and fulfilling contracts involving property, the part-time office of solicitor was established. For most of this early period the solicitor derived his income not from salary but from fees paid by individuals requiring his services in their dealings with the company. Nathaniel Ingersoll Bowditch, the eldest son of Dr. Bowditch, served as solicitor from

1827 to 1861, when he was succeeded by his younger brother, William.[41] At the September meeting a messenger was hired.

A system of controls had also to be established. The directors provided for a rotating committee of three directors, one of whom was to be replaced each month, to assist the actuary in his day-to-day operations. This committee was to advise him on matters of policy and to check his accounting records, reporting to the Board of Directors at each monthly meeting. Since the company would be faced persistently with the problem of investing money to advantage and with security, the directors also appointed a special Committee of Finance.[42] As the company grew, this committee became the central committee in the operation of the company. The consistently high caliber of its membership made it a very valuable resource for the actuary. Both of these committees, established in August and September, 1823, undoubtedly had their prototypes in the practices of banks and insurance companies in Boston and elsewhere.

A third control established subsequently upon the actuary, the annual committee of examination of the Board of Control, has already been mentioned. Its novelty lies not in its annual audit — a common enough function in banking and insurance firms — but in the fact that it was comprised, in the majority, of vice-presidents who were sufficiently remote from the day-to-day affairs of the company as to make about as close to an outside audit as one could get in these times antedating the growth of public accounting firms.

One other important item remained, the matter of profit-sharing. Since no one could foresee the course of needs of the company during its early years, the directors felt that the profit-sharing feature should be postponed. Consequently, the directors sought to postpone the first settlement until January 1, 1829, in return for accepting the Hospital's claim that profits arising from all aspects of the company's business should be shared.[43] An agreement along these lines was reached by December 1. The trustees of the Hospital agreed to the postponement, and the directors accepted an amendment to the Massachusetts Hospital Life charter which, in mid-January, 1824, embedded in law the Hospital's definition of the scope of profit-sharing.[44]

This close relationship between the two institutions was in many ways a decided benefit to both. Since the company became a success, the Hospital gained not alone substantial extra income from profit-sharing in the years ahead but also one-tenth of all profits paid stockholders through its ownership of 10 per cent of the company's stock. It also gained in other ways. It received a fair income from its special or occasional surplus funds on deposit with the company. From time to time the Hospital also borrowed additional funds from the company, secured either by mortgage or note.[45] The income derived from the company by the Hospital is shown in Table 1, with figures given by decades until the reorganization of the company in 1949.[46]

TABLE 1

Income Derived by Massachusetts General Hospital as a Result of Special Provisions in the Original Charter

PERIOD	FROM DIVIDENDS	FROM PROFIT-SHARING	TOTALS
1824–1830	$ 11,000	$ 687	$ 11,687
1831–1840	38,000	40,000	78,000
1841–1850	47,000	85,000	132,000
1851–1860	46,000	80,000	126,000
1861–1870	54,000	115,000	169,000
1871–1880	53,000	115,000	168,000
1881–1890	49,000	95,000	144,000
1891–1900	49,000	95,000	144,000
1901–1910	40,000	50,000	90,000
1911–1920	47,000	85,000	132,000
1921–1930	65,500	177,500	243,000
1931–1949	35,500	52,500	88,000
	$535,000	$990,687	$1,525,687

In part, the early success of the company can be credited to the widespread esteem it received because of its connection with the Hospital. The company's unique status also proved a useful protection when popular feeling at times — as in the Jackson era — ran strong against financial institutions.[47] Nathaniel Bowditch, for one, valued highly the company's link with the Hospital.

Nor was the value of the relationship lost to his successors. A later actuary, Charles G. Loring, in 1867 wrote concerning the profit-sharing provision: [48]

But as we do not look upon this company as a money-making machine for the benefit of the stockholders, but as a great Charity for the safe-keeping and prudent care of the property of those who cannot manage it for themselves, or who desire such place of deposit — we do not count this any loss — on the contrary, I think that it strengthens the institution in public confidence and sympathy, and makes the management of it a more honorary and agreeable duty than it otherwise might be. It is also a useful breakwater against the occasional surging of legislative jealousy and prejudice, which always breaks out more or less frequently against great moneyed institutions of any sort. . . . Upon the whole I should say that if I were seeking the establishment of an institution *for the same general purpose* which *this now accomplishes* I should as a matter of policy, advise the insertion of some similar provision in favor of some great *unequivocal* public charity.

Apart from the company's formative period, however, the relationship with the Hospital probably was more harmful than helpful. The company failed to develop an aggressive spirit. The profit-sharing provision, the Hospital as by far the largest single stockholder, and the widely held concept of the company as a charity, seem responsible for this deficiency. The cumulative result of these factors was an early established conservatism. This conservatism blinded the company's officials to new developments, practices, and opportunities which they might have seized to advantage. A pioneer in two fields, life insurance and trust deposits, the company had lost out in the first and was beginning to lose its pre-eminence in the second by the time Loring wrote the letter quoted above.

◆ III

THE BOWDITCH ERA

1823-1838

If the main impetus to the establishment of the Massachusetts Hospital Life Insurance Company was the Massachusetts General Hospital and its loyal supporters, the main force in its early and great success was Dr. Bowditch. Bowditch was just 50 years of age when he joined the company as its actuary. With the exception of two successors, he was the youngest man to be appointed to that office. He served the company from 1823 to 1838. So inseparably did he become associated with his company in the public mind that, more frequently than by its own mouth-filling name, the company became known simply as the "Bowditch office," or "Dr. Bowditch's office." [1]

Dr. Bowditch's life had been the sort of success story of which New England could be particularly proud.[2] The son of a none-too-prosperous sea captain and of a mother whom he had lost by the time he was 10, he had had little formal schooling. After his mother's death, he had been apprenticed in a Salem ship chandlery from which, on becoming of age, he had graduated to the sea. Thereafter he had made the normal progress of a bright New England boy from clerk to supercargo to ship's captain. In 1804 he left the sea to become president of the newly established Essex Fire & Marine Insurance Company of Salem.

What distinguishes the career of Nathaniel Bowditch from many another was that in addition to his business career and despite his scant schooling he was scholar as well. A voracious reader, he had been his own teacher and had thoroughly mastered mathematics, astronomy, and several foreign languages. His early great achievement, a by-product of his sea voyages, had been his *New American Practical Navigator* (1802). This work, remarkable for its accuracy in comparison with prior attempts, contained in tabular form the results of thousands of mathematical calculations. It enabled sea captains to determine their longitude without a chronometer, an item few thrifty New England shipowners felt they could afford.[3] This was a type of scholarship which merchants in particular were prepared to appreciate. For his *Navigator* Bowditch had been honored with a Harvard M.A., and for later achievements with the LL.D.

Throughout his period of service as actuary Dr. Bowditch continued to combine the dissimilar activities of scholar and businessman. In each activity he found a release from the other, and in both, satisfaction for his New England conscience. At the time he was offered the actuaryship, he was beginning to translate and annotate Laplace's *Celestial Mechanics*, the first great attempt to synthesize astronomical theory since Newton. His son stated later that a potent force in inducing him to move to Boston for a salary more than three times his former pay was the use to which he could put the additional income in financing this work. The translation grew in time to four volumes.[4] In 1829 Bowditch succeeded John Quincy Adams (who in nature he somewhat resembled) as president of the American Academy of Arts and Sciences.

With characteristic keenness, energy, and meticulousness, Dr. Bowditch worked at his new job. Combining his personal experience with the legal knowledge of the distinguished lawyers of the Massachusetts Hospital Life board, he introduced a series of contract forms for the insurance and trust business which endured almost without change for more than half a century and with but minor changes for half a century more.[5] He drew up a system of internal accounting controls. It included four major series of accounting records: the cash or "waste" book, a daybook indicating by major accounts monies received or paid out, as well as a journal series and a ledger series. A special series of records was kept listing all mortgages, and another listing all collateral loans, as well as a monthly listing of all interest payments due from whatever source. Summary statements of monthly activity and of the company's property holdings were also drawn, as well as annual profit and loss statements and balance sheets. Not the least of his contributions to good office practice was a series of tables calculated to show interest at 6 per cent for any number of days in both regular and leap years, thus both promoting accuracy and saving a vast amount of repetitious calculation.[6]

Committees of examination of the Board of Control repeatedly commented on the clarity and accuracy of the accounting records and the success with which the new venture had been launched. One committee said of the trust business in 1832: [7]

> It was an experiment, and the individual who had the principal agency in putting it into operation was without a precedent to guide him. In the nine years that have elapsed since it was organized, numerous and considerable sums have been intrusted to its management by citizens in different parts of the country, which proves that such an institution was needed, while it shows the confidence the public have in its stability as well as in the justice and liberality of its dealings.

But central though Dr. Bowditch was to the success of the company, his leadership was not the only factor. The real basis for the growth of the company lay in the manner in which it was able to manage money so as to secure an attractive yield on the deposits in trust and yet maintain security of investment. The Board of Directors was a great help to this end, but even more the company's success was due to the Committee of Finance, which had been set up to advise the actuary. Members of this committee usually served for a considerable time and were the most regular in attendance at the monthly directors' meetings. Of the three original members, Amos Lawrence served to within two months of the death of Dr. Bowditch in March, 1838. Ebenezer Francis was succeeded in February, 1831, by the prominent merchant, Daniel P. Parker, who served until February, 1843. The other member, Patrick Tracy Jackson, served until February, 1825, when he was succeeded by the attorney, Samuel Hubbard, first solicitor of the company, who was in turn succeeded by John Bryant of the mercantile firm of Bryant & Sturgis in February, 1828. Mr. Bryant continued to serve until 1838. Dr. Bowditch consulted frequently with this committee, particularly with respect to matters of policy and any large investments. The pooling of talents of this caliber with that of the actuary assured the company of first-quality guidance in investments.

As early as 1826, it was evident that the company was a success. In January, 1827, a 7 per cent dividend was declared on the stock,[8] inaugurating a series of annual dividends which was to continue unbroken until 1939. In January, 1829, the Massachusetts General Hospital received its first payment under the profit-sharing provision.[9] These payments, too, continued each year without a break until 1932. By contrast, the other activity, the Commercial Insurance Company, over which Dr. Bowditch and Moses L. Hale were presiding as president and secretary, respectively, was doing none too well, the result of some serious marine insurance losses. Consequently, in 1826 the Commercial Insurance Company was placed in liquidation.[10] Beginning in 1827, both Dr. Bowditch and Moses Hale received their salaries solely from the Massachusetts Hospital Life. These salaries of $5,000 and $2,000, respectively, subsequently raised to $6,000 and $3,000, compared favorably with the $5,000 to $6,000 being paid to treasurers of the larger textile factories, or the $3,700 and $3,000, respectively, being paid the Governor and Chief Justice of the Commonwealth.[11] As the business of the company continued to grow, a "receiver," or cashier, George F. Flint, was appointed in November, 1832. This brought the full-time staff to four in number.[12] No other employee was hired during the incumbency of Dr. Bowditch.

As has been noted, business was solicited in the first instance by a booklet of *Proposals* showing the nature of the contracts — life insurance, annuities, and deposits in trust — in which the company was prepared to engage.[13] Beginning in 1825, the Board of Control authorized the actuary to advertise each week in two Boston papers "the several descriptions of contracts which this Corporation are accustomed to enter into" and once every three months in some one paper in Providence, Rhode Island, Portsmouth, New Hampshire, and Portland, Maine.[14] Dr. Bowditch reported that this advertising, which was maintained throughout the later 1820's, was extremely beneficial, especially in the Boston newspapers. Further means of publicizing the company were the annual reports of the committees of examination of the Board of Control, which were uniformly and properly laudatory. But, particularly in its trust business, the company was not anxious to receive money from any and all comers. Viewing the company primarily as a charitable institution, its officers wished to receive funds only from those dependent members in society in whose interest the company had developed its trust powers. Consequently, as the company became better known and increased in size, it ceased to advertise.

Since the company was nonaggressive in spirit, it is not surprising that public desire for its services determined its pattern of growth. This was mainly in deposits in trust – or, as they were called, "annuities in trust" – rather than in insurance and life annuities. Bowditch told the Board of Control with equanimity in January, 1826, "The business of Life Insurance and Life Annuities is at present very small and the whole force of the institution tends toward the trust establishment." At that time the company was administering 190 deposits in trust of various types amounting to $1,084,094. Forty-two insurance policies were then in force, putting approximately $72,000 at risk, and 20 annuities of a cash value of $21,127.[15] By the close of the year 1830 the company was administering 1,123 deposits in trust amounting to $4,865,254. At the same time it had 95 insurance policies in force for a total risk of $184,650, and 53 annuities, then valued at $63,285. With $500,000 of its own capital, at the end of 1830 the company was administering a fund amounting to approximately $5,500,000.[16] Although the pace of growth thereafter slowed markedly, at the end of 1837 the company was administering a fund of more than $6,200,000.[17] The company was little affected by the panic of 1837.

Some indication of the relative size of the Massachusetts Hospital Life may be gathered from the fact that in June, 1830, all 70 of the commercial banks in Massachusetts had total holdings in mortgages, loans, and investments of but $27,987,000.[18] During the booming 1830's, as new banks were founded and old ones expanded, this amount grew. In February, 1838, the 124 banks in the Commonwealth had holdings totaling $52,800,000. The State Bank of Boston ranked first among these banks, with mortgages, loans, and investments amounting to $2,225,000. Since savings banks at this time were few and small, and fire and marine insurance companies had also but small funds to invest, one can safely say that by far the largest single institutional source of funds in New England in this period was the Massachusetts Hospital Life.[19]

Toward the end of 1837, Dr. Bowditch fell ill of cancer. In spite of this, he worked through the heavy business period of year-end settlement, figuring interest, posting the books, and preparing the annual report. He continued to come to the office until the middle of February and thereafter to conduct some of the business of the office at his home. He spoke of the company as the child of his affections and had its staff witness his will. Dr. James Jackson of the Massachusetts General Hospital was the physician in attendance.[20]

Nine days before his death, Bowditch sent his final message to the directors. In part, he wrote, "Providence has seen fit signally to bless our efforts and make it an Institution of public record. I am not aware of any change, the introduction of which into the present system of management I should desire or recommend." [21] The directors responded with an expression of their warm esteem. At a special meeting after his death, the Board of Control passed resolutions indicating their loss.[22] Wrote William Appleton in his diary, "I most sincerely regret his death, he was one of the most valuable men in society. . . . I fear it will not be easy to fill his place to the satisfaction of the public. The usefulness of the Institution much depends on there being active confidence in the management of it." [23]

A number of prominent Bostonians have been appointed chief executive of the Hospital Life in the 115 years since Bowditch's death, but none has surpassed him either in public prestige or in devotion to his company.

Life Insurance and Annuities

The business of the Massachusetts Hospital Life fell into two main divisions: life insurance and annuities, and deposits in trust. In one sense a unity existed between the divisions: The company was concerned with the creation or the preservation of estates chiefly for the economic protection of dependent members — women, children, and the aged — in society. The purchase of insurance made possible the creation of a modest estate on the death of the insured for the benefit of his family or creditors. The purchase of a life annuity assured a fixed dollar income for the duration of the life of the annuitant. The placing of a deposit in trust made possible an income, normally fluctuating within narrow limits, so long as the money was left on deposit with the company. There were various types of contracts under each of these heads, with those of insurance and life annuities requiring the company to take into consideration the duration of life in the fixing of rates.

At the time of the founding of the Massachusetts Hospital Life Insurance Company, life insurance and annuities as a private business had progressed considerably further in Europe than in the United States, but even in England the conduct of an insurance and annuity business on any large scale hardly predated the founding of the Equitable Life Assurance Society in 1762.[24] In the United States the Pennsylvania Company for Insurance on Lives and Granting Annuities had been in operation since 1813.[25] In his planning, Dr. Bowditch had the limited experience of the Pennsylvania Company to guide him. He also had a number of books describing English experience and including various mortality tables for England and Sweden in the eighteenth century.[26] He could not be sure, however, how closely any of these records would forecast New England experience, though presumably the Pennsylvania experience was closest to the mark. Dr. Bowditch took the Pennsylvania Company data as his best guide. These two companies kept in close touch with one another during their early years, and shared their experience for their mutual benefit.[27]

In its *Proposals*, the Massachusetts Hospital Life offered the following types of policies: life insurance, life annuities, deferred life annuities, and endowments. Of the last, only three policies were issued in the company's history. For each type a written application was required. Any misinformation on the application (e.g., on such a crucial matter as age) could lead to voiding the policy and forfeiture to the company of any funds paid in. The company levied a charge of $1.00 for issuing each policy.

The terms of the annuity contracts were flexible. They provided for payments on a quarterly, semiannual, or annual basis, and for an option whereby an annuity could be written for two or more lives. At the will of the applicant, both annuity and endowment contracts could be written with an inalienability clause protecting the individual in any payments received under a contract from the claims of his creditors. Beginning about 1873, a similar inalienability clause was written into the deposit in trust contracts.

Because the company was a pioneer in life insurance, it naturally sought to restrict its contract in various ways to minimize risk. The company, for example, would grant no very large policy unless the applicant's physician submitted answers to a series of questions pertaining to the health of the applicant. Frequently, the applicant was required to make a personal appearance at the company's office. No life was insured for more than $5,000, and no policy was sold to any individual beyond the age of 60. In the case of a policy written for life, as opposed to a term of years, a fixed-level premium was charged, and a portion of the premium received in the earlier years was set aside as a reserve for the years ahead.

Since the company wished to base its policies on as close to a unity of experience as possible, neither insurance policies nor life annuities, providing for payments to others beginning on the death of the purchaser, were sold to individuals who intended to reside outside New England. Nor was travel viewed with favor. In addition to the to-be-expected restrictions voiding the policy if the insured met death by suicide, duelling, or "the hands of justice," the policy was also void if the insured died at sea or upon any of the Great Lakes. If the policy was to remain in force, the insured had to receive the previous consent of the company before venturing beyond the settled limits of the United States, or beyond Nova Scotia and New Brunswick in Canada, or before visiting south of the southern boundaries of Virginia and Kentucky, or before entering military or naval service.

The terms governing payment of premiums were also restrictive. No period of grace was permitted. A policy which had lapsed could be revived only within 15 days from the date when the premium was due. In such cases payment of a penalty of 10 per cent of the premium was required in addition to payment of the premium.[28]

The attitude of the company was not to push its wares, but rather to wait for the customer. On occasion, various individuals suggested that a greater business in annuities and insurance could be had through the use of agents, but to no avail. Frederick Packard, the company's mortgage agent at Springfield, wrote in August, 1825, that he had had several inquiries about annuities and insurance which he was ill-equipped to answer. He pointed out that the expense of going from the Connecticut Valley to Boston for insurance was equivalent to a substantial increase in the premium and would deter many people from seeking insurance who might do so if the mortgage agents were permitted to issue policies.[29] A year later Lewis Phillips, secretary of the Howard Fire Insurance Company in New York, proposed himself as agent in that city.[30] A large Philadelphia bookseller made a similar proposal. He felt a good opportunity existed there because the Pennsylvania Company was so passive.[31] In a brief reply to the bookseller, Dr. Bowditch wrote, "The Directors have not allowed any Agents whatsoever." [32] Probably the risk in doing an insurance business remote from Boston and the belief that the company's mission was to serve the Boston community were the reasons responsible for this attitude.

From the beginning, rates on life annuities were somewhat higher to annuitants than those of the Pennsylvania Company. Despite this fact, the annuity business of the Massachusetts Hospital Life showed a loss of $14,634 during the first 15 years.[33] While the Pennsylvania Company used a 5 per cent yield on the annuitant's principal in computing its rates, Dr. Bowditch estimated a 4 per cent yield. In 1829 the rates on annuities above age 50 were increased about 10 per cent.[34] Despite this increase, there were more years of loss than of gain in the 1830's, indicating either that the number of annuitants was too small for an adequate sample or that New Englanders were too long-lived for tables based on experience outside New England! The large majority of annuitants were women. The average age was between 65 and 70; few were under 50. Prior to 1830 the largest sum payable to an annuitant was $400. The names of many of the annuitants suggest membership in New England's first families. Probably in a number of instances elderly women of these families were given an annuity to supply them with a small personal income. By the end of 1840 a total of 91 annuities had been issued, of which about 60 were then in force.[35]

Compared with annuities, insurance was a more important and profitable part of the company's business. Here the company started with premiums identical with those of the Pennsylvania Company. These premiums were reduced in 1832, but the company sought to maintain a loading charge in its premiums equivalent to about one-sixth beyond its mortality experience.[36] In the first 15 years of the company, the insurance business showed no loss in any year and a total profit of $53,238. This profit was more than sufficient to cover the loss on annuities to that time and to take care of the profit-sharing payments ($35,688) to the Hospital. Insurance policies, in contrast to annuities, were generally written on the lives of men and for round sums — $500, $1,000, $2,000, $3,000, and $5,000. Most were term policies, with one-year and seven-year policies being most common. As in the case of the annuitants, the list of insured contains many of Massachusetts' finest names, including Daniel Webster.[37] A little more than half of the policies were payable to the estate of the insured. In most other cases the policy seems to have been taken out at the instance of a creditor of the insured, with the creditor designated as beneficiary.[38]

By the end of 1840 a total of 756 insurance policies had been issued, of which 189 were then in force.[39] About twice as many policies per year had been issued in the 1830's as in the average of the company's first 6½ years. This gradual increase caused the committee of examination of the Board of Control early in 1837 to hope "that as our citizens become more familiar . . . and better understand the nature of the contracts, and the benefits to be derived from them to families, and to individuals in particular situations, they will come into more general use." [40] Such was indeed to be the case in the next decade. But the quiet methods of the Massachusetts Hospital Life were not responsible for this development. Credit belongs to the new mutual life insurance companies who hired agents and campaigned aggressively for customers.

Trust Deposits and Depositors

At the time the Massachusetts Hospital Life began operations, there were individuals in the Boston community who were managing the funds of others, but as yet their level of performance did not match that of the later, highly skilled "Boston trustee." The Massachusetts Hospital Life entered this field. As the company grew in its trust business, so did private trusteeship, with many Boston trustees playing a guiding role in its affairs. It was a later actuary, Francis C. Lowell, who stated in 1847 as the main policy of the company, "The office would wish to be governed by the same rules of law, equity and honor which would govern private trustees." [41]

In receiving funds from a large number of sources within the community, the Massachusetts Hospital Life was pooling the risk of investment for the individual depositor and minimizing it through careful management. The company took deposits, together with its own capital, insurance premiums, and funds from life annuities, and invested the common fund in mortgages, notes, and securities, gaining for the individual depositor the advantages of diversification as to number, type, and location of its investments. It thus made the individual depositor a co-adventurer with the stockholder. The depositor shared in the income from investments on the same basis as the stockholder, except for an annual deduction from the income of the fund sufficient to make his earnings ½ of 1 per cent less than the average rate of interest earned on the investments in each year. Thus if the return on the fund as invested averaged 5½ per cent, each depositor would receive 5 per cent on his principal as his proportionate share. Any income not distributed annually was held in a "Reserved Interest Account," from which an additional payment was declared once in five years if warranted by the size of the account.

The ½ of 1 per cent deduction or "fee" (the charge also made by nearly all investment companies today) was a service charge. In addition to the fee, the earnings of the company were made up of the proportionate share of the income of the total fund due on the capital accounts and the gains or losses resulting from the insurance and life annuities business.

In addition to deposits of money, for the same fee the company also offered to accept "such stocks as they are authorized to hold in trust." This service was little used, however, for only in the case of the children of David Sears were such trusts ever established.[42]

In its *Proposals* the Massachusetts Hospital Life claimed it had certain advantages over private trusteeship. The ½ of 1 per cent fee, it asserted, was less than that usually charged by a private trustee, and the terms of its contracts permitted the depositor to escape the probate fee which could occur under private trusteeship. Moreover, the depositor avoided the hazards arising from the resignation or death of trustees or imprudent management, a not infrequent result of the practice of some trustees of merging their trust funds with their personal funds.

The company also stressed that its trust operations were entirely separate from all its other activities, including profit-sharing. Gains or losses from its life insurance and annuities business were computed from the difference between income from insurance premiums and life annuity sales and the payments made on those contracts. Such gains or losses were a charge or profit to capital alone. Nor did profit-sharing with the Hospital affect the income of depositors, for profits were shared, not on the basis of income from the total fund, but solely on the earnings of the stockholders.

Dr. Bowditch, in alluding to the Hospital Life's trust business, on one occasion referred to the company as "a species of Savings Bank for the rich and middle class of Society." [43] The Massachusetts Hospital Life accepted no deposits of an amount less than $500 nor for a term of less than five years, except in the case of a minor who would come of age within that period. Presumably the $500 minimum was set in the belief that the Provident Institution for Savings was a more logical place for any lesser sum. The officers may also have believed that the fee received on any lesser sum offered too small a return for their efforts.

The Massachusetts Hospital Life offered five different types of trust contracts.[44] The most popular, the "G" form, was a five-year deposit arrangement, renewable by the depositor for additional five-year terms. This form was used most frequently by a depositor who placed money in his or her own name. The interest was payable to the depositor, as was the principal also at the end of the five years. In the event of the death of the depositor, the principal was payable to the depositor's estate or to some party or parties designated in the contract. The company also received "G" deposits from organizations and societies, but only through a designated officer of the organization or society to whom the interest and principal were payable. The company never accepted deposits unless there was a clearly designated person or estate to which the money would be payable. Unlike modern trust companies, it refused to have anything to do with settling estates or performing any agency services.

Much of the money which came to the company under the "G" and other forms of contract was deposited by administrators, executors, and trustees under wills. Typically, in this period a trustee made a deposit in the name of the individual in whose behalf he was acting. However, interest was made payable to the trustee, as was the principal, at the termination of the five years or on the death of the individual named in the contract. Such an arrangement permitted a trustee or guardian to maintain control of funds designated for the care of another person. In other contracts, while the trustee was the depositor, both interest and principal were made payable to the individual named in the contract or to his or her estate.

Two forms of contract were stricter variants of the "G" form, one for women and the other for men. Under each form money was deposited for the duration of the life of the named individual without privilege of withdrawal. At his or her death the money was payable to the estate of the deceased or to some specified party or parties. These contracts provided a means of securing an income to the named man or woman during his or her lifetime without risking dissipation of the principal. The "strict female" form, at the option of the applicant, could also contain an inalienability provision which, among other things, specified that the income was "for her separate use, free from the debts, control, or interference by any husband she now has, or may hereafter have. . . ."

The remaining two forms, the endowment in trust and the deferred annuity in trust, were designed for children. Under the first form, money was deposited in the name of the child and the interest was permitted to accumulate as new capital until the principal was due and payable. Provision was made for payment of the principal to the child or some other designated person on the child's attaining his majority, or in the case of a girl, perhaps on her marriage. An inalienability clause was added to the endowment contract if the applicant desired. The deferred annuity in trust was a contract in which the interest was cumulative as new capital until a specified date, usually a child's coming of age. After that time interest was payable to that individual, but the principal was maintained intact either for his estate or for some other named individual.

Thus, while all these contracts hinged upon a specific life, there was a great deal of leeway as to how they were written — as to who might make the original deposit, as to the recipient of the interest, and, finally, as to the recipient of the principal. There was also leeway as to whether the interest would accumulate, or would be paid annually, semiannually, or quarterly. In the early years more than one-quarter of the depositors under the "G" annuity contract form permitted the interest to accumulate.[45]

The principal, "or such part thereof as shall not have been lost by bad debts or otherwise, without the actual fault of" the company, became payable 60 days after the death of the individual on whose life the deposit contract had been written. According to the contract, payment was to be made "in Real Estate, Stocks, Notes, Bonds, or Mortgages" belonging to the company, "all, any, or either of them, at the pleasure and direction of the Directors, at the prices at which the same shall stand charged on the Books of the company" at the time of the death. No past practice is known for the origin of this repayment clause, although from 1817 to 1842 the Provident Institution for Savings did have a bylaw permitting its trustees, in cases of withdrawals of more than $100, to pay the excess over $100 in investments at their value upon the books of the institution.[46]

An extract in the *Proposals* further explained that the payment could be made "in money, or stocks, or property, at the pleasure of the Directors. . . ." In the degree to which payment was made in stocks, the directors would consider "an equitable share of those stocks which may be worth more, as well as those which may be worth less" than the values at which they were carried on the company's books. If the payment was made wholly or partly in money, the company would make "such reasonable allowance for any increase or decrease in the price of the common property, as the Directors shall judge equitable." The effect of the provision in the deposit contract was to protect the company in times of crisis from the threat of having to liquidate its investments at ruinous prices in order to pay off its contracts in cash. The effect of the further explanation in the *Proposals*, which was also printed in fine print at the bottom of the contract, was to make the depositors co-adventurers sharing equitably in the gains or losses of the company. It is upon the basis of the common fund and these provisions for repayment that the Securities & Exchange Commission has found the Massachusetts Hospital Life to be a pioneer of the modern investment company.[47]

Despite the description of the means of repayment, from the beginning depositors were always paid in cash. Nor did any instance occur during the nineteenth century when a depositor was paid either more or less than his principal and accrued interest. The company's investments were mainly in mortgages and notes, on which capital gains were not possible. Losses on the investments were rare and insignificant. Only during the Civil War, when for a period most of the funds of the company were in government securities, did the question of capital gains arise. The officers decided against the claim made at that time.[48]

In the case of the "G" (five-year term) deposits, repayment was occasionally made short of the term of the contract, though at a penalty to the depositor. The penalty was usually a ½ of 1 per cent per annum charge against the principal to the terminal date of the contract.[49] The justification for the charge was that early repayment put a requirement on the cash of the company beyond normal expectancy. If repayment were permitted at any time without penalty, the result could be damaging to the investment policy of the company and to the interest of those whose money remained with the company. Normally, no other barrier was placed in the way of repayment, especially if interest rates in the money market were high. On occasion, however, an actuary did express reluctance, particularly if he felt money released to the depositor would soon be dissipated to the detriment of the welfare of the depositor.[50]

Dr. Bowditch and the directors were gratified at the speed with which the trust business grew and with the status of most of their clients. The flow of funds was at a maximum in 1827 when the gain in trust funds amounted to more than $100,000 per month. The depositors were mainly society's dependents or those inexperienced in business – widows, orphans, children, single women, the aged, teachers, ministers, and naval officers. At the end of 1828 Dr. Bowditch made the compilation shown in Table 2.[51] It was the category marked "Others" in Table 2 that he watched with care, for it was not the intent of the company to manage money for those whose position in life was such that they should be able to accept the risks of management. In several cases Dr. Bowditch refused such deposits.[52] After the panic of 1837, when investment of funds was more difficult, a committee of examination recommended to the Board of Control that the company accept no new deposits "except so far as may be found necessary to enable it to fulfill the benevolent purposes for which it was incorporated." [53] For a brief period the actuary vigorously followed this policy, causing a slight decline in the total amount of deposits.

Nor did the company desire to receive deposits from outside New England. A few were accepted, but especially after the first two or three years Dr. Bowditch discouraged individuals in New York and elsewhere from seeking to place their funds with the company.[54] The company was viewed as a regional institution offering a special service to certain types of individuals rather than as a national enterprise.

TABLE 2

Trusts Held in 1828

SIZE	$500– 1,000	1,001– 2,000	2,001– 5,000	5,001– 10,000	10,001– 25,000	25,001– 50,000	50,001– 100,000	TOTAL
Females	177	106	108	42	30	6	1	470
Minors	34	20	18	6	1	1	1	81
Executors & trustees	10	6	8	13	8			45
Clergy & instructors	23	9	6	1	1			40
Charitable institutions	16	11	13	3	4	2		49
Old men	8	11	8	3	1			31
Navy officers		4	3	1				8
Others	17	14	9	9	6	2	2	59
Total	285	181	173	78	51	11	4	783

By the end of 1830 the first great period of growth in deposits was over. At that time the Massachusetts Hospital Life had funds in the six trust categories shown in Table 3.[55] Many of the names in each category suggest that the company in its trust business was in large part performing a service function for the mercantile family groups of the Boston area who had brought it into being.*

* Thus 51 of the 77 "EG" endowment policies in force at this time were for members of the following families: twelve for members of the Shattuck family, six for an Appleton, six for a Gray, five for a Blanchard, four for a Barrett, four for a Carlisle, three for a Phillips, three for a Russell, two for a Coolidge, two for a Bannister, two for a Lee, and two for a Perkins. The 42 deferred annuities then in force included the following: eight for a Sears, five for a Perkins, four for a Lowell, three for a Cruft, two for a Lawrence, two for a Dana, two for a Thorndike, two for a Curtis, and two for a Wales. Likewise, among the 60 strict female contracts these names appear: Hooper five times, Lawrence three times, and Appleton, Bigelow, and Blanchard twice each. Three Perkins and three Lawrence deposits comprised six of the twelve in the strict male category. Of the 922 "G" deposits for individuals in force at the end of 1830, nearly one-fifth (176) grouped within 14 family names: Appleton 9, Belknap 12, Cabot 9,

Of the 308 "G" deposits made by individuals in the years 1828 and 1829, more than 40 per cent (125) were made by widows and single women. An additional 66 were placed by trustees, administrators, and executors, and 25 by guardians. Aside from four by wives, the balance were made by men, distinguished only as including eight

TABLE 3

Amounts Held in Trust at the End of 1830

Endowments "EG"	$ 170,768
Deferred annuities "D"	168,594
Strict trust for females for life "SF"	379,284
Strict trust for males for life "SM"	316,907
Public institutions "G"	389,696
Individuals "G"	3,440,005
Total	$4,865,254

deposits by ministers and two by Army officers. The average life of these deposits was about 15 years. This suggests that, on the average, they may have been with the company even longer than endowments in trust. Geographically, Boston was responsible for about 55 per cent and the North Shore (Salem, Beverly, and Newburyport) for 20 per cent. Various Massachusetts localities supplied the remainder except for 7 per cent from other states, principally in New England.

The institutional deposits were made almost exclusively by civic, religious, educational, and charitable organizations directed by Boston's leading families. They included, among others, churches and organizations of the Congregational and Episcopal faiths, the American Academy of Arts and Sciences, the Boston Athenaeum, the Handel & Haydn Society, Harvard College, the Boston Dispensary, the Massachusetts Charitable Eye and Ear Infirmary, Massachusetts General Hospital, Massachusetts Medical Society, Boston Female Society, Boston Marine Society, Boys Asylum, Bunker Hill Monument, Franklin Fund, Greene Foundation, Provident Institution for

Channing 8, Danforth 10, Eliot 8, Greene 20, Lee 21, Newman 18, Perkins 11, Pickman 10, Phillips 17, Richardson 15, and Tucker 8. More than one-third (12 of 31) of the "G" deposits for individuals amounting to more than $20,000 each were made by members of these families.

Savings, Savings Bank of Newburyport, and the Salisbury Savings Bank. The Union Insurance Company (Thomas H. Perkins, president) on three occasions under specially drawn contracts placed money at issue in court cases.[56] But this novel venture into the field of corporate trust services had no further development.

Of all these deposits, the Franklin Fund is the one in which the Massachusetts Hospital Life has taken most pride.[57] This deposit grew from one of two bequests in the will of Benjamin Franklin. He gave £1,000 each to Boston, city of his birth and youth, and to Philadelphia, city of his adult years, to be held in trust, principal and income, for a century. During this period Franklin prescribed that money from the fund could be lent to young married artisans under the age of 25 to help them get a start in life, provided they were willing to pay interest at 5 per cent and obtained the signatures of two sureties. This phase of Franklin's plan was little used. Franklin also provided that at the end of a century 100/131 of the total sum should be spent for some useful public work. The remainder was to be held in trust, principal and interest, for another 100 years and then be divided equally between the city and the state for use in whatever ways the respective governments chose.

Franklin's bequest to Boston came into the Massachusetts Hospital Life through the trustee of the fund, William Minot. A first deposit of $10,000 was made on January 28, 1827, and subsequent deposits totaling $5,950 were made through July 7, 1865. When the first distribution took place in 1894, three years beyond the centennial, the Franklin Fund amounted to $427,544. The City of Boston used $329,300 to set up the Franklin Union, a technical school for boys. The balance continued at interest with the Massachusetts Hospital Life. In December, 1931, $423,661 was paid to the treasurer of Boston, and an additional $50,000 was paid in December, 1937. At the end of 1953, the sum of $125,229 still remained with the company and was invested in its Massachusetts Life Fund. The growth of the Franklin Fund is an enlightening example of the effect of compound interest.

The people of Philadelphia were by no means so fortunate in the investment of their £1,000. Their fund had grown only to $89,000 by 1891. At that time approximately $70,000 was earmarked for some useful public work and in 1908 was given, plus interest, to the building fund of the Franklin Institute. The balance of the fund has continued at interest. At the end of the year 1953 it amounted to $228,529.[58]

The rapid growth in deposits through 1830 and the slowing down thereafter raises the interesting question why the earlier pace of growth was not maintained. No clear answer can be given, nor is there any evidence that the officers of the company ever gave the matter consideration. It may be that the pace slackened because the company had met most of the existing needs for service. The mercantile families, too, may have been investing more of their capital directly in new business opportunities. The heavy investments in the textile industry and in railroads after 1830 could well have left less money available for the Massachusetts Hospital Life than in such years of depression as 1828 and 1829. Or it may also be that in the Boston community a sort of competition was growing (between person and institution for the management of funds) in which the Massachusetts Hospital Life was passive and not always the victor. The "Boston trustee" pattern developed more clearly following the decision of *Harvard College* v. *Amory* (1831) delimiting the responsibility of trustees. The many new companies in finance, transportation, and industry also offered these trustees larger opportunities for investing the funds placed with them. Whatever the cause or causes, the amount of the company's deposits did not again double until about the time of the Civil War.

Investment Policy

The nature of the company's depositors determined its general investment policy, which was to make as near riskless investments as possible. The officers felt their responsibilities keenly. As the booklet of *Proposals* put it, the directors would have "always in view the safety of the Capital, rather than the greatness of the income." [59]

In managing Massachusetts Hospital Life funds, Dr. Bowditch and the Committee of Finance had available three broad categories of investment: mortgages, collateral loans, and securities. The statute of incorporation and the amendment did, however, impose certain restrictions. Mortgages were confined to property within the Commonwealth of Massachusetts; loans on collateral and ownership of securities were limited to the indebtedness of the United States or Massachusetts and the stock of the Bank of the United States or of any bank incorporated in Massachusetts. Except for a large block of United States Bank stock in 1835–1836, ownership of securities was not important as a means of investment during the Bowditch regime. The bulk of Massachusetts Hospital Life funds was invested in mortgages, or loaned on collateral, or deposited with Boston commercial banks. The amount of funds invested in mortgages was normally greater than that in collateral loans and deposits. In the boom of the early 1830's, however, when interest rates rose, for a few years collateral loans and deposits were larger in amount than mortgages.

During the company's first years, Dr. Bowditch and the Committee of Finance faced the problem of putting the rapid inflow of deposits to work quickly and safely. On numerous occasions deposit-in-trust contracts specified a waiting period of as much as 60 days before the deposits began to draw interest. The investment problem was made considerably easier by the fact that the banks of Boston were anxious for deposits, so that the Massachusetts Hospital Life was able to share responsibility for the ultimate investment of a substantial proportion of its funds.

After 1830 no longer was investment quite the problem it had been. While there was still a net cash inflow, this flow was much smaller. Liquidity, while no serious problem, became a matter of more concern. For a first time, in 1832, interest payments due depositors amounted to more than the net cash inflow from trust deposits. There was also the possibility that deposits might be withdrawn owing to deaths or the end of five-year terms in greater degree than new money was received. When state law forbade commercial banks to pay interest on deposits, except from savings banks, after October 1, 1834, for a brief period the Massachusetts Hospital Life was faced with a recurrence of its earlier problem. The demand for credit at this time proved so great, however, that the company was able, with relative ease, to invest the funds formerly placed with the banks.

The company made its initial investments during the fall of 1823 by placing just under $100,000 in 25 mortgages. Nearly all these mortgages were in and around Boston, and $35,000 of the amount was on the property of the Massachusetts General Hospital. This loan must have been useful to the trustees of Massachusetts General in meeting the first assessment of $10,000 on the hospital's 500 shares of stock.[60]

Before many months had passed, it became apparent that the company would require more outlets for its funds than the Boston community could immediately provide. In the spring of 1824 Dr. Bowditch began to tap the demand for mortgages among the farmers of western Massachusetts, especially in Franklin County. Here there was less competition among lenders and a greater need for credit. Consequently, there seemed to be an opportunity to "cream" the mortgage market through the careful selection of risks. In several past instances the Commonwealth had sought to supply greater credit to the western counties by provisions in bank charters requiring the banks to place varying proportions of their funds in farm mortgages. This the Massachusetts Hospital Life found desirable not because of legislative prescription but because of the sudden magnitude of its funds.[61]

During 1824 the company placed 323 new mortgages amounting to $401,122. Of this number, 166 were located in Franklin, 50 in Hampshire, and 10 in Hampden counties, all in the Connecticut Valley, and three in Berkshire County beyond. An additional 17 were in Worcester County, 15 in Middlesex County, and four each in Essex and Norfolk counties. Of the 54 in Suffolk County, 48 were in Boston. The Boston mortgages (averaging $3,500) were considerably larger than those elsewhere (averaging $800), but the total value of the Connecticut Valley mortgages alone was greater than the total in Boston.[62] This venture into western Massachusetts mortgages was of considerable, though diminishing, importance to the company in placing its funds during the next 15 to 20 years.

The method the company used to select and watch these mortgages shows clearly its intense concern with security. The first problem facing the company was that of selecting suitable agents in the western part of the state. By the end of 1824 it had four agents forwarding desirable mortgage applications.* All four were attorneys and prominent men in their communities. Three of them were

* They were: Elijah Alvord of Greenfield, Franklin County; Lewis Strong of Northampton, Hampshire County; Frederick Packard of Springfield, Hampden County; and Rejoice Newton of Worcester, Worcester County.

well-known in Boston as members or former members of the Massachusetts legislature.[63] These men also served the company in lesser degree in collecting interest.

The fees of the agents came not from the company but from the applicants, which in itself suggests the favorable market for mortgages in the western counties. Dr. Bowditch commonly regarded the fees charged as no concern of the company. Nor did he feel that this arrangement endangered the company through encouraging the agents to an excess of zeal in forwarding and perhaps falsifying applications in order to collect fees, for he hedged the application procedure with a series of limitations which were designed to permit only the best mortgages to sift through.[64]

Rural mortgages could not be written for more than one-third the value of the property (in contrast to the two-thirds maximum for the city of Boston).[65] This limitation seems to have had a double significance, for it made foreclosure unlikely and, if foreclosure did occur, made a ready sale possible. Because of the large amount of funds available, in the early years the company sought mortgages of $500 or more.[66] It did not, however, encourage mortgages on expensively built homes, which might prove difficult to sell if foreclosure occurred.[67] Nor in general did it accept mortgages on small business or factory property, which might decline too rapidly in value, nor on religious, educational, or charitable property outside Boston.[68] It preferred to have its mortgages based on the value of land. If buildings figured in any great degree under the mortgage, the company required that a fire insurance policy payable to the company be maintained by the mortgagor.[69] The company wrote no second mortgages, no mortgages on property the title of which was clouded for any reason, including dower rights, and no mortgages to women, unless there were sureties. Mortgagors had to be of good character (e.g., not intemperate), for the company wished to lend only to responsible persons who would maintain their property.[70] For a similar reason the company accepted mortgages only from residents of Massachusetts.[71] Each mortgage had to be recorded with the Register of Deeds for the particular county in which the property lay.

Mortgages were normally written for one year. So long as the interest was paid promptly and the property well maintained, a mortgage was automatically renewed from year to year.[72] Interest began on the date the mortgage was written rather than on the date the mortgagor received his money. Mortgage payments, either in full or in part, were permitted only on the anniversary date. Partial payments were not encouraged and were accepted in even hundreds of dollars only.[73] Interest and principal were payable in specie, Boston money, or in such money as the Boston banks would accept without discount.[74] At this time the company was depositing with the Suffolk Bank.

The cumulative effect of these requirements caused one of the agents to write: "There are several gentlemen in this town who have been, for several years, and now are in the practice of loaning largely on mortgages, whose terms are more favorable to the borrower than yours. . . . Under the circumstances, I am apprehensive that few applicants will appear who ought to be recommended." [75] Another agent wrote, "I presume I have rejected 50 offers, during my agency, where I have taken one." [76] But it was the few of highest quality that Dr. Bowditch wanted. When an agent slipped in the quality of the applications he submitted, he heard about it at once.[77]

If a client seemed to meet the requirements for a mortgage, the agent helped him prepare an application. This involved: a full description of the property offered for mortgage, signed by the applicant; a certificate from the Register of Deeds of the county that the title was clear and free from encumbrance; and an appraisal by a qualified individual. The agent also signed a personal statement that the title was good and free from encumbrance, and that the word of the appraiser could be relied upon.[78] In the case of one mortgage for $6,000, Dr. Bowditch required two independent appraisals and a certificate that the property was unencumbered from each sheriff in the county.[79] If the amount was small and the security adequate, Dr. Bowditch forwarded the money and mortgage form at once. Larger requests were reviewed by the Committee of Finance. Even after the mortgage had been approved, Dr. Bowditch urged the agents to withhold the money if they had any doubts about subsequent payment, principal or interest.[80]

Dr. Bowditch required that mortgagors in arrears in their interest payments be dealt with sharply and summarily. In such cases the solicitor and the agent each usually wrote the delinquent warning him of court action unless the interest was paid. A flat charge of $2.00 was made for the solicitor's letter, and Dr. Bowditch wished the agent to charge sufficiently more to be equivalent roughly to interest on the overdue interest. "I wish all who have loans to understand fully that it will always cost them money if the interest is not punctually paid," he wrote to an agent.[81] On another occasion, he wrote: ". . . fine him well . . . make him smart. . . ."[82]

In cases of delinquency, the company usually pressed for the reduction or liquidation of the mortgage. If reduction or liquidation proved impossible and arrearage of interest continued, the company sought to assign the mortgage to another, preferably to one who had an interest in the property.[83] In no other instance would the company consider assignment of a mortgage without the consent of the mortgagor. As a last recourse, the company would institute foreclosure proceedings, though it sought always to avoid court action if possible. When property was acquired through foreclosure, the policy of the company was to sell it as quickly as a satisfactory price could be gained.[84]

By 1830, mortgages in the western counties were beginning to be of less importance in the total Massachusetts Hospital Life investment pattern. The gradual change in the following years was the result of a number of factors: a diminishing flow of funds into the company; attractive opportunities for mortgages, collateral loans, and bank deposits in the Boston area; and increasing competition for the better mortgages in western Massachusetts itself. As early as the middle of 1829 Bowditch was advising that no new mortgages be written in Berkshire County at that time, in part because of the ease with which available money could be placed in or near Boston.[85] In 1834 he was pointing out that money could be placed in Boston on top security for from three to five years at 6 per cent; the company therefore was interested in only the best farm mortgages, if at all.[86] Two years later, in declining a large mortgage application, Bowditch wrote, "It appears as if you had so many rich money lenders in Northampton and its vicinity that the company has no chance of making any loans except in times of great pressure. . . ."[87] Moreover, he believed these loans were likely to be picked off at their anniversary dates by western financial institutions or wealthy individuals who would offer loans representing a higher percentage of property value and better terms than the Massachusetts Hospital Life cared to make. Consequently, when the company did make loans on western Massachusetts property, it declined to accept short-term mortgages so that it would not be faced with the necessity of reinvesting after a brief period.[88]

At Bowditch's death in 1838, the greatest number of mortgages was still in western Massachusetts, but the bulk of the funds invested in mortgages was in Boston. Of the 282 mortgages on which interest was due in March, 1839, 63 were in Boston. These Boston mortgages averaged $3,650, in contrast to $630 for those elsewhere. Those counties having the greatest number of Massachusetts Hospital Life mortgages were Franklin 124, Suffolk 64, Berkshire 51, and Worcester 12. Not one of the other six counties had as many as 12.[89] It is worth noting that the two western counties with the most mortgages were Franklin and Berkshire. Franklin, the most northern of the three Connecticut Valley counties, had no large town, as had Hampshire County (Northampton) or Hampden County (Springfield). Berkshire, the most western county in the Commonwealth and the last to be settled, also had needs for credit it could not as yet supply.

Many of the mortgages on the books in 1839 had been long in existence. Of the above sample of 282, 38 had been written prior to the beginning of 1825; 98, before 1830; and 56 were taken before 1835. The oldest mortgages tended to be small mortgages which had not been picked off by competitors in the western counties. An early act of Joseph Tilden, Bowditch's successor as actuary, was to survey the western mortgages. Thereafter they were rapidly thinned out.[90] After 1840 few new mortgages were written in the west, except in Berkshire County.

If Massachusetts Hospital Life mortgages during these years created a considerable amount of agricultural credit in the western counties and served a variety of needs in Boston, its collateral loans and bank deposits mainly served business and financial interests in the Boston community. Most of its loans in this period were to banks, financial houses, and business firms rather than to individuals. In cases where loans were made to individuals, the greater proportion undoubtedly were for business purposes. The extraordinary success of the Massachusetts Hospital Life resulted in a more readily available pool of capital in the Boston community than would have been possible had the funds remained in private hands.

Loans to individuals were mainly to the merchant group responsible for founding the company. The most frequent borrower prior to 1840 was William Appleton, who borrowed some 30 times.[91] Enterprises in which he was interested were also borrowers, including textile companies, a real estate company, and a sugar refinery. Second in number of loans was the capitalist David Sears (22 loans), who was frequently associated with William Appleton in business ventures. The Massachusetts Hospital Life had no rule forbidding loans to its directors, or even to members of its Committee of Finance. Something of the character of the company's officers and directors is indicated by the fact that in more than a century the company suffered no loss from such loans.

Another group of borrowers were financial houses and banks. Brokerage firms like S. & G. Williams Company and Dana, Fenno & Henshaw were frequent and large borrowers. Of greater consequence, however, were Boston's commercial banks. During 1824–1826 the company had discounted a few notes for banks or had placed sums on deposit. After 1826 most transactions recorded in its loan book were with the banks as shown in Table 4.

TABLE 4

Number of Loan Transactions, 1826–1835

YEAR	TOTAL NUMBER	WITH BANKS
1826	56	5
1827	125	46
1828	165	98
1829	122	73
1830	133	92
1831	135	95
1832	204	166
1833	251	216
1834	163	98
1835	78	2

In time nearly all of Boston's commercial banks (23 of the 29 in existence in 1834) were sharing responsibility with the Massachusetts Hospital Life in the ultimate placement of its funds. The company most frequently made loans and deposits in favor of the City, Commonwealth, Globe, American, Atlantic, Columbian, State, Merchants, Traders, Oriental, Eagle, and Commercial banks. Having greater resources than any of these, the Massachusetts Hospital Life made possible a substantial increase in their resources. On occasion the sums advanced were secured by a note of the bank, but more frequently they were secured by a deposit book. The company also made loans to or deposits with four banks in Salem and the Railroad Bank of Lowell. The rates received from the banks varied between 4 and 6 per cent depending on the date of the loan or deposit, its duration, and the particular institution. By the early 1830's most of these loans and deposits were yielding the company 5 per cent or more.

Depositing with the banks reached its climax in October, 1834. After this date the Commonwealth forbade the commercial banks to pay interest on deposits except on those made by savings banks.[92] The law stemmed from a fear that deposits would pile up, encouraging the banks to lend less wisely in order to pay interest and thereby endanger their stability. Since the Hospital Life could no longer receive interest on money deposited in commercial banks, it substantially reduced its transactions with these banks. In the five years ending January 1, 1835, 667 of the 885 transactions recorded in the loan book were with banks; in the next five years, only 45 out of 425 were with banks.

In later years the Massachusetts Hospital Life was to be more intimately associated as a source of credit with the textile industry than with any other industry. This was natural, for many of the founders of the company were also "Boston Associates" — the term so frequently used to designate those Boston capitalists who made important textile centers of such places as Lowell, Lawrence, Holyoke, Chicopee, and Manchester.[93] In these years one may see the beginning of this important credit relationship. Although credit had been advanced earlier to two small textile companies (to one through a mortgage), the first significant textile loan occurred in 1826.[94] At that time $20,000 was advanced to the Boston Manufacturing Company in Waltham on its note, endorsed by Patrick Tracy Jackson and Nathan Appleton, and five shares of stock in the Suffolk Bank. This note began a credit history lasting more than a century with the pioneer mill of the Boston Associates. A far larger borrower in this period was the Dover Manufacturing Company, of Dover, New Hampshire, in which William Appleton and David Sears were interested. In a series of four loans, the Dover company borrowed $200,000 in 1827 and 1828.[95] Other companies of the Boston Associates borrowing from the Massachusetts Hospital Life prior to 1840 were the Amesbury Flannel Company, Boott Cotton Mills, Eliot Manufacturing Company, Hamilton Manufacturing Company, Proprietors of the Locks and Canals on the Merrimack River, Lowell Manufacturing Company, and Merrimack Manufacturing Company. Six of these companies were located at Lowell.[96] In the later 1830's their borrowings were nearly as important as loans and discounts to banks in the placement of Massachusetts Hospital Life funds.

Miscellaneous but important borrowers were the Massachusetts General Hospital, the City of Boston, and the Commonwealth of Massachusetts. The Massachusetts General Hospital, ubiquitous in its relationship with the Hospital Life as profit-sharer, stockholder, depositor, and mortgagor, borrowed sums as large as $50,000 on its capital stock in the company on 10 different occasions prior to 1840. Notes of the City of Boston and the Commonwealth of Massachusetts generally ran for a year or less, although in one instance the company held Boston notes totaling $97,500 for three years. These notes of Boston and Massachusetts were probably obtained through brokers.

Collateral most frequently offered the company in the early years consisted of shares in the second Bank of the United States or in Boston commercial banks. This was in conformity with the statutory prescription limiting acceptable collateral to securities of the United States Government or of Massachusetts, or stock of the Bank of the United States or of banks incorporated in Massachusetts. However, on its own initiative the company gradually broadened the types of acceptable collateral. The company probably did this to obtain more adequate outlets for its rapidly increasing funds. By 1824 it was lending on shares of several Boston insurance companies, and in 1826 on notes of the City of Boston. Its first two textile loans, to the Salisbury Woolen Manufacturing Company and to the Boston Manufacturing Company, were guaranteed by three shares of the Eagle Bank and five shares of the Suffolk Bank, respectively, which were completely inadequate as security. The main security for the first loan lay in the pledged capital stock of the Salisbury company, and in the second in the note of the Boston company endorsed by Patrick Tracy Jackson and Nathan Appleton. In lending a total of $200,000 to the Dover Manufacturing Company in 1827 and 1828, the company was lending to a concern operating in New Hampshire, and on collateral which could not meet the legislative prescription except for a token 10 shares of stock in the Boston bank and five shares in the Bank of the United States. Loans to individuals likewise were frequently based on stock of the new textile companies and other nonbanking companies.[97]

These practices (except for loans to companies operating out of state or acceptance of their stock as collateral) were finally sanctioned by an amendment to the statute of incorporation in March, 1839.[98] This amendment permitted the company to invest its funds in railroad securities and to make loans to cities and towns of the Commonwealth and to other corporations and individuals on the basis of railroad, manufacturing, or other corporate securities issued within the Commonwealth. Loans to no one corporation or individual on the basis of such collateral were to exceed one-third of the capital stock of the company. Thereafter the company normally acted within the terms of law, although in rare instances, especially with textile companies, it made loans in excess of the limitation of one-third of its capital. Why it did not seek an earlier amendment is not known. The company's practices, meanwhile, had been responsible for a considerable investment of funds which it might not otherwise have been able to place so advantageously.

Bank stock had a preferred status as collateral, however. Loans on bank stock were usually written for 90 per cent of the par value without reserving any right to call for additional security if the price of the stock declined. In the case of insurance or manufacturing stocks, loans were made for about two-thirds of the market value, and the right was reserved to call for additional security if the market value declined. If additional collateral was not forthcoming or the loan was not reduced, the company auctioned off the pledged stock to recover its funds.[99] This occurred in a few cases during the depressed years for the textile industry of 1828 and 1829.[100]

Except for loans to the banks, which frequently were for terms of less than a year, most notes in this period were written for one year. Other notes, secured chiefly by nonbank stocks, were written on a "demand" basis. These were left outstanding at the will of the borrower, so long as the interest was regularly paid and the collateral maintained its value. Of 12 such notes written in 1830, only two were paid in a year or less. Six of these were in existence for four years or longer. The average duration of all loans and deposits made in that year was about 15 months. The average deposit with banks during the year was just over $17,000; the average loan to an individual was $12,000.

Ownership of securities was of little importance in these years. Although bank stocks were legal investments, the company preferred the lesser risk of loans and deposits, especially since the dividends of Boston banks were hardly better than 6 per cent during this period. Securities of the Commonwealth and of the United States were on the market in but limited amounts and at relatively low yields. Intermittently the company did buy federal securities, but in small quantities. At maximum in 1831 the Hospital Life held a little better than $250,000 in United States bonds, which yielded about 4 per cent. These securities had been bought mainly through the brokerage firm of Prime, Ward & King of New York City, with William Appleton as agent.[101] This investment was gradually liquidated in 1832–1833.[102]

Of greater importance was the substantial and lucrative investment Dr. Bowditch made in the spring of 1835 in the stock of the Bank of the United States. This occurred at a time when the company was still transferring to other uses funds it could no longer deposit at interest in commercial banks. Defeated in its battle with President Jackson for recharter, the Bank of the United States ceased lending early in March, 1835, and presumably was preparing for orderly liquidation. At that time the bank had first-class assets of better than $70,000,000 and outstanding liabilities of but $26,000,000.[103] With a capital of $35,000,000 and its stock in March at no more than 108, the stock seemed an attractive investment in terms of its prospective liquidation. Again through William Appleton, who was president of the Boston branch of the Bank of the United States, and Prime, Ward & King, the Massachusetts Hospital Life bought 5,350 shares at prices ranging between 107⅞ and 114 from March to May, 1835. The stock continued to rise in price. It made a further gain as the bank seemed to be moving successfully to recharter as a state bank in Pennsylvania early in 1836. During the month of February, 1836, William Appleton liquidated the holdings of the company at prices ranging between 124½ and 127¾. As a result, the company netted just over $75,000, or 12.6 per cent, on an investment lasting from nine to eleven months.[104] This successful coup provided a good share of the income for the company's first extra dividend of $6.00 per share plus $15,000 for the Massachusetts General Hospital in 1840.[105]

The first great test of the company's investment policies occurred during the panic of 1837. In January of that year, the annual committee of examination had reported to the Board of Control that in the 13 years since the company began operations there had been only five cases of foreclosure in 3,000 mortgages and that no debt had been lost, either mortgage or collateral loan.[106] A year later Dr. Bowditch stated that in more than six months before the suspension of specie payments by the Boston banks in mid-May, 1837, the company had not felt it necessary to call for additional collateral on any of its notes. Thereafter it had made a number of such calls, including requests for additional securities in five loans secured by bank stocks. As a result of the panic, in January, 1838, Bowditch was anticipating a small loss on one note.[107] Interest payments were in arrears on approximately $420,000 of the company's $6,000,000 in mortgages and notes. Because of the value of the property or of the collateral, however, Bowditch believed that in no instance would the company fail to recapture its investment.

During the summer and fall of 1837 when the panic was most intense, the company permitted a number of its borrowers to regain their collateral. This collateral was worth more than the amount loaned and, when sold, could yield enough money to repay the Massachusetts Hospital Life and still leave a margin for settling other debts. This action permitted borrowers to regain securities valued in excess of $400,000.[108] At the same time the company had no difficulty in investing repaid funds in new loans, some of which were written for as long as three years. The only immediate effects of the panic on the loan policies of the company were slight. A change was made in the language of notes secured by bank stocks providing for the right to call for additional collateral if the value of the stock declined. There was also a greater tendency to write notes on "demand."

Judged by whatever yardstick – security, yield, or liquidity – the investment policies of the Massachusetts Hospital Life were exceptionally successful in the early years. Its conservative mortgage loans consistently yielded nearly 6 per cent. Its bank deposits, collateral loans, and security investments, while normally not quite so high in yield, had provided investments of minimal risk and a liquidity it had never needed. Although the yield to the company depositors dropped briefly as low as 4½ per cent in 1831, by 1836 the rate was 5½ per cent, a rate that was maintained throughout the depression until 1845. Meanwhile the $7.00 per share dividend, first declared in 1827, was increased to $8.00 in 1829 before again lapsing to $7.00 in each of the next three years. The $8.00 rate, regained in 1834, was maintained (plus extras) until after the Civil War, when it was further increased. This return closely approached the record of the most profitable of the Boston banks, the Suffolk Bank, during the same period.[109] After 1829 the company also paid the Massachusetts General Hospital $2,500 for each dollar of regular dividend above $6.00 and $2,500 for each dollar of extra dividend, in addition to the dividends paid to the Hospital on its 500 shares of stock.

Influence on Other Companies

By 1830 the success of the Massachusetts Hospital Life Insurance Company was attracting considerable attention. One can readily trace its impact on a series of life insurance and trust companies, organized to the number of about 25 in the course of the next two decades.[110] Only one of these, the Connecticut Life Insurance & Trust Company, chartered in 1833, was established in New England. The Hospital Life probably had its greatest significance in its impact on the practices of the emergent private trustees, who were to figure so largely in the administration of private funds in the New England area. This is difficult to document, but it at least seems reasonable that an institution outstanding for its careful management of funds should have had an influence, directly or indirectly, on individuals handling funds for others in lesser amounts. Some of these individuals in turn influenced the company through membership on its boards.

The impact of the Massachusetts Hospital Life on another institution may be seen in the creation and organization in 1830 of the New York Life Insurance & Trust Company, the most outstanding of the companies to be influenced by it. This institution, the first life insurance and trust company to be chartered in New York, exists at present as one of the three institutions merged into the Bank of New York & Fifth Avenue Bank. The Bank of New York itself is the oldest bank in New York, having been founded by, among others, Alexander Hamilton. The bank operates today under the charter of the New York Life Insurance & Trust Company.

This company originated from the interest of William Bard, a member of the New York financial community, who thought he saw an opportunity in New York for an institution similar in nature to that earlier established in Boston. Among those to whom Bard wrote in his preliminary planning was former United States Senator James Lloyd of Massachusetts. Senator Lloyd replied enthusiastically. Of the Massachusetts Hospital Life, he wrote, "I know not how public confidence could be more unreservedly reposed in, or expressed in favor of any institution public or private, than has been, and continues to be and is, I believe, most deservedly manifested toward this company." This letter was among the evidence submitted to the New York legislature. The Assembly Committee, to which the matter was referred, reported favorably. It took special notice of the Massachusetts Hospital Life as a main reason for its decision: [111]

> Your committee have had before them proof that, in the city of Boston, a company has for many years existed, with the power of insuring lives, granting annuities, and receiving money in trust. They have also had before them satisfactory evidence of the great utility that company has been to the citizens of Massachusetts, and that it now commands the confidence of the people of that state, manifested by the property which the citizens, with feelings of entire security, are constantly entrusting to its management and care.

The charter of the New York Life Insurance & Trust Company varies from that of the Massachusetts Hospital Life in the more specific character of its provisions relating to trusts, for as the name of the company indicates, the acceptance of trusts was more clearly in mind at the time of its origin. In its organization, this company showed the same sensitiveness to the problem of securing maximum public confidence in the institution. To this end the charter provided for a board of 30 trustees.[112] As in the case of the Massachusetts Hospital Life, every effort was made to enlist the support of outstanding figures in New York business, financial, and civic circles.* Initially no stockholder was permitted to hold more than 100 shares ($10,000 of the $1,000,000 capital),[113] though this ban was later removed.

Before the New York Life & Trust began business in June, 1830, William Bard, its president, visited Dr. Bowditch to study the procedures and practices of the Boston company. Thereafter he was occasionally in touch with the Boston executive. In one case, at the request of his trustees, he carefully inquired as to the experience of the Massachusetts Hospital Life in using unpaid agents in gathering applications for mortgages.[114]

Lacking the philanthropic background of the Massachusetts Hospital Life, the New York company became more aggressive. It was the first American insurance company to use agents and to pay them commissions. By 1840, it had built up by far the largest life insurance business in this country. In its trust business the company desired to receive funds from all comers and to find new means for using its trust powers. It would accept deposits of as little as $100 and for as brief a period as two months, and it promised repayment in cash.[115] The New York company had hardly been organized before its officers were seeking the surplus funds of the Erie Canal as deposits from the legislature.[116] It accepted deposits from business firms and broadened its activities well beyond those of the Massachusetts Hospital Life in other ways. In 1833 it at least considered keeping and probably agreed to keep the stock transfer books of the Camden & Amboy Railroad.[117] Some years later it agreed to act as trustee in receiving annually from the Tioga Navigation Company (a railroad) 2 per cent of the face of its $100,000 bond issue for in-

* Among the original trustees were John Jacob Astor, Philip Hone and Cadwallader Colden, former mayors of New York City, James Kent, former chancellor of the New York Court of Chancery, Charles Wilkes, president of the Bank of New York, Nathaniel Prime, of Prime, Ward & King, Peter Lorillard, Gulian C. Verplanck, all of New York City, and Stephen Van Rensselaer and Erastus Corning of Albany. By the terms of the charter this board was made self-perpetuating.

vestment and management.[118] In 1836 and 1837 it was seeking to raise funds in Europe for investment either through trust deposits or by direct loans.

Like the Massachusetts Hospital Life, the New York company emphasized its trust business. Within three years of its founding its deposits in trust amounted to approximately $2,500,000. These deposits continued to increase rapidly until 1837; thereafter a marked decline occurred. The terms of deposit made the deposits of the New York Life & Trust considerably more volatile than those of the Massachusetts Hospital Life and their fluctuations were quite in contrast to the steady growth in the Massachusetts company. As late as the end of the 1890's the New York Life & Trust Company had a lesser volume of trust deposits than did the Massachusetts Hospital Life.[119] Interest rates on these deposits were fixed, not on the basis of sharing in proportion to investment in the income of a common fund, subject to a management fee, but on the basis of set rates increasing with the length of term of the deposit.[120]

By the terms of the charter, all capital funds of the New York Life & Trust had to be invested in first mortgages, with at least half this amount outside New York County. Other funds of the company could be invested with few restrictions. In no instance, however, could the New York Life & Trust own stock to the extent of more than $25,000 in any private incorporated company. The investment pattern of the two companies roughly approximated each other, though in the 1830's the New York Life & Trust Company invested in mortgages to a greater degree than did the Massachusetts company. The New York company also tended to be a little more liberal in its mortgages, for it lent to half the value of the property in areas outside New York County.[121] Its loans on collateral tended to be of a shorter term than those of the Massachusetts Hospital Life, probably reflecting the greater volatility of its deposits. The company did not make deposits in commercial banks to any great extent, but in the later 1830's it was a minor stockholder in several of the New York banks.[122]

Although its resources were smaller than those of the Massachusetts Hospital Life, the New York company was, during its early years at least, considerably more profitable. This was probably due both to the more favorable maximum legal interest rate in New York

State and to a clear-cut profit orientation on the part of its officers. Since the legal rate in New York was 7 per cent, payable semi-annually, as opposed to 6 per cent in Massachusetts, the opportunity for profits for its stockholders was correspondingly greater. By 1834 the New York Life & Trust was paying 9 per cent per year dividends and 12 per cent by 1836. Except for an 18 per cent payment in 1838, the 12 per cent rate was maintained until 1842, when it became necessary to suspend dividends for two years because of the secretary's embezzlement of about $350,000.[123] From 1844 until the Civil War, dividends fluctuated between 7 per cent and 10 per cent.[124]

Other important companies to be influenced by the Massachusetts Hospital Life and by the immediate and striking success of the New York Life & Trust were the Ohio Life Insurance & Trust Company (1834) and the Girard Life Insurance, Annuity & Trust Company of Philadelphia (1836).[125] The Ohio company is better known for the loose use to which it put its power of paper money issue than for anything done under its insurance, annuity, and trust powers. It was in touch with the Massachusetts Hospital Life in 1835 in regard to its insurance program.[126] In 1836 the Pennsylvania Company for Insurance on Lives and Granting Annuities, which as early as the beginning of 1827 had considered following in the path of the Massachusetts company, successfully sought an amendment to its charter permitting it to accept trust deposits.[127] Fully half of the life insurance and trust companies established in these years were in the southern states, and most of the rest were in Pennsylvania. By the 1840's fewer were being organized, for the rise of the mutual insurance companies rapidly drove most proprietary companies from life insurance, leaving them almost exclusively in the trust field. Those which survived, like the New York Life & Trust, were aggressive institutions which sought actively to expand their range of trust activities.[128] Almost universally they were money-making ventures, free from any hint of philanthropy.

One other company should be mentioned here, the Rhode Island Hospital Trust Company of Providence. This first trust company in Rhode Island was chartered in May, 1867, nearly 50 years after the Massachusetts Hospital Life. It is today the largest banking institution in Rhode Island. Although life insurance and annuities were never a part of its business, the Rhode Island Hospital Trust was directly influenced in its origin by the Massachusetts Hospital Life. A letter solicited from Charles G. Loring by Robert H. Ives, a founding director of the Rhode Island Hospital Trust, had great influence in determining the pattern of organization of the latter company. Much of this letter was quoted toward the end of the preceding chapter.[129]

The charter of the Rhode Island Hospital Trust provided that that institution would pay annually to the Rhode Island Hospital one-third of all net profits earned above 6 per cent on the capital stock, so long as the same requirement was placed in the charter of all trust companies subsequently organized in Rhode Island. This provision lapsed in 1880, when the Rhode Island Hospital agreed to its abrogation in return for a stock interest of $100,000 in the company.

From the beginning, the Rhode Island Hospital Trust did both a general banking and a trust business. Its trust business in its early years was quite minor, for in the first 24 years after its charter the company accepted only 191 trusts. The company was willing to broaden its field of service from the lesser limits of the Massachusetts Hospital Life, however, and thus was laying a base for a more substantial trust business in this century.

During its earlier years the Rhode Island Hospital Trust also showed the influence of the Massachusetts Hospital Life in the so-called "participation accounts" in its banking department. Deposits left with the Rhode Island company at least three months prior to the semiannual settlement of the company's books were entitled to interest at the average net rate earned on the investments of the company, less ½ of 1 per cent. This liberalized adaptation from Massachusetts Hospital Life practice in regard to deposits in trust brought $3,281,000 in participation accounts to the Rhode Island company by June, 1874. Although the term "participation account" was maintained as late as 1928, when it was changed to savings account, the practice of permitting holders of these accounts to share in the earnings with the stockholders, subject merely to a ½ of 1 per cent disparity, had lapsed long before. The practice had been abandoned owing to the continued pressure downward on interest rates during the last quarter of the nineteenth century.

Aside from this late instance of the Rhode Island Hospital Trust, the influence of the Massachusetts Hospital Life in its home area is of more intangible nature and more difficult to adduce. That but one company modeled after its type was founded in New England during a period when a considerable number were being founded elsewhere may suggest that the size of the Massachusetts Hospital Life was a deterrent to imitation in its home area. Or perhaps there were too few large urban centers apart from Boston to offer much opportunity for a life insurance and trust company. So little imitation does not mean that the company was without influence in developing standards and practices in the management of funds in New England, however.

Historically, to a greater degree than in any other area the management of private funds in a trust capacity in New England has been the province of the private trustee as opposed to trust institutions. At the time of the founding of the Massachusetts Hospital Life the care of funds by private trustees was in its infancy. Some individuals active in the founding of the company were in a limited way in their own right private trustees – for example, Nathaniel Bowditch, Ebenezer Francis, William Sturgis – and they performed their trustee functions with a high sense of responsibility. But not all individuals acting in a trustee capacity were so capable or so scrupulous. In fact, in its *Proposals* of 1823 the company pointed out shortcomings present in private trusteeship as then practiced by some trustees as arguments for placing deposits with the Massachusetts Hospital Life. It seems reasonable to presume that the presence of a large institution so ably administered must have had a salutary effect on the practices of the more lax private trustees, else the institution quite probably would have grown at a more rapid rate than it did in the 1830's and thereafter.

A landmark in the growth of private trusteeship was the decision in the case of *Harvard College* v. *Amory* in 1831. In this decision, Justice Samuel Putnam, the father-in-law of John Amory Lowell (son of John Lowell), enunciated what has come to be known as the "prudent man" rule. This was a liberating and clarifying decision for private trustees, for the judicial decision favored the trustee defendants in declaring: "All that can be required of a private trustee to invest, is, that he shall conduct himself faithfully and exercise a sound discretion. He is to observe how men of prudence manage their own affairs, not in regard to speculation, but in regard to the permanent disposition of their funds, considering the probable income, as well as the probable safety of the capital to be invested." [130] Dr. Bowditch had put the emphasis a little differently in his *Proposals* of 1823. He had said that the directors would have "always in view the safety of the Capital, rather than the greatness of the income." Both statements, however, focus on the interest of the passive investor, who, entrusting his funds to the care of another, normally does so to get as good an income as possible consistent with the safety of the principal.

In the years ahead, as we shall note, the story of the Massachusetts Hospital Life is interlinked with the growth of private trusteeship. Members of such famous private trustee families as Bowditch, Minot, Codman, Dexter, and Loring are present repetitively among its officers and are a part of its history. Toward the end of the nineteenth century a prototype of the modern Massachusetts-type investment company emerges, the Boston Personal Property Trust (1893), the creation of private trustees. In this pattern of investment company, developed into the Massachusetts mutual investment funds of the twentieth century, we find a simple capital structure and a common fund, in the principal and income of which all shareholders share in proportion to their holdings, subject to a small management fee. Management of the fund is vested, under a declaration of trust, in a group of trustees who invest the fund and distribute the income to the shareholders. The shareholder is guaranteed the right of liquidating his holdings at their proportional value to the total fund, usually subject to a small discount.[131] There are differences between the old Massachusetts Hospital Life pattern of trust deposits and investments and that of the modern investment fund, notably in the absence of any capital interest in the modern fund apart from the general shareholders and in the greater ease with which a shareholder may liquidate his interest; nevertheless, the similarities are striking.

The Massachusetts-type open-end trusts also indicate their heritage in their advertising. Thus the trustees of the George Putnam Fund stated in a leaflet published in 1943: "More attention is given to capital protection and income than to stock market speculation." In its prospectus, published in 1942, the State Street Investment Corporation declared: "In selecting investments the question of immediate income is given careful consideration, but a greater amount of time and thought is directed to the study of how to conserve and secure the growth of purchasing power of the principal." [132] The Massachusetts Hospital Life Insurance Company, reorganized and modernized in 1949 as a mutual fund investment company, it might be added, is again using the language of Dr. Bowditch quoted above as expressing the central policy on which its operations are based — "having always in view the safety of the Capital, rather than the greatness of the income." [133]

IV

IN THE MOLD OF THE FOUNDERS (1838–1878)

The history of the Massachusetts Hospital Life Insurance Company between the death of Dr. Bowditch in March, 1838, and the resignation of the company's fifth actuary, George T. Bigelow, almost exactly 40 years later, is that of an institution kept steadily on the course set for it by its founders. Until the later 1860's a diminishing number of the founders were still active in company affairs. When Nathan Appleton died in August, 1861, he was president of the company and a member of its Committee of Finance. His cousin, William Appleton, a vice-president since 1845, died in 1862. They were followed in death in 1863 by William Sturgis, a long-time member of the Committee of Finance, and in 1864 by John Bryant, Josiah Quincy, and Thomas Motley. In 1868 Moses Hale resigned as secretary of the company after 45 years of service, during which time he had seen four actuaries come and go and a fifth installed. The last of the original stockholders, David Sears, a vice-president since 1823, resigned in January, 1870. At that time he wrote, "The deep interest I have always felt in this Corporation, believing it would work good in the community and provide a needed security for the helpless, is confirmed, and the experience of nearly half a century has verified the fact." [1]

For a decade more the company was influenced by three individuals who had been closely tied to the founders. Two of them, John Amory Lowell and J. Ingersoll Bowditch, were sons of founders. John Amory Lowell, son of John Lowell, had been a director of the Massachusetts Hospital Life Insurance Company for 45 years at the time of his resignation in January, 1879,[2] when he was succeeded as director by his son, Augustus Lowell. Because of the range of his business and civic interests, especially in textiles, education, and philanthropy, John Amory Lowell could vie with anyone for the title of first citizen of Massachusetts in the third quarter of the nineteenth century. J. Ingersoll, the second son of Dr. Bowditch, had served as director for 42 years at the time of his resignation in 1881. On three occasions he had served as acting actuary, and since 1856 he had been a member of the Committee of Finance. J. Ingersoll Bowditch was succeeded as director by his son, Charles P. Bowditch. The third of the trio, Ignatius Sargent, had started his career in the counting room of Thomas H. Perkins, another of the merchant founders. At the time of his resignation in January, 1879, he had been a director for 36 years and a member of the Committee of Finance for 15. His son, Charles Singer Sargent, professor of horticulture at Harvard College and first director of the Arnold Arboretum, served as a vice-president of the company from 1885 until his death in 1927.

It was thus the old merchant group, though now no longer dominantly of the sea lanes, and their associates and descendants who maintained control of the company. Of the 105 active stockholders in 1865, 78 lived in Boston, and all but five of the rest were in the immediate vicinity. None of the five — two in Newport, Rhode Island, and three in New York City — was important in the affairs of the company.[3] Although the great days on the sea had passed, the idealization of the merchant endured. In 1847 Francis C. Lowell wrote scathingly to one who was waiting for the last possible moment to redeem his property which the company had foreclosed, "This appears to me a very strong ground for a merchant to take, that he would not fulfill his engagements because no legal penalty would be inflicted on him for not doing so." [4] And in the 1850's Augustus Lowell, T. Jefferson Coolidge, and Arthur T. Lyman, after their graduation from Harvard College, thought joining firms in the East India trade was a proper way to begin their business careers.

Administrators and Administration

Leadership in the company after the death of Dr. Bowditch was much more the result of group effort. There was no hand as strong as his, nor, with the possible exception of Charles G. Loring, any actuary whose interest in the company was so intense.

Joseph Tilden, first of the four actuaries in this period, was Bowditch's personal choice.[5] At the time he became actuary, Tilden was 59 years of age. Bowditch and Tilden had long known each other as fellow directors of the Massachusetts Hospital Life Insurance Company and as fellow members of the American Academy of Arts and Sciences, of which Dr. Bowditch was president in his later years and Joseph Tilden, treasurer. Like three of these four Bowditch successors, Tilden had a Boston mercantile heritage. While not one of the outstanding Boston Associates in the rapid expansion of the textile industry, Tilden was nonetheless an important member of that group. He was, for example, a director of the Suffolk Manufacturing Company at Lowell, a proprietor of the Locks & Canals, a director of the Boston & Lowell Railroad and, in the later 1840's, president of the Amoskeag Company at Manchester, New Hampshire. When he became actuary of the Massachusetts Hospital Life Insurance Company in March, 1838, Tilden resigned as treasurer of the Locks & Canals, the central company of the Boston Associates in the creation and the industrialization of Lowell. From May, 1824, until August, 1837, he was also president of one of Boston's larger commercial banks, the Columbian Bank.

The range of Tilden's interests in contrast to the singleness of Dr. Bowditch's devotion to the company, suggests another reason, beyond the impact of the panic of 1837, why the directors took a more active interest in the affairs of the company during the early years of his regime. More directors attended the regular monthly meetings, and a few minor administrative changes were made. Their cumulative effect was to make the Tilden era the most notable for change in this near-changeless institution down until the 1880's. A new clerk was hired, bringing the number of full-time employees to five, a number not again increased during the nineteenth century. The actuary's salary was reduced to $5,000, and perhaps because of his many interests Tilden accepted this reduction; the secretary's salary was increased to $4,000.[6] William Prescott, continuing as president until his resignation early in 1843, served as chairman of a committee to revise the bylaws.[7] Slightly modified and recodified, they were not again changed until the late 1880's. In 1838 the company bought its first building, a building formerly owned by the Boston Marine Insurance Company and located where the company still has its home (50 State Street).[8]

Steps were taken to re-examine existing mortgages and to establish firmer controls over the company's mortgages. Virtually all loans were written on a "demand" basis, though with a clear understanding as to their probable duration. In 1839 the amendment to the statute of incorporation, previously described, was secured from the legislature.[9] But the basic outlook of the company under Tilden remained the same as under Dr. Bowditch. In resigning in February, 1845, Tilden wrote: [10]

> The moral influence of the institution has ever been before me, believing as I do that the faithful care of property belonging to others contributes to the independency and self-respect so important to a community. Most of the property now deposited has gone through the Probate Courts, or was the earnings of persons unused to making investments for future support. In the midst of cares and responsibilities which more or less must be incident to the duties of an Actuary, there will always be great support to him in a faith that the institution was established for protection.

Tilden's successor, Francis C. Lowell, actuary from 1845 to 1854, was the most distinguished in lineage of all the actuaries and also the youngest. At the time he became actuary Lowell was 42 years old. He was the son of Francis Cabot Lowell, founder at Waltham of the first successful textile mill of the Boston Associates, nephew of John Lowell, and cousin of John Amory Lowell. Lowell possessed a comfortable inheritance, which grew under his care. Starting out as a merchant in partnership with his cousin, John Lowell Gardner (subsequently a president of the Massachusetts Hospital Life Insurance Company), Lowell also early turned to the textile industry. In 1825, at the founding of the Hamilton Company at Lowell, he became clerk, a position he held until 1829. Following the dissolution of his partnership with Gardner in 1836, he accepted the position of treasurer of the Merrimack Manufacturing Company, oldest of the textile companies established by the Boston Associates at Lowell. This position he held two years. Simultaneously, he was interested in the establishment of the Stark Mills and the Manchester Mills of Manchester, New Hampshire. In the first of these he was an incorporator and in both a substantial investor. In 1845 he was one of a group of investors who brought the Essex Company into being, the central company in the creation of the city of Lawrence and its various textile enterprises. Lowell also served as a director of the Columbian Bank and of the New England Mutual Life Insurance Company.[11]

Although, unlike Tilden, Francis C. Lowell had had no official connection with the Massachusetts Hospital Life Insurance Company before he became actuary, he was related to a number of its officers either in a personal or business capacity. His period as actuary through 1854 is notable for the sharp transition toward investment of the company's funds in the textile industry and the scant increase in the total funds available for investment. New trust deposits and new annuities on lives were less numerous than in earlier years, and the life insurance business was dwindling toward nothing. For a period of a year and a half, 1851 to 1852, Lowell was away on a European tour. J. Ingersoll Bowditch served as acting actuary. It is perhaps indicative of the routine into which the company's activities had fallen that Bowditch estimated he could take care of the major duties of the office in about two hours per day.[12]

Like Francis C. Lowell, Charles G. Loring had had no official connection with the company prior to becoming actuary, but, like Lowell also, he was well-known to the group who controlled the institution.[13] Although son of a distinguished merchant, he had followed the law and had become a leading lawyer in New England. He had begun his study of law in the office of Charles Jackson and Samuel Hubbard. The former, a justice of the Supreme Judicial Court and brother of Patrick Tracy Jackson and Dr. James Jackson, was a vice-president of the Massachusetts Hospital Life for 30 years dating from its founding, while Samuel Hubbard was the first solicitor and a director and vice-president for almost as long as Jackson. Thereafter Loring had been for a time law partner with Franklin Dexter, a son-in-law of William Prescott. Loring's second wife was a daughter of Justice Samuel Putnam, famed for his "prudent man" decision. Throughout his career Loring was distinguished for his brilliance at law and for his sincerity and his earnestness in fighting for causes in which he deeply believed. Before becoming actuary of the Massachusetts Hospital Life Insurance Company he had twice refused interim appointments to the United States Senate. He had also refused opportunities to become a member of the Supreme Judicial Court of Massachusetts. His career is the more remarkable because throughout it he had been burdened with ill health, having been virtually blind for several years and intermittently racked with rheumatism and neuralgia.

Charles Loring had passed his sixtieth birthday before he became actuary. His friends considered his appointment as mutually desirable both to the company and to himself, for they believed that the company would benefit from his earnestness and from his familiarity with the principles and practices of trusts and that he would benefit from work less taxing in nature than his former career at law. Having only civic interests apart from his position with the company, like Bowditch he labored diligently in the company's cause. Loring had the satisfaction of watching the company grow again fairly rapidly for the first time since the days of Bowditch and of viewing the results of the company's fortunate investment policy during the Civil War. Loring also shared Bowditch's view of the company and of the actuary's role, for as William Amory aptly observed in a eulogy after his death, Loring regarded it "very properly as an Eleemosynary Institution, and himself as the guardian and friend of every depositor. . . ." [14]

Like Loring, his successor, George T. Bigelow, came to the company from the field of law. In fact, part of his legal education had been gained under Charles G. Loring. Following several terms in the state legislature, Bigelow became a judge of the Court of Common Pleas, then a justice of the Supreme Judicial Court of Massachusetts and, in 1860, Chief Justice. From the last position he resigned at the end of the year 1867 to become, at the age of 57, actuary of the Massachusetts Hospital Life Insurance Company. Like Loring, he accepted the actuaryship in part because of ill health, for he had left the court on account of attacks of the gout and increasing deafness. Said his memorialist, George B. Chase, "He accepted this position of dignity, responsibility, and ease, and held it till his last illness." [15] After seeing the company through the panic of 1873, he resigned at the end of March, 1878.

Distinguished though these men were, each of them came to the position of actuary from other interests. Each of them, with the exception of Francis Lowell, came into office quite late in life. In their rather brief periods of tenure they either retained other interests (Tilden and Lowell) or suffered in some degree from ill health

(Loring and Bigelow). The result, accentuated by their view of the company as a passive institution working well enough in the mold set by the founders, was to make for weak executive leadership.

In this situation the Committee of Finance became relatively more important. This was true partly because of the character of the men who served on the committee and partly because of their long periods of service. These men thus helped to give a continuity to company management which the actuaries could not have given. Their names and periods of tenure appear in Table 5.

With the exception of Bowditch, these men had started their careers as merchants and in greater or less degree had become interested in the textile industry. Because of their interests, with the possible exceptions of Austin and Bowditch, all may be properly

TABLE 5

Membership of the Committee of Finance in the Period 1838–1878

YEAR	COMMITTEEMAN	COMMITTEEMAN	COMMITTEEMAN
1838	Daniel Parker (since 1831)	Nathan Appleton	Abbott Lawrence
1842	William Sturgis	Nathan Appleton	Abbott Lawrence
1850	William Sturgis	Nathan Appleton	Ebenezer Chadwick
1855	William Sturgis	Nathan Appleton	J. Ingersoll Bowditch [a]
1861	William Sturgis	Edward Austin	J. Ingersoll Bowditch
1863	Ignatius Sargent	Edward Austin	J. Ingersoll Bowditch
1878	Ignatius Sargent	Edward Austin (until 1880)	J. Ingersoll Bowditch (until 1881)

[a] Abbott Lawrence returned to serve for a brief period in 1855, before the election of J. Ingersoll Bowditch.

listed as Boston Associates. The whole group was interlinked by business ventures outside the Massachusetts Hospital Life Insurance Company.[16]

Daniel P. Parker, the oldest member of the group, had been a partner in an importing firm with the brothers Nathan and Ebenezer Appleton before the War of 1812. In 1818 he had joined with Nathan Appleton and others in founding the Suffolk Bank. Though never a large investor in textiles, Parker had been among those who founded the Appleton Company in Lowell in 1828.

Nathan Appleton, who served longer on the Committee of Finance than any other during this period except for J. Ingersoll Bowditch, ranked with Abbott Lawrence in importance in the New England textile industry.[17] He was an investor in the original mill of the Boston Manufacturing Company at Waltham, and it was his firm, B. C. Wark & Company, that pioneered as the mill's selling agent for the Waltham mill. The pattern thus set became characteristic for nearly all the mills of the Boston Associates. Until 1851, Nathan Appleton was a partner in J. W. Paige & Company, selling agents for a number of important mills. He was also an investor and frequently a director or officer in a series of mills important in New England textile towns, including the Boston Manufacturing Company of Waltham; Locks & Canals, Merrimack Manufacturing Company, Hamilton Company, Appleton Company, Boott Cotton Mills, and Prescott Manufacturing Company of Lowell; the Cabot Manufacturing Company of Chicopee; the Amoskeag Company, Stark Mills, and Manchester Mills of Manchester, New Hampshire; and the Essex Company of Lawrence. Appleton achieved national fame for his advocacy of sound money. In addition to being a founder of the Suffolk Bank, he was also a director of the Boston Bank and of the American Insurance Company.

Abbott Lawrence succeeded his elder brother, Amos, as a member of the Committee of Finance.[18] Like Nathan Appleton, he possessed an ample personal fortune. This fortune grew partly from the mercantile firm of the two Lawrence brothers, A. & A. Lawrence & Company which became the largest textile agency in New England. And it grew partly from investments in textile companies, for after their initial venture in the Tremont Mills of Lowell in 1830, the Lawrence brothers (especially Abbott) became large-scale holders of textile securities. Abbott was a stockholder in the Tremont, Suffolk, Boott, Lawrence, Massachusetts, and Lowell companies of Lowell, and in the Essex Company, the Atlantic Cotton Mills, and the Pacific Mills of Lawrence. In addition, he was a founder of the Suffolk Bank, a director of the Merchants Insurance Company, and a promoter and investor in the Western and the Boston & Providence railroads.

When Lawrence went to London in 1850 as American minister to the Court of St. James's, he was succeeded on the Committee of

Finance by Ebenezer Chadwick. Like Nathan Appleton and Abbott Lawrence, Chadwick was intimately connected with the Boston Associates, though in lesser degree. In 1839 he succeeded Francis C. Lowell as treasurer of the Merrimack Manufacturing Company, a post he held for the next 15 years. Chadwick was an important investor in the Hamilton and Middlesex companies and the Atlantic Cotton Mills. He served as a director of the Boston & Lowell Railroad, the Merchants Insurance Company, and the Suffolk Bank.

William Sturgis was another prominent mercantile capitalist who turned from the sea lanes to the New England textile industry. Although his firm Bryant & Sturgis was active in the East India trade as late as 1840, Sturgis had been investing substantial sums in the textile industry ever since the establishment of the Hamilton Company in 1825. In time he became an investor in the Hamilton, Appleton, Lowell, and Prescott companies of Lowell, the Perkins Mills and Dwight Manufacturing Company of Chicopee, a director of the Boston & Lowell, Boston & Worcester, Eastern, and Boston & Providence railroads, and an incorporator of the Essex Company. Sturgis was also a pioneer private trustee, investing funds for friends and associates, as well as lending his experience to the Massachusetts Hospital Life Insurance Company.

Ignatius Sargent began his independent career as a merchant partner with Peter C. Brooks, Jr., but soon switched his interests to the textile field.[19] He concentrated in the Chicopee-Holyoke area along the Connecticut River, where he was a major investor in the Hadley Falls Company, the company which developed Holyoke as a textile center. Sargent served as director of the Cabot Manufacturing Company, Chicopee Manufacturing Company, and Perkins Mills, and as president of the Dwight Manufacturing Company. He was also president of the Hamilton and Lawrence companies and a director of the Middlesex Company, president of the Globe Bank, a director of the Boston Insurance Company, and a director of the Western, Boston & Albany, Boston & Providence, Hartford & New Haven, New Haven & Northampton, and Connecticut River railroads.

J. Ingersoll Bowditch and Edward Austin had somewhat more modest business careers. The former was president of the American Insurance Company from 1836 to 1864 and continued as director until his death 20 years later. He was also an important early private trustee. Edward Austin was from a Boston mercantile family. He succeeded his father, Samuel Austin, as a director of the Massachusetts Hospital Life Insurance Company in 1859. His major interests, apart from his mercantile business, included directorships in the Suffolk Bank, the American Insurance Company, and the Western Railroad.

Presidents of the company during the period after the resignation of William Prescott in 1843, included Peter C. Brooks, 1843–1848; Nathan Appleton, 1849–1861; George W. Lyman, 1862–1871; and Peter C. Brooks, Jr., 1871–1879. Three of the four had been elected to the presidential office from vice-presidencies, while Appleton had been a director since the founding of the company.

Peter C. Brooks retired from the marine insurance business in 1803 with a substantial fortune and never invested in great degree in the new industrial enterprises.[20] George W. Lyman, of a prominent mercantile family, turned to textiles as early as 1825 when he became an investor in the Hamilton Company. In the course of the next half-century he probably was an officer of more New England textile mills than any other man, even John A. Lowell. Lyman's associations as investor and frequently director and officer included the Merrimack, Hamilton, Appleton, Suffolk, Boott, and Lowell companies of Lowell; the Hadley Falls, Chicopee, Cabot, Lyman, and Perkins Mills of the Chicopee-Holyoke area; the Essex Company and Pacific Mills of Lawrence; the Lancaster Mills of Clinton; and the Stark Mills of Manchester, New Hampshire. Peter C. Brooks, Jr., like his father, had little interest in the textile industry. A merchant in his early years, he subsequently took little part in business affairs, although he was a director of the Chicopee Manufacturing Company and the Massachusetts Mutual Fire Insurance Company.

Such a concentration of talent was certainly at least equal to that at any other period in the company's history. Consequently, it is not surprising that the company was well and conservatively managed throughout this period. In only six years (1845–1851) of this period were the returns to depositors in trust as little as 5 per cent. Thanks to the company's fortunate investment policy during the Civil War, these returns were 6 per cent or better for a dozen years after 1864. Stockholders and the Massachusetts General Hospital found themselves similarly favored. After 1838 the stockholders regularly received $8.00 per share, plus, at each five-year interval, an extra dividend, usually $6.00 but on occasion $8.00 or $10.00 per share. In 1866 and 1867, the rate was $12.00 per share and then consistently $10.00 per share into the 1880's, plus an extra dividend in 1876 of $6.00 per share.

Although these figures indicate a very satisfactory internal condition, externally the company was beginning to lose that pre-eminence among financial institutions it had so rapidly acquired under Dr. Bowditch. Commercial banks, for example, grew much more rapidly in resources during this period than did the Massachusetts Hospital Life. In 1838 the company had resources equal to one-sixth of the resources of the 32 banks in Boston. Twenty-five years later this ratio was one-eleventh, and it continued to decline.[21] As the banks began to lend for longer periods of time, they offered increasing competition to the Massachusetts Hospital Life, especially in collateral loans.

Savings banks likewise showed a more rapid increase in resources than did the Massachusetts Hospital Life. In 1836 the resources of the company had been half again as large as those of all 28 savings banks in the state. Thirty years later, owing to the increase in the number of savings banks and the increase in size of the maximum deposit, the resources of savings banks were approximately six times those of the Massachusetts Hospital Life. One of them, the Provident Institution for Savings, in 1865 had deposits of $8,061,000. By 1880, with deposits of $21,559,000, it had greater resources than the Massachusetts Hospital Life.[22] As the savings banks grew and their maximum permissible deposit increased in amount (to $3,000 following the close of the Civil War), they began to offer the Massachusetts Hospital Life a competition for smaller trust deposits which in other circumstances might have come to the company. A major factor in this competition was the relatively lenient withdrawal provisions of the savings banks in contrast to the minimal five-year term prescribed by the Massachusetts Hospital Life. As the savings banks grew, the company experienced greater competition in the lending of funds to textile companies and in the placing of mortgages.

Even in the trust field, the company was beginning to be challenged. In 1869 the New England Trust Company was chartered. By the middle 1870's the Boston Safe Deposit & Trust Company and the Massachusetts Loan & Trust Company were also bidding for business. As the New England Trust Company began operation in 1871, it advertised a wide range of activities characteristic of the modern trust company. These included receiving and holding "moneys and property in trust and on deposit from courts of law or equity, . . . executors, administrators, assignees, guardians, trustees, corporations, or individuals. . . ." It also advertised that it would "act as agent for the purpose of issuing, registering, or countersigning the certificates of stock, bonds, or other evidences of debt, and for the payment of dividends of and interest of any corporation, association, municipality, State, or public authority, and also act as agent or attorney for the care and management of invested property and transact all other business usually done by Trust Companies." Deposits on a demand basis were accepted, and interest was paid on the daily balances.[23] The other two companies advertised approximately the same pattern of services.[24]

From the beginning of their existence these companies were competitors of the Massachusetts Hospital Life. In the endeavor to attract trust deposits from individuals they offered somewhat better and more flexible terms. The fee for management charged by both the New England Trust and the Boston Safe Deposit & Trust companies was only 5 per cent of the gross income per year. If the return to the depositor was 5 per cent upon his capital, this charge was equivalent to 1/4 of 1 per cent per year as opposed to the 1/2 of 1 per cent charged by the Massachusetts Hospital Life. Their trust contracts, like those of the Massachusetts Hospital Life, provided that trust funds invested in the common fund would be paid the depositor either in a proportionate share of the investments of the fund or in money equivalent to that proportionate share, at the option of the directors. A depositor could also specify that his trust funds be invested individually, however. In the latter case the depositor would receive the investments made with his funds at the time of the termination of the contract. The time periods of deposit for trust funds required by these companies were also somewhat more flexible. In addition, these companies included a range of corporate trust services which were beyond the interest of the Massachusetts Hospital Life.[25]

Apparently, the Massachusetts Hospital Life was unconcerned.

These companies were not of its type, for they were aggressive, profit-seeking institutions without any charitable orientation. In fact, no sharp area of conflict seems to have been foreseen. The first president of the New England Trust Company was Amos A. Lawrence, a son of Amos Lawrence and son-in-law of William Appleton. He was himself a stockholder in the Massachusetts Hospital Life. The majority of his 15-member Board of Directors were also either stockholders or were members of families in which there were stockholders. The relationship with the Boston Safe Deposit & Trust Company was not so close, but at least one of the directors, Richard S. Fay, was a stockholder of the Massachusetts Hospital Life. Several other directors were members of families in which there were stockholders, and one vice-president, Samuel C. Cobb, was shortly to succeed George T. Bigelow as actuary. The relationship of the New England Trust Company to the Massachusetts Hospital Life is indicated in another way; its chief executive officer was called "Actuary," even though the New England Trust Company did no insurance business. It is also interesting to note that, in language closely paralleling the Massachusetts Hospital Life rule for the disposition of shares, each of these companies required stockholders, selling their shares, to offer them first to their boards of directors.[26] Though small in their early years, these companies in time were to surpass the Massachusetts Hospital Life in size. Their aggressiveness and their larger range of activities were important factors in this achievement.

In another phase of its business, life insurance, the Massachusetts Hospital Life lost out to more specialized institutions, the mutual life insurance companies, during this period. The business of life annuities was maintained, but it continued to be of minor importance.

Trust Deposits, Life Insurance, and Annuities

Deposits in trust under the four successors of Dr. Bowditch grew from $5,690,462 at the end of 1838 to $14,403,066 at the end of 1877. The bulk of this increase came during and after the Civil War, for in 1860 these deposits amounted to $8,338,226. The increase in amount of funds was not paralleled by any such substantial increase in the number of deposit contracts, for the 1,341 deposits at the end of 1838 had grown to only 1,486 in 1860 and to 1,617 at the end of 1877.[27] The size of the average deposit increased from about $4,250 in 1838 to $5,600 in 1860 and to $9,000 in 1877. This increase in size suggests the greater proportion of "strict male" and "strict female" forms of contract – normally representing larger deposits – in the total number. It also indicates that the Massachusetts Hospital Life was not receiving as many small deposits, proportionately, as in the earlier period.

Deposit contracts were written under the same five forms, with the "G" (five-year term) contract continuing to dominate. The rule was maintained that contracts would be written only with some person clearly designated as the ultimate recipient of the funds, for the company refused to be troubled by such matters as determining eligible heirs or performing services beyond the actual care of funds.[28] Nor in normal circumstances would it accept funds from individuals residing outside Massachusetts.[29] Since it was more difficult to place money at interest following the panic of 1837, the term before new deposits were permitted to draw interest was increased to four months.[30] This waiting period was maintained even after the Civil War.

There had been also little change in the basic attitude with which the Hospital Life received and judged its deposits. The company was ready and willing to accept deposits for society's dependents, for charitable, educational, and civic organizations, and for those exceptionally innocent in matters of business, but it viewed with disfavor funds from any other source. Loring expressed the company's attitude when he wrote on one occasion: "While the company refuses to receive deposits from living persons competent to manage property, it has always felt bound to take those bequeathed." [31] Actually the barrier was not always quite so high.

After the panic of 1857 a determined effort was made again to reduce the volume of new deposits, especially from individuals who were competent to manage their own funds. At the end of 1858 the Board of Control appointed a special committee to make an analysis of the deposits. Three founders of the company, William Sturgis, William Appleton, and David Sears, the actuary, Charles G. Loring, and George Ticknor, who over a 30-year span had served first as a director and later as a vice-president, comprised the committee. It reported a total of $8,554,416 held in trust under the seven categories shown in Table 6.[32]

TABLE 6

Amounts Held in Trust at the End of 1858

Trust for minors	$ 190,000
Strict trust for females for life "SF"	1,901,000
Strict trust for males for life "SM"	1,550,000
Deposited by trustees under wills, principally for females	2,891,000
Charitable institutions, etc.	582,000
Clergymen, military and naval officers	130,000
Individuals for themselves	1,309,416
Total	$8,553,416

The seventh category of deposits – made by individuals for themselves – the committeemen felt should be watched. They held this attitude not because they believed it was beyond the ability of the company to take care of more funds, but because their New England Puritan heritage put an emphasis on individual responsibility. They did not wish their institution to serve individuals who ought to be able to serve themselves. Consequently, at their request the board voted, "That the Finance Committee and the Actuary be invested with discretionary power to accept or decline deposits under general rules or by especial action in the case presented, as they shall think proper. . . ." [33]

In 1866 George Peabody, the distinguished American international banker, very seriously considered placing $1,500,000 in trust with the Massachusetts Hospital Life for some 20 people. He finally decided not to do so, principally because the maximum legal interest rate of 6 per cent in Massachusetts offered too low a return in comparison with rates elsewhere. Peabody's decision was used by Loring the next year in getting the Massachusetts legislature to raise the legal rate to 7 per cent on the ground that money was being lost to New York where the legal rate was higher. While Loring would obviously have liked the banker's trust funds, he replied to Peabody, "Our deposits are already so large that we have no desire to increase them, tho' not feeling authorized to decline any proposal within the rules of the Institution." [34]

The first important stimuli to consideration of changes in the terms of the deposit contracts came from the abnormal business conditions existing during the Civil War and after the panic of 1873. A result of the war was to channel the bulk of Massachusetts Hospital Life funds into United States government bonds. As interest on these bonds was high in rate and payable in gold, such investment proved very profitable. This was particularly true after gold sold at a premium owing to the greenback paper money issues. In the resulting inflation, the market price of government and certain other securities held by the company climbed above par, and the company's fixed investment in its office building, carried on its books at the prewar figure of $90,000, was greatly undervalued.

In this situation a depositor for the first time requested that his deposit be paid off in a pro rata share of the company's investments, for he claimed that the interest paid upon the principal of his deposit had been less than his fair share of the income and appreciation on the investments. There would certainly seem to have been a basis for discussion of the claim because of the description of the methods of payment contained in the *Proposals* and printed at the bottom of the deposit contract, but Loring refused to consider the request. He held that it was almost impossible to figure accurately capital gains which had been unrealized: "In the vast amount of property we hold . . . a precise valuation of every item would be impracticable; and the mode adopted is to estimate them at the prices paid for them." He also argued that no unreasonable amount of earnings was being withheld from depositors. "The whole principle upon which the Institution is based and has been administered is that of investment and division of the whole income as nearly as possible. Accumulation of principal on the deposits forms no part of the plan of operations; and when an excess remains of income after payment of the utmost which is considered safe, it is considered a reserved fund to constitute a guarantee to keep the assets whole." [35]

Because of this dispute, which took place early in 1864, and the continuing rapid accumulation of income in the reserved fund as a result of sales of gold interest payments at a premium, Loring made two recommendations to the Board of Directors in May, 1865. The first was that an extra dividend of 15 per cent on the stock and an additional 3½ per cent on deposits which had been with the company during the year 1864 be paid from the reserved fund. Fearing further disputes in paying off depositors, he also recommended that the board consider eliminating from future contracts the provision calling for payment of the deposit as a proportionate share of the total assets at the time the payment was made.[36] The effect of this proposal, had it been adopted, would have been to increase the similarity between the company and a savings bank and to minimize the similarity which had existed, on paper at least, to the modern investment company.

The committee appointed to consider these proposals recommended an extra dividend of 10 per cent for stockholders and a retroactive 2¾ per cent on deposits held by the company during 1864, payable as of January 1, 1866. Its recommendations were accepted by the board. Similar, though smaller, payments from the reserved fund were made into the middle 1870's – so long as the company held bonds providing for payment of interest in gold and so long as gold was at a premium.

On the second proposal the committee took no action. The committee obviously differed with Loring. They expressed their opposition to any change which would "deprive the policyholder [depositor] of a legal claim to a full share in the common property." They pointed out that the option remained with the directors, "absolutely, finally, whether the division shall be made in kind or in money." Nor did they think that valuation of the investments posed an insuperable problem. They pointed out that the statement in the *Proposals* indicated the use of "market value" as the basis of valuation and that "substantial justice" rather than "mathematical accuracy" was indicated in determining the amount to be paid a depositor, which might be the exact amount of his principal on deposit or more or less than his principal.

Although the question was not then at issue, the committee further considered whether a depositor withdrawing his funds at that time deserved an additional payment beyond his principal and accrued interest. This question the committee decided in the negative. They recognized that the United States government securities held by the company bearing interest at 6 and 7.3 per cent, payable in gold, were worth considerably more than the figure at which they were carried on the books, but they also expressed the belief that the company's notes and mortgages bearing only 6 per cent interest and not payable in gold were correspondingly worth less.[37]

The effect of this decision was to preserve intact the contract established by the founders in which, theoretically, principal as well as interest could vary up and down, even though in no case to that time had either more or less than the principal and accrued interest been paid a depositor. Perhaps the committee felt that the unusual situation in which so much of the company funds was invested in government bonds would soon pass and that nearly all the funds would again be invested in mortgages and notes, on which capital appreciation was not possible. In such a situation the question of an increment to principal would be academic. Yet the directors would continue to have a way of sharing losses, which Loring claimed was the original basis for the inclusion of the provision in the contract. The phraseology of this distinctive feature in the company's deposit contracts, foreshadowing the modern investment company, was thus maintained.[38]

The other and less important stimulus to change in the terms of the deposit contracts was the stringency just prior to and during the panic of 1873. In this panic a number of individuals for whom the company held trusts, including a son of Nathan Appleton, went bankrupt. As a means of protecting trust funds from creditors, first in the "strict male" contracts and subsequently in other forms, the company adopted an elaborate but optional provision designed to protect the deposit, both as to principal and interest, from claims of creditors. Under this provision the beneficiary of the trust deposit could designate his child or children or some other person to be the subsequent recipient of the interest on the deposit and, in time, of the deposit itself.[39]

As in the earlier period, the company's trust deposits during the mid-nineteenth century showed a high stability and, in general, they were made by individuals whom the company desired to serve. An analysis of 178 "G" deposits – presumably the most volatile – made during 1858 and 1859 indicates that the average deposit was with the company for a term of almost 20 years.[40] In about 10 per cent of these cases, interest on the deposit was permitted to accumulate with the company as new capital. Of the 304 "G" deposits made between 1856 and 1859, more than one-third (105) were made by widows and single women and an additional 16 by or for wives. Sixty-four deposits were made by trustees, 34 by guardians, 29 by charitable and civic organizations, eight by ministers, and one by a military officer. Of the 47 other deposits made by males, some may have been in the names of minors or for the benefit of a second party not named. Slightly over half of these deposits (154) were made from Boston. Approximately 10 per cent were from out of state, but nearly all were from New England. The balance were from eastern Massachusetts. The North Shore was no longer so important a source of funds as it had been in the days of Dr. Bowditch.

The old family names and institutions still continue among the depositors, with a startling exception here and there. One deposit of $500, placed in 1857, was by a Mary Ann Rooney. When this deposit was withdrawn in December, 1909, it had accumulated to $5,553.[41] Institutional depositors included, among others, the Massachusetts Society for Promoting Agriculture, the Widows and Orphans Fund of Trinity Church, the Widows Society of Boston, and Mt. Auburn Cemetery. An unusual series of deposits were those of $18,300 deposited annually between 1856 and 1872 by J. Thomas Stevenson, Trustee of the Sinking Fund of the Boston & Lowell Railroad. These deposits undoubtedly occurred because, to a considerable extent, the officers and directors were the same for both the railroad and the company. But this departure which might have served as the basis for the company's gradual entrance into a new, large, and lucrative field of trust activity stands alone.

The "strict female"[42] and "strict male" trusts show in even greater degree than the "G" deposits the presence of money from the old families. One especially interesting trust of $37,000 was established in March, 1846, for Daniel Webster by David Sears, William Amory, and Ignatius Sargent. The deposit contract was written so that on the death of Webster the money reverted to the donors. In the meantime Webster received an annual payment of nearly $2,000 per year from this distinguished trio in industry and finance.[43]

In comparison with the trust business, life annuities were a minor source of funds, and life insurance in time provided almost nothing. The cause for the decline in life insurance was the competition of the mutual companies and the inability or lack of desire on the part of the Massachusetts Hospital Life to match their aggressiveness.[44]

The oldest of these companies, the New England Mutual Life Insurance Company, had been chartered in 1835. It did not commence business, however, until December, 1843, for it feared the effect on its operation of the profit-sharing provision with the Massachusetts General Hospital in its charter.[45] Since it was a mutual and not a stock company, it did not know how "profits" would be construed. It feared an interpretation jeopardizing the reserve fund it would need to establish to fulfill its contracts as they became payable in larger numbers in later years.[46] With the resolution of this difficulty, the New England Mutual began its illustrious career in insurance. As it began operation, it also found another competitor in the field, the Mutual Life Insurance Company of New York, which had issued its first policies in February, 1843.

The mutual companies were distinguished not so much by more favorable terms in their policies as by their lower rates and their more aggressive spirit. The New England Mutual policy was more favorable than that of the Massachusetts Hospital Life in permitting its policyholders to travel on the Great Lakes and to be in the South between the months of October and May. If the policyholder lived south of the southern borders of Kentucky and Virginia for more than a month between May and October without the consent of the company, the policy was void. In rates, the contrast was much more marked. According to the tables of premiums in force during 1843 and 1844, those of the New England Mutual tended to be lower than those of its New York rival, but, except for rates for people close to 60 years of age, both mutual companies had rates considerably lower than those of the Massachusetts Hospital Life. In some cases the disparity was as great as 30 per cent. There was also the prospect of a dividend for the policyholder of a mutual company. Moreover, these companies used agents selling on commission and in their sales literature stressed vigorously the arguments why individuals ought to be insured.[47]

In these circumstances it is not surprising that the insurance business of the Massachusetts Hospital Life fell away rapidly. In 1843, its peak year, the company placed 62 policies and had $344,780 of insurance in force; the next year the number of new policies had declined to 26, and the amount of insurance in force fell off one-third. By contrast, during its first year the Mutual Life Insurance Company of New York sold 470 policies, placing at risk $1,640,718.[48]

Sooner or later all four of the important early stock life insurance companies – the Pennsylvania Company for Insurance on Lives and Granting Annuities, the Massachusetts Hospital Life, the New York Life & Trust, and the Girard Life Insurance, Annuity & Trust Company – were forced from the life insurance field. The first to go was the New York Life & Trust in 1865, the last the Girard company in 1878. The Massachusetts Hospital Life sold its last life insurance policy in 1867.[49] These companies fell before a combination of rate competition, profit-sharing with the policyholders, and the aggressive use of agents in soliciting business as practiced by the mutuals. None could match the mutuals on all three points, though all made some effort to stay in the field.

In 1844, probably through Abbott Lawrence, the Massachusetts Hospital Life sought the assistance of Elizur Wright. This able mathematician and antislavery leader, after having insured his life with the New England Mutual Life Insurance Company, was about to embark for England to try to free himself from debt incurred in translating and printing an edition of La Fontaine's *Fables.* He hoped to sell his remaining copies in England. The Massachusetts Hospital Life gave him a collateral assignment to interview Joshua Milne, head of the Sun Life & Fire Office in London, and others, in the endeavor to establish a more satisfactory rate structure. Although a result of the trip was to make Elizur Wright aware of serious abuses in the field of life insurance and eventually to open a career for him in life insurance reform, the information with which he returned proved of little help to the Massachusetts Hospital Life in meeting the competition of the mutuals.[50]

Late in 1845 the company adjusted and reduced its rates on the basis of the experience of 17 of the English companies. These reductions were made principally for ages 40 and lower, where the rates were most out of line with the mutuals, but the company sought to maintain a 20 per cent spread above expected risk. The result was that the rates of the Massachusetts Hospital Life continued to be higher than those of any other company. Said a committee of the directors in November, 1845, "This business the committee think is not likely to be very considerable for the future – should it become large, however, it must be safe, and the larger the more safe, if well conducted." [51] Aside from a further reduction in 1855,[52] no other effort was made to combat the mutuals. The idea of mutualizing the insurance business of the Massachusetts Hospital Life was broached to Joseph Tilden by Hyman Gratz, president of the Pennsylvania Company, whose company did inaugurate a scheme of profit-sharing with its policyholders.[53] But the company refused to consider such a drastic adjustment; neither is there any evidence that it gave thought to the use of agents to solicit business.[54]

Between 1831 and 1840 the Hospital Life had issued 531 policies; between 1841 and 1850, 291 policies; between 1851 and 1860, 65 policies; and after 1860, one policy. Thus the second American company to enter the life insurance field, for lack of resolute action, removed itself from competition after the middle 1840's. When one considers the company's basic orientation, its ineffectual reaction to the new competition is understandable, but thereby it forsook a field of enormous potentiality virtually without a struggle. It is of some interest that among the 11 directors of the New England Mutual Life in the middle 1840's were Francis C. Lowell, actuary of the Massachusetts Hospital Life, George H. Kuhn, a director, Robert Hooper, later a vice-president, Charles P. Curtis, and George Howe. They helped shape an aggressive institution in association with Willard Phillips, president of the New England Mutual Life, but they sought no similar goal in the Massachusetts Hospital Life, in which they were all stockholders.

In the life annuity field, the Massachusetts Hospital Life was not faced with such intense competition, yet throughout this period its life annuity business was of minor importance. This business increased at about the same rate as the trust deposit business. In 1838 the company had 60 life annuities in force and in 1877 the number was 85.[55] Like the individual trust deposit, the size of the average life annuity increased, especially after the Civil War. Of the 41 life annuity contracts written between 1875 and 1877, 13 were for annual payments of at least $400, the maximum annual payment required on any annunity in force in 1830. The two largest were for $1,000 each. More life annuities were written for women than for men, though the disproportion was not quite so great as in the earlier period. The average age of the annuitant at the time of the writing of the contract continued high, being about 70. The names of important Massachusetts families were no longer readily apparent on the lists of annuitants, although in a number of instances individuals important in business and financial circles were purchasing annuities, perhaps for aged servants.[56]

But though the life annuity business continued small and the insurance business rapidly diminished, they were normally conducted at a profit. Life annuities, which had been the unprofitable part of the company's business prior to 1838, were still subject to violent fluctuations in profit and loss, owing to the small number of annuitants. Yet in all but 11 of the 40 years this branch of business showed a profit. In 1845, influenced by Elizur Wright's interview with John Finlaison, actuary of the National Debt of Great Britain, the company made an attempt to put life annuities on a more sound actuarial basis. In line with Finlaison's research proving that female annuitants tended to live longer than male annuitants, the company adopted separate tables for men and for women in contrast to the former single table.[57] The profits realized from life annuities and insurance during these 40 years amounted to approximately $111,000 for annuities and to $88,000 for insurance.[58]

Investment Policy

Since in resources the Massachusetts Hospital Life continued to be, until almost the end of the period 1838–1878, the largest financial institution in Massachusetts,[59] the company is of interest for what it did with its relatively large pool of capital. Possessed of remarkably stable deposits, its liquidity needs were light. It therefore was in an excellent position to make loans running for a year or longer. The same three categories of investment – mortgages, collateral loans, and security ownership – continued to exist for the company. At various times each looked most attractive. The lending powers granted in 1839 sharply influenced the development of the company's investment pattern during these years. In some degree the investment pattern was influenced by the grant made also in 1839 permitting the company to own Massachusetts railroad and municipal securities, in addition to Massachusetts and federal securities and stock of banks chartered in Massachusetts.

As in the Bowditch era, mortgages were the most important type of investment for the funds of the company. In the early 1840's approximately 70 per cent of the company's total investment was in mortgages. Thereafter this figure declined as the size of the company's investments increased elsewhere, especially in government bonds and in loans to textile companies. At the end of the Civil War the mortgage portfolio was but 30 per cent of the total, its minimum for the period. As the securities of the national government, in which the company had invested heavily, were either sold or called, the funds acquired again went mainly into mortgages. At the end of 1877 mortgages were once more about 70 per cent of the total investment.

But the location and size of the mortgages tended to change during these years. No longer was the company a heavy investor in western Massachusetts mortgages. By 1850 more than half the mortgages were in Suffolk County (Boston) where, in the words of one committee of examination, "the value . . . is generally known or easily ascertained by the Actuary and the Directors." [60] Of 176 mortgages on which interest was payable in June, 1850, 96 were located in Suffolk County. Thirty-three were in Franklin County and 24 in Berkshire County. Fewer than 10 were located in each of four other counties: Hampshire, Worcester, Hampden, and Middlesex. The mortgages in Boston averaged about $2,900 each; those outside about $600.[61]

This shift in location, which had begun as early as 1830, was accelerated after the panic of 1837 by the higher rate of default in mortgage interest payments both in western Massachusetts and in Boston. If mortgagors were to default, better that they be at the doorstep of the company than in more distant areas. According to the Solicitor's Book, about 4 per cent of all mortgages were in default in the eight years following the panic of 1837. This was about twice the rate for the five years previous to the panic. The resulting administrative burden prompted the board of directors to give the actuary greater independence in assigning to other parties mortgages on which interest was in arrears and in releasing mortgages on which satisfaction had been given.[62] The board also encouraged Joseph Tilden to institute a careful survey of all western mortgages in 1840. The survey was intended to provide a basis for weeding out the less desirable mortgages and for reducing the principal of larger mortgages which had been long outstanding.[63] A similar survey was proposed after the panic of 1857, and one was made of Berkshire County mortgages in 1865.[64]

When mortgages were granted in the western part of the state, the procedures established by Dr. Bowditch were followed. Applications continued to be funneled through agents, with all costs borne by the mortgagor. The mortgages were usually granted solely on land and for no more than one-quarter of its value. They were rarely made for an amount greater than $500 or for a term longer than one year.[65]

The shift in mortgages toward Boston became even more marked in the later 1840's, as the company's money flowed increasingly into the textile companies. Thereafter few mortgages were accepted outside the immediate Boston area. An analysis of the 67 mortgages on which interest was received in June, 1870, shows that 52 of these were in Boston. They averaged just under $13,000 in size. Of the other 15 mortgages, which averaged about $760, only one had been granted as late as 1845.[66]

Most mortgage loans were made to individuals and for purposes which undoubtedly included home or farm ownership and business needs or opportunities. A few prominent Bostonians may be recognized among the mortgagors, but these are not typical and are not so frequent as later in the nineteenth century. A few industrial mortgages were also made, especially after the 1857 debacle in the textile industry. In 1858 loans to the Hampden and Lyman mills of Holyoke and to the Middlesex Mills of Lowell were converted into mortgages. The amount of industrial mortgages was thus increased to $468,000, or about 10 per cent of the total in mortgages.[67] This amount was rapidly reduced, however, during the next few years.

Approximately 70 per cent of the company's funds were invested in mortgages in the early 1840's at a time when that medium of investment no longer looked so attractive. It seemed undesirable to put a larger proportion of funds into real estate loans. Business and personal loans had been the other great area for investment earlier, but in the years following the panic of 1837 there was intense competition for the smaller volume of these loans. Joseph G. Martin, historian of the Boston stock market, records that in June,

1843, Boston banks were discounting notes at 3 per cent, "an almost unheard of figure." Even then the banks could hardly keep their funds occupied.[68] In these circumstances the company embarked on a sustained program of ownership of securities. It turned to investment in the securities of the national government and of the Commonwealth of Massachusetts in the hope of maintaining earnings.

The impact of the panic of 1837 and the subsequent depression on the revenues of the national government had created new opportunities for investment in government securities. From 1838 to 1840 the company had purchased small quantities of Treasury notes through Abbott Lawrence,[69] but it did not make any large-scale purchases of bonds until the spring of 1843. At that time the company had three federal loans from which to choose: the Loan of 1841, of which $5,700,000 in bonds at 5½ per cent and 6 per cent redeemable on January 1, 1845, had been issued; the Loan of 1842, which had resulted in the sale of $8,300,000 in 20-year 6 per cent bonds; and the Loan of 1843, a funding issue of $7,000,000 in Treasury notes into 10-year bonds bearing interest at 5 per cent.[70]

While the company bought small quantities of both the 1841 and 1843 loans, it concentrated on bonds of the 6 per cent loan of 1842. Between June, 1843, and September, 1844, it acquired $1,374,000, or roughly one-sixth of this issue, in 40 different purchases. These purchases were made principally through the Boston brokerage houses of John E. Thayer & Brother, Dana & Henshaw, and Pelham W. Warren. Unfortunately, these purchases were not made at the time of issue, when the credit of the United States was temporarily at a low. Instead of buying these bonds when they were at par or slightly below, the company did not begin the purchases until June, 1843, when the bonds were selling at a premium of 13½ per cent. Subsequent purchases were made at prices ranging between 112½ and 116¼. At maximum, the investment of the company in the Loan of 1842 was $1,666,000.[71] Yield on the bonds ranged between 4.9 and 4.75 per cent, which, except for 1831, was less than the rate of interest the company had yet paid its depositors.

At about the same time – between April, 1843, and June, 1844 – the company purchased $631,000 in long-term Massachusetts 5 per cent dollar and sterling bonds at or slightly below par.[72] These bonds had been issued mainly to help finance railroad construction in the state.[73] The result of these activities was to boost the percentage of company funds invested in securities to approximately 33 per cent at the end of 1844 as against the earlier peak of approximately 10 per cent in 1835.

These bonds were entered on the books of the company at the price purchased, if purchased at par or below. Bonds purchased at a premium were recorded in either of two ways. In every case but one in 1843, bonds purchased at a premium were recorded at par, with the premium being charged to the interest account. Thereafter, bonds purchased at a premium were entered at the market price. Adjustments of 1 per cent downward were made by the Committee of Finance at the end of each year, and the difference was charged to the interest account. This latter pattern of adjustment seems to have been in rough conformity to the statement made by the company in its original *Proposals,* "If a premium be paid for bank or other stock (on account of the capital not being liable to reimbursement for a number of years) such premium must be deducted from the interest, in annual portions, so that at the time of the reimbursement of the capital, it may stand charged on the books of the company at par." [74]

As business revived in the years following 1844, the company gradually divested itself of most of its securities, principally through James G. King & Sons of New York, and made large sums available for loans, especially to the Massachusetts textile companies. In the case of the 6 per cent United States government bonds, this meant exchanging a security, bought at a premium and bearing 6 per cent interest until the end of 1862, for the note of a private company or private individual bearing 6 per cent interest for a shorter term. That such an exchange was in the best interest of the Massachusetts Hospital Life may well be questioned, especially since the bonds were selling at considerably less than the premium prices which the company had paid for them. In liquidating these bonds, the company lost about $104,000 in principal. Its losses were at a maximum when almost one-third of the total investment was sold in November, 1847. These sales were made in order to help cover $500,000 in loans in the same month to five major companies in the textile field.[75] The Essex Company, Lawrence Manufacturing Company, and Tremont Mills — linked closely to Abbott Lawrence — received loans totaling $350,000. The other two, the Hamilton and Appleton companies, were companies in which Nathan Appleton had a strong stock interest.[76] During the next six weeks these United States government bonds dipped sharply from 105½ to 97¾, but within seven months they were selling at 111 or above. By contrast, the company made a slight gain on the Massachusetts 5 per cent bonds, bought at par or slightly less, as these bonds were also gradually sold.

From 1844 until the outbreak of the Civil War the funds of the company were channelled in great degree into the Massachusetts textile industry, either on the notes of the companies directly or on pledged collateral of individuals active in that industry. At the beginning of these years the last mills were developed and expanded in Lowell. Expansion also occurred in the Holyoke-Chicopee area, but the period is chiefly marked by the boomlike development of Lawrence.[77] The Essex Company was chartered in 1845; during the next decade the great Atlantic, Bay State, Pacific, and Pemberton mills were also constructed. Funds of the Massachusetts Hospital Life were at work in all these textile centers, frequently in loans running for a term of several years. Of the 163 loans made in the five-year period from the first of the year 1845, 51 were to textile companies. In the next five-year period, 117 of 244 loans were made to textile companies, and between 1855 and 1860, 72 out of 136 loans.[78]

In the 11 years from the beginning of 1845 until the end of 1855, when loans were at a maximum, the amount of such loans increased from $311,000 to $3,927,000. This amount in 1855 was just short of 50 per cent of the total invested fund of the company. Two-thirds of this sum ($2,615,000) had been borrowed directly by companies in or associated with the textile industry. Their notes were endorsed by their selling agents, by the treasurers of the respective companies, or by one or more important stockholders. So close-knit were the Boston Associates that any classification of the companies overlaps, but nearly all the companies may be grouped around four great selling agencies, A. & A. Lawrence & Company, Lawrence, Stone & Company, Charles H. Mills & Company, and J. W. Paige & Company. The interests of Amos and Abbott Lawrence were most closely linked with the first and largest of these companies. Their younger brother, Samuel, was the most important partner in the second of these companies, and the interests of George W. Lyman were most closely associated with the third. Nathan Appleton was a partner in J. W. Paige & Company from its origin in 1828 until his resignation in 1851. Table 7 shows loans of the Massachusetts Hospital Life which were outstanding to textile companies at the end of the year 1855. When no firm is listed as guarantor, linkage to a group may be inferred from the individuals (listed in parentheses) who endorsed the notes of the respective companies.[79]

According to the Massachusetts census of 1855, capital invested in the cotton textile industry in that Commonwealth amounted to $31,961,000, and to $7,305,500 in the woolen textile industry. Capital of the above companies engaged in cotton textile manufacture amounted to $16,020,000 in 1855. If we include the Lowell Manufacturing Company as a woolen textile company, since it was manufacturing primarily woolen cloth and carpets by 1855, the percentage of the woolen textile industry borrowing from the Massachusetts Hospital Life is still higher, for the combined capitals of the Middlesex Company, Bay State Mills, and Lowell Manufacturing Company amounted to $4,800,000.[80] The capitals of the Essex Company and the Hadley Falls Company, which were the parent companies established for the development of Lawrence and Holyoke, respectively, are not included in the above totals, nor are the capitals of the Lowell Machine Shop, Lawrence Machine Shop, and Ames Manufacturing Company, which manufactured textile machinery. The mills of the Boston Associates were, in general, by far the largest textile mills in Massachusetts. It is also of interest that the mills associated with the Lawrence family tended to be the heaviest borrowers.

One should not make the assumption that these companies borrowed solely from the Massachusetts Hospital Life, however. An examination of several of these companies' financial records stored in Baker Library of Harvard University shows that their sources of funds also included private individuals, savings banks, other textile companies, the selling agent firms, and commercial banks.[81] Usually loans by the selling firms were for no more than six months, and loans by other textile companies and discounts by

TABLE 7

Outstanding Loans to Companies in or Associated with the Textile Industry, December 31, 1855

COMPANY	LOCATION	CAPITAL (000 *omitted*)	NO. OF LOANS	AMT. OF LOANS (000 *omitted*)	DATE OF EARLIEST OUTSTANDING LOANS	SELLING AGENT GROUP
Mass. Cotton Mills	Lowell	$1800	7	$300	Mar. '49	A. & A. Lawrence & Co.
Atlantic Cotton Mills	Lawrence	1800	1	200	Sept. '49	A. & A. Lawrence & Co.
Boott Cotton Mills	Lowell	1200	6	200	Jan. '49	A. & A. Lawrence & Co.
Lowell Mfg. Co	Lowell	2000	2	200	Jul. '49	A. & A. Lawrence & Co.
Middlesex Co.	Lowell	1000	6	195	Aug. '45	Lawrence, Stone & Co.
Tremont Mills	Lowell	600	3	150	Jun. '53	A. & A. Lawrence & Co.
Hadley Falls Co.	Holyoke	1470	5	145	Sept. '52	(George W. Lyman)
Bay State Mills	Lawrence	1800	3	130	Jan. '51	Lawrence, Stone & Co.
Essex Co.	Lawrence	1500	3	122	Feb. '53	(Abbott Lawrence, *et al.*)
Appleton Co.	Lowell	600	2	100	Aug. '53	J. W. Paige & Co.
Hamilton Co.	Lowell	1200	2	100	Jun. '53	J. W. Paige & Co.
Lawrence Machine Shop	Lawrence	900	2	100	Sept. '53	(Abbott Lawrence, *et al.*)
Lowell Machine Shop	Lowell	600	4	100	Jul. '54	(Abbott Lawrence, *et al.*)
Suffolk Mills	Lowell	600	2	100	Nov. '54	J. W. Paige & Co.
Lyman Mills	Holyoke	1470	2	90	Jul. '55	Charles H. Mills & Co.
Chicopee Mfg. Co.	Chicopee	700	2	70	Jun. '53	Charles H. Mills & Co.
Lancaster Mills	Clinton	900	3	70	Aug. '51	(G. W. Lyman, *et al.*)
Boston Mfg. Co.	Waltham	450	4	60	Apr. '54	J. W. Paige & Co.
Dwight Mfg. Co.	Chicopee	700	1	50	Apr. '54	Charles H. Mills & Co.
Perkins Mills	Chicopee	1000	1	50	Apr. '53	Charles H. Mills & Co.
Merrimack Mfg. Co.	Lowell	2500	1	48	Jun. '54	J. W. Paige & Co.
Pemberton Mills	Lawrence	500	1	20	Feb. '54	Lawrence, Stone & Co.
Ames Mfg. Co.	Springfield	250	1	15	Dec. '55	Charles H. Mills & Co.

commercial banks were for no more than three or four months. Savings banks and private individuals were direct competitors of the Massachusetts Hospital Life in making loans for a year or longer. The records of the Lawrence Manufacturing Company show that it was borrowing from the Provident Institution for Savings and the Suffolk Savings Bank, among others, in the middle 1850's, as well as from the Massachusetts Hospital Life. The Hamilton Manufacturing Company was also borrowing a small amount from the Salem Savings Bank. In 1846 the 38 savings banks in Massachusetts held total deposits of $10,681,000 in comparison with the $7,703,000 fund of the Massachusetts Hospital Life. A decade later there were 81 savings banks in Massachusetts with total deposits of $30,373,000, and the Massachusetts Hospital Life fund amounted to $7,978,000.[82] As savings bank deposits increased and commercial banks began to lend for longer terms, these institutions became keener competitors of the company in the textile loan field, but the Massachusetts Hospital Life probably continued to be the greatest single source of credit for the textile companies at least as late as the end of the nineteenth century. This was due to the continuing close relationship of many of its board members with the textile industry, as well as the terms under which the company would lend.

Funds borrowed by individuals during these years were very frequently secured by textile stocks pledged as collateral. There was a substantial coincidence between textile companies who were themselves major borrowers and textile companies whose stocks were held in considerable amounts by the Massachusetts Hospital Life as collateral for personal loans. Thus the Massachusetts Hospital Life, as of December 31, 1855, had outstanding in loans to the Massachusetts Cotton Mills and the Atlantic Cotton Mills sums equivalent to 16.7 per cent and 11.1 per cent of their capitals, respectively. As of May 2, 1856, the company also held 12.8 per cent of the stock of the former and 14.9 per cent of the stock of the latter company as security for loans made to individuals. Shares in textile companies held by the company as collateral in May, 1856, are shown in Table 8.[83] Individual borrowers who pledged collateral of a par value of $25,000 or more in return for Massachusetts Hospital Life loans are listed in Table 9. The relatively small group of families among the borrowers, and the especial significance of the Massachusetts Hospital Life to members of the Lawrence family are clearly indicated. In cases where more than $10,000 (par value) of the collateral was in the stock of a particular company, that company has been specified.[84]

TABLE 8

Stock of Companies in or Associated with the Textile Industry: Held as Collateral, May 2, 1856

COMPANY	LOCATION	CAPITALIZATION (000 *omitted*)	NO. OF SHARES (00 *omitted*)	MHL HELD	% HELD BY MHL
Atlantic Cotton Mills	Lawrence	$1800	18	268	14.9
Pemberton Mills	Lawrence	500	5	70	14.0
Mass. Cotton Mills	Lowell	1800	18	231	12.8
Suffolk Mills	Lowell	600	6	69	11.5
Dwight Mfg. Co.	Chicopee	700	7	78	11.1
Middlesex Co.	Lowell	1000	10	107	10.7
Tremont Mills	Lowell	600	6	54	9.0
Boott Cotton Mills	Lowell	1200	12	101	8.4
Lowell Mfg. Co.	Lowell	2000	29	230	7.9
Lowell Bleachery	Lowell	300	15	105	7.0
Bay State Mills	Lawrence	1800	18	119	6.6
Lawrence Mfg. Co.	Lowell	1500	15	96	6.4
Lowell Machine Shop	Lowell	600	12	76	6.3
Merrimack Mfg. Co.	Lowell	2500	25	140	5.6
Hamilton Co.	Lowell	1200	20	67	3.3
Lancaster Mills	Clinton	900	20	67	3.3
Essex Co.	Lawrence	1500	150	460	3.1
Lyman Mills	Holyoke	1470	147	418	2.8
Appleton Co.	Lowell	600	6	14	2.3
Hadley Falls Co.	Holyoke	1470	147	263	1.8
Chicopee Mfg. Co.	Chicopee	700	7	11	1.6
Ames Mfg. Co.	Springfield	250	5	4	0.8
Boston Mfg. Co.	Waltham	450	6	4	0.7
Hampden Mills	Holyoke	400	4	19	4.8
Essex Steam Mills	Newburyport	100	?	10	?
Salisbury Mfg. Co.	Salisbury	661	?	1	?

As economic tension increased in the years before the panic of 1857, the Massachusetts Hospital Life reduced its outstanding loans. In December, 1855, Loring wrote letters to the Massachusetts Cotton Mills, Boott Cotton Mills, Atlantic Cotton Mills, Middlesex Company, Bay State Mills, Hadley Falls Company, and Chicopee Manufacturing Company, asking that they decrease their indebtedness by an aggregate of $440,000.[85] This reduction foreshadowed no wholesale cessation of lending, however, for 34 loans to the textile industry were concluded in 1856. Some of these loans were written to run for three years or more. When the panic of 1857 broke, two of the four important selling agents, Lawrence, Stone & Company, and Charles H. Mills & Company, went bankrupt. The Middlesex Company, Bay State Mills, Pemberton Mills, Lawrence Machine Shop, and Hadley Falls Company likewise failed, and a number of other companies, including the Lyman Mills and Hampden Mills of the Holyoke area and the Atlantic Cotton Mills and Pacific Mills of Lawrence, were in danger of failure.[86] Though the company continued to lend to the textile mills during the crisis, most of the loans were written for periods of less than a year until the crisis had passed.

As a result of the panic the company was faced with the necessity of protecting its loans to textile companies and to selling agents which had failed or were in danger of failure. All the loans were ultimately paid by the textile companies, but interest on the loans to the Bay State Mills was lost for two years. In the case of three companies, loans were converted into industrial mortgages for greater security. Actuary Loring participated actively in the receivership of the Bay State Mills. After having offered to settle in full for 80 per cent of the principal and accrued interest, Loring subsequently agreed to accept payment of 25 per cent of the principal in cash and the other 75 per cent in voting rights in the stock of the Washington Mills, which had been organized from the properties of the Bay State Mills.[87] Through this means, the company was able to recapture its investment by the end of 1862. Only on its loans to the firm of Lawrence, Stone & Company and to two individuals (one of whom was Samuel Lawrence) did the Massachusetts Hospital Life take a loss.[88] The losses sustained amounted to approximately 1½ per cent of all loans exclusive of mortgages. Nor were the losses on mortgages large. This record, the committee of examination for 1857 believed, was better than that made on the average by those directors of the company who also were private trustees.[89] Thereafter more money was shifted into mortgages, but both individuals and companies in the textile industry continued to be large borrowers.

TABLE 9

Borrowers with Pledged Collateral of $25,000 or More (Par Value), May 2, 1856

BORROWERS	COLLATERAL (Company specified when over $10,000 par value)
Estate of Abbott Lawrence [a]	$225,000; Mass. Cotton Mills; Suffolk Mills; Atlantic Cotton Mills; Boott Cotton Mills
William Amory; [a] son-in-law of David Sears; treas., Amoskeag Mfg. Co., Stark Mills	$155,000; Lowell Mfg. Co.; Lancaster Mills; Hadley Falls Co.; other textile, insurance, railroad securities
Lawrence, Stone & Co.	$109,000; Middlesex Co.; Bay State Mills; Pemberton Mills
Amos A. Lawrence; [b] son of Amos Lawrence	$108,000; Boott Cotton Mills; Lawrence Mfg. Co.; Lowell Machine Shop; Middlesex Co.; Bay State Mills; Suffolk Mills
Samuel Lawrence; partner in Lawrence, Stone & Co.; brother of Amos and Abbott Lawrence	$85,000; Middlesex Co.; Bay State Mills; Pemberton Mills
John A. Lowell; [a] son of John Lowell	$77,000; Merrimack Mfg. Co.; Mass. Cotton Mills; other textile stocks
J. H. Wolcott; [b] partner in A. & A. Lawrence & Co.	$75,000; Mass. Cotton Mills; Tremont Mills; Lowell Mfg. Co.; Boston Gas Light Co.; other textile stocks
James K. Mills [b] and Charles H. Mills; partners in Charles H. Mills & Co.; James K. Mills, treas., Hadley Falls Co.	$73,000; Lyman Mills; Dwight Mfg. Co.; Chicopee Mfg. Co.; railroad securities
George W. Lyman [b]	$71,000; Lowell Mfg. Co.
Samuel Cabot; [b] son-in-law of Thomas H. Perkins	$69,000; Mass. Cotton Mills; Boott Cotton Mills; Dwight Mfg. Co.; other textile stocks
Augustus Thorndike; son of Israel Thorndike; brother-in-law of Ebenezer Francis	$62,000; Lowell Mfg. Co.; Merrimack Mfg. Co.; other textile stocks
Patrick T. Jackson; partner, Charles H. Mills & Co.; treas., Hampden Mills; son of P. T. Jackson; son-in-law of Charles G. Loring	$59,000; Hadley Falls Co.; Hampden Mills; other textile stocks

BORROWERS	COLLATERAL (Company specified when over $10,000 par value)
Francis C. Gray;[b] dir., Merchants Natl. Bank; original stockholder, Western Railroad	$50,000; Essex Co.; Merrimack Mfg. Co.; Suffolk Mills; other textile stocks
William Gray;[b] treas., Atlantic Cotton Mills	$45,000; Boott Cotton Mills; Atlantic Cotton Mills; Mass. Cotton Mills
James Lawrence;[b] partner in A. & A. Lawrence & Co.; son of Abbott Lawrence	$42,000; Essex Co.; Lawrence Mfg. Co.; other textile stocks
Benjamin S. Rotch; son-in-law of Abbott Lawrence	$42,000; Lowell Mfg. Co.; Mass. Cotton Mills; Lawrence Mfg. Co.; other textile stocks
Francis C. Loring; lawyer; bro. of Charles G. Loring	$40,000; Mass. Cotton Mills; Middlesex Co.; Dwight Mfg. Co.; other textile stocks
Caleb W. Loring;[b] son of Charles G. Loring	$38,000; Bay State Mills; other textile and insurance stocks
W. S. Bullard;[c] merchant	$36,000; Lowell Mfg. Co.; other textile stocks
William R. Lawrence; son of Amos Lawrence	$36,000; Atlantic Cotton Mills; other textile stocks
J. Ingersoll Bowditch;[a] son of Nathaniel Bowditch	$34,000; textile and insurance stocks
Franklin H. Story;[b] treas., Dwight Mfg. Co.; treas., Perkins Mills	$33,000; Dwight Mfg. Co.; other textile stocks
J. Pickering Putnam; treas., Boott Cotton Mills; treas., Boston Mfg. Co.	$30,000; Pemberton Mills; Essex Co.
Samuel Austin;[a] merchant	$28,000; Lancaster Mills; other textile stocks
Thomas H. Perkins; son of Thomas H. Perkins	$27,000; Lowell Mfg. Co.; Middlesex Co.; insurance stocks
Charles T. Appleton; treas., Lowell Bleachery; nephew of Joseph Tilden	$26,000; Lowell Bleachery; other textile stocks
H. H. Hunnewell;[b] capitalist; banking, railroads	$25,000; various textile stocks

[a] Director, Massachusetts Hospital Life.
[b] Stockholder, Massachusetts Hospital Life.
[c] Vice-President, Massachusetts Hospital Life.

The magnitude of the debacle in Massachusetts in 1857 drew public attention sharply and none too favorably toward the textile industry. The Massachusetts Hospital Life stood revealed as a very important center of its financing. One irate critic of the Boston Associates, Dr. James C. Ayer of patent medicine fame, charged that the Massachusetts Hospital Life was a powerful financial institution which used its loans and interlocking directors to dominate various textile companies. In the reorganization of the Middlesex Company and the Bay State Mills, Ayer claimed, the Massachusetts Hospital Life had used its power "to dictate who should be made the officers of those companies . . . and it was threatened that immediate demand for payment of its claims would be made, unless officers acceptable to its Trustees [i.e., Directors] were chosen." [90]

There is no evidence in the records of the Massachusetts Hospital Life to substantiate this charge. It is true that a number of important figures in the textile industry were directors or officers of the Massachusetts Hospital Life and were in a position to direct funds toward particular textile companies. But it is very doubtful whether these individuals, so many of whom viewed the Massachusetts Hospital Life primarily as a charity, ever considered the company as an instrument of control over various textile companies. If they had, they would probably have been more aggressive in seeking funds for that institution. Their presence there as officers or directors was mainly a sign of community service, even though the company funds (as in the case of the Lawrences) did serve their primary interest in textiles. The holdings of the Boston Associates in the individual textile companies were, in general, sufficient for purposes of control. Consequently, the Associates did not develop the idea of using a financial institution as a means of controlling an industry, as that idea was to develop in the later nineteenth century. Dr. Ayer, after becoming treasurer of the Tremont and Suffolk Mills of Lowell in 1870, himself made that company an important borrower from the Massachusetts Hospital Life.

As the bonds of the United States government were sold rather rapidly in the late 1840's, and those of the Commonwealth of Massachusetts were sold at a somewhat slower pace, the security portfolio of the Massachusetts Hospital Life was sharply reduced. It did not again increase for a decade, and then rather modestly. The venture into governments in the 1840's had paved the way for investment in other securities, however. In 1847 the company made its first venture into the field of municipal securities when it bought $200,000 of 5 per cent water bonds of the city of Boston at slightly less than par. Abbott Lawrence, of the Committee of Finance, had been a vigorous advocate of public ownership of the city's water supply system, and this purchase may have been in part in support of his belief. These bonds were payable in 1859. In that and the succeeding year the company bought a total of $229,000 of Boston 5 per cent bonds at slightly more than par. In 1861 the company disposed of the larger portion of its Boston bonds, but it also bought $148,000 of 5 per cent bonds of the city of Roxbury.[91]

Meanwhile the Massachusetts Hospital Life began to invest in railroad securities. In 1847 it purchased 1,000 shares (at $100 par) of the stock of the Pittsfield & North Adams Railroad. This line had been leased in 1841 for 30 years by the Western Railroad, which had guaranteed an annual return of 6 per cent upon its stock. During 1849 it purchased $50,000 of 6 per cent bonds of the Old Colony Railroad, and, during 1851, $137,000 of 6 per cent bonds of the Boston & Providence Railroad. In 1856 it bought $100,000 of 6 per cent bonds of the Boston & Lowell Railroad. By the end of 1861 the company had $585,000 invested in the securities of five Massachusetts railroads: the Pittsfield & North Adams, Boston & Providence, Boston & Lowell, Connecticut River, and Eastern railroads. Boston Associates were present on the boards of all these roads. Such financial support as the company gave the railroads during this period was done primarily through ownership of their securities. Only 28 of the 1,321 loans made by the company between 1835 and 1875 were made to railroads. These were short-term loans, in rare instances lasting more than a year and at maximum a little more than two years.

Following the outbreak of the Civil War the Massachusetts Hospital Life again became a large-scale owner of government securities. Owing to war conditions, the normal channels of investment were narrowing. The cotton textile industry, depressed for lack of fiber,[92] was no longer a heavy borrower, and the number and value of loans to individuals, so frequently secured by textile company stocks, also declined. Throughout the period of the war the company's investment in mortgages showed a gradual, though persistent, decline, which can be attributed in part to the war-induced prosperity. While it seems reasonable to assume that the company could have met its problem of reinvestment by lending to enterprises called into being or swollen by war contracts and by lending to individuals upon the securities of these enterprises, the company in fact made few such loans. Instead of accepting the risks involved in loans of this type, the company chose to place large orders for government bonds and notes, at the time of their issue.

The first order was placed in April, 1861, immediately after the surrender of Fort Sumter.[93] By the end of 1862 the Massachusetts Hospital Life had $2,685,000 invested in United States government securities. Five hundred thousand dollars of this was in Treasury notes bearing 7.3 per cent interest, and the balance bore interest at 6 per cent. At the end of 1865 the investment in governments had increased to $4,879,000, and at maximum at the end of 1867 to $4,949,000.[94] At that time this investment amounted to 47 per cent of the total resources of the company.

This investment helped create the highest return gained on the total fund in the company's history and at no sacrifice of security. As Loring had pointed out, "if reinvestment could have been made in mortgages or loans upon stocks, the security would not be substantially better," for the law making greenbacks legal tender meant that these mortgages and loans could be paid in greenbacks. Moreover, the bonds of the government bore interest payable in gold, which commanded a substantial premium during and after the Civil War.[95] In 1864 this premium amounted to a little better than 100 per cent; as late as 1870 it was about 17 per cent, and in 1876 about 10 per cent. As a result of the premium, the yield on these bonds was increased by approximately $1,000,000 or about one-third more than the stated interest.[96] These profits from sales of the gold coupons were larger during the Civil War and in the later 1860's when the amount of bonds held was greatest and the gold premium highest. Thereafter, as the gold premium declined, a new source of income was created by sale of the bonds at a premium. In December, 1871, however, the company lost approximately 30 per cent ($1,430,000) of its total holdings of government bonds when these bonds were called at par. Except for $670,000 in bonds which it held to maturity in 1881 and 1882, it sold the balance between 1868 and 1875 for a premium of $383,000.[97]

Company income was further swelled during the years 1868–1873 owing to the increase in the legal interest rate to 7 per cent authorized by the legislature in March, 1867. Since these years offered good opportunities for lending, the company was able to make most of its new mortgages and loans at 7 per cent. Mortgages were confined almost exclusively to the Boston area, while loans were again directed chiefly into the textile industry. At the beginning of 1873 the value of mortgages was more than double the loan portfolio. Of the loans, almost three-fourths of the total were to the 16 textile companies shown in Table 10.[98]

While it is difficult to compare these figures with the similar table compiled for 1855 in an exact fashion, it seems evident that by the early 1870's the Massachusetts Hospital Life had fallen from its former position in financing the Massachusetts textile companies. Its loans tended to be to the old companies of the Boston Associates and to be larger in the total amount per company, but loans were made to fewer companies. These companies, moreover, represented a much smaller percentage of the total capital invested in the Massachusetts textile industry. In 1855 companies possessing more than half the capital invested in the textile industry in Massachusetts were borrowers from the Massachusetts Hospital Life. By 1875 the total capital invested had increased to $63,845,000 in cotton textile companies and to $17,210,000 in woolen textile companies.[99] In the early 1870's the Massachusetts Hospital Life was lending to companies which possessed no more than one-sixth of this total capital. Perhaps the fact that the textile industry had been splintered among a considerable number of selling agents in comparison with the group of four in the earlier period may have had something to do with the decline of the company as a source of capital. An examination of the financial records of certain of the companies to which the Massachusetts Hospital Life was lending, e.g., the Dwight Manufacturing Company and the Hamilton Manufacturing Company, also indicates very clearly that savings banks and commercial banks were giving the Massachusetts Hospital Life increasing competition.[100]

The panic of 1873, like the earlier crises, caused the company

TABLE 10

Outstanding Loans to Companies in or Associated with the Textile Industry, December 31, 1872

COMPANY	LOCATION	CAPITAL (000 *omitted*)	NO. OF LOANS	AMT. OF LOANS (000 *omitted*)	DATE OF EARLIEST LOAN OUTSTANDING	ENDORSERS OF NOTES
Pacific Mills	Lawrence	$2500	5	$340	Dec. '67	James Little & Co.
Atlantic Cotton Mills	Lawrence	1500	4	200	Dec. '63	William Gray
Hadley Co.	Holyoke	1470	2	200	Jul. '65	G. W. Lyman *et al.*
Hamilton Co.	Lowell	1200	2	200	Dec. '67	Frothingham & Co.
Dwight Mfg. Co.	Chicopee	1200	2	200	Mar. '69	Minot, Hooper & Co.
Tremont and Suffolk Mills	Lowell	1200	2	200	May '69	George C. Richardson & Co.
Lawrence Mfg. Co.	Lowell	1500	2	200	Dec. '71	George C. Richardson & Co.
Washington Mills	Lawrence	1650	2	150	May '69	E. R. Mudge, Sawyer & Co.
Boston Mfg. Co.	Waltham	600	3	150	Jul. '69	Wheelright, Anderson & Co.
Appleton Co.	Lowell	600	2	100	Nov. '71	George C. Richardson & Co.
Lowell Machine Shop	Lowell	600	2	50	Aug. '62	J. Thomas Stevenson & George H. Kuhn
Lyman Mills	Holyoke	1470	1	50	Mar. '70	George R. Minot & N. Hooper
Everett Mills	Lawrence	800	1	50	Dec. '71	George C. Richardson & Co.
Mass. Cotton Mills	Lowell	1800	1	50	Dec. '72	Frothingham & Co.
Indian Orchard Mills	Springfield	600	1	40	Dec. '70	J. C. Howe & Co.
Hampden Mills	Holyoke	400	1	25	Jan. '65	P. T. Jackson, Caleb W. Loring

little harm. The stability of its deposit structure was again clearly evident. In fact, between the end of 1873 and the end of 1877, its total resources increased from $12,795,000 to $15,296,000. Nor did it suffer any major losses on its investments. At the end of 1876 the committee of examination reported, "The Committee are impressed with the favorable condition of the investments, and especially those connected with the mortgages of Real Estate, showing the good policy of this Corporation in not exceeding a moderate per centum of the proper value of real estate as collateral security for its loans." This sanguine conclusion was reiterated by the committee appointed for 1878.[101]

The security of the funds held by the company was maintained, but its income position was by no means so satisfactory. Money could no longer be readily lent at 6 and 7 per cent. Business loans in particular declined both in volume and rate. Several loans made to railroads in 1876 for terms of six months or less were written for 4 per cent. Old borrowers, instead of permitting a note to run at the will of the company for a period of years beyond the term for which it was written, paid off the old note and negotiated a new loan at a lower interest. In 1877 the rate of return to depositors fell to 5 per cent, as low as the rate paid in 1862. The following year the rate of 4¼ per cent was the lowest the company had yet paid.[102]

The pace of growth at a time when satisfactory investment was difficult, created problems in investing new money. During the late 1870's and 1880's in particular, Boston capital was suffering from intense competition in its home area. The national banks of Boston at this time, for example, had a greater total capital than did those of New York.[103] The Massachusetts Hospital Life had its old areas of investment, but it faced a much heavier competition from savings and commercial banks.

In the area of security ownership, which had proved so profitable during the Civil War period and after, the company was particularly constricted. The great opportunity for investment in governments was over. Much of the indebtedness of the national government had been paid off, and the funded debt, reflecting the government's improved credit, bore only 4 per cent interest. The company's other categories of ownership, limited to securities of Massachusetts banks, railroads, municipalities, and the Commonwealth, were not sufficiently broad for satisfactory investment. At the end of 1877 the company owned securities worth $1,469,500. This was just under 10 per cent of its total fund. More than one half of this amount was in United States government bonds which were due and payable in 1881. The balance was divided between bonds of the cities of Roxbury and Fall River ($129,000) and stocks and bonds of seven Massachusetts railroads ($490,500).[104] As this very successful period of investment came to a close, it became obvious that the company's investment powers would have to be enlarged if its earnings in the future were to approach the record of its earlier years.

V

A SLIGHT TRANSITION

(1878–1901)

For at least its first half century the Massachusetts Hospital Life was consistently motivated by the charitable orientation of its founders. By contrast, after 1878 the charitable aspect is evident only historically and in the payments made regularly to the Massachusetts General Hospital. The company is rarely, if ever, referred to by its officers and directors as a charitable institution. Neither is there that same sense of warm regard for the institution and pride in its achievement so characteristic of the founders and their immediate successors. To its officers and directors in the late nineteenth century the Massachusetts Hospital Life seems to have been merely an important and historic Boston financial institution. It was no longer even the largest, for by the turn of the century the Provident Institution for Savings, the New England Mutual Life Insurance Company, the National Shawmut Bank, and the Boston Five Cent Savings Bank had larger resources.[1]

For at least its first half century the officers and directors had also conducted the company's operations in a pattern very close to that set down by Dr. Bowditch and his associates. Over time, however, changes must be made in any institution. The changes that occurred in the period 1878 to 1901 were not changes that basically altered the pattern of the company's operations, but they were necessary adjustments. Thus legal provisions had to be altered so that the company might find more varied and satisfactory outlets for its funds at a time marked by a severe secular downtrend in interest rates. The forms of contract in some ways were becoming outdated. A number of minor adjustments were also made in the internal operation of the company. In particular, its accounting and auditing procedures, which had gone so long unchanged, were re-examined. In calling upon professional accountants, the company was in step with the historic development in business, in the later nineteenth century, of seeking aid from outside specialists in various aspects of business activity.

Administration and Business Policy

Top management of the Massachusetts Hospital Life continued in the same group which had controlled the company from the beginning. The men in this period were further removed from the mercantile origins of their ancestors, but in their financial strength they were as dominant in Boston as their ancestors had ever been. Almost without exception they were men of broad financial interests, and a number of them were professional Boston trustees.

Four of the 13 directors of the company in 1900 were grandsons of founder-stockholders. Each had succeeded his father as a director of the company. Most of the other directors were members of families in which there had been predecessor stockholders. In fact, the names of the executives and directors suggest that office-holding in the company had become almost a matter of inheritance.

Three actuaries served as chief executives during this period: Samuel C. Cobb (1878–1891), the younger Abbott Lawrence (1891–1893), and Charles F. Choate (1893–1901). Of the three, Samuel Cobb was by far the most important both because of his longer service and because most of the changes mentioned above occurred while he was actuary. Son of a Taunton lawyer, he had early established himself as a successful merchant with wide commercial interests in the Mediterranean, the Baltic, and Brazil. In his early years he had operated as partner, first with J. Henry Cunningham and then with Josiah Wheelwright, but after 1858 he had conducted his business under his own name. Between 1873 and 1876 he had been mayor of Boston. As mayor he had given Boston notably efficient government, so much so that taxes were reduced almost three million dollars during his term of office. After a trip to Europe and a brief period as president of the Revere National Bank, at the age of 52 Cobb became actuary of the Massachusetts Hospital Life in April, 1878. This position, said his memorialist, James M. Bugbee, was one of "much dignity and responsibility, but by no means one of ease in these days of accumulated capital competing for investment." Bugbee also records that in 1870 Cobb suffered a serious illness from which he never fully recovered.[2]

Samuel Cobb had had some prior acquaintance with trust companies, for he had been a vice-president of the Boston Safe Deposit & Trust Company. He resigned from this position in 1878. While actuary in the mid-1880's he also joined with others to form the Bay State Trust Company. This company showed the influence of the Massachusetts Hospital Life in that its chief executive officer was called actuary and that Cobb, Abbott Lawrence, and two other Massachusetts Hospital Life directors were on its 13-member board. Like the New England Trust and the Boston Safe Deposit & Trust companies, the operations of the Bay State Trust Company ran the full gamut of trust company activity.[3]

Cobb's successor, Abbott Lawrence, served but two years, a briefer span than any other actuary. He was the youngest son and namesake of Abbott Lawrence and son-in-law of James W. Paige; consequently, he had his roots deep in the Massachusetts textile industry. In spite of these roots and his presidency of the Pacific Mills and of the Essex Company of Lawrence, he had taken little part in business, preferring to devote himself to literature and philanthropy. Among his philanthropic interests were the Massachusetts General Hospital and the Boston Dispensary. At the time Lawrence became actuary he had served on the Committee of Finance for 11 years and on two brief occasions had been acting actuary during Samuel Cobb's absence. Lawrence was 65 when ill health forced his resignation early in 1893.[4]

Like Abbott Lawrence, Charles F. Choate, the last of this group of actuaries, had had a prior connection with the Massachusetts Hospital Life, for he had been a director of the company since 1889. Since 1887 he had also been one of three vice-presidents of the New England Trust Company. This position Choate retained until his death in 1911. Choate's main career had been in law and in the railroad field, however. He had been counsel of the Old Colony Railroad in Massachusetts from 1865 to 1878 and served as its president from 1878 to 1900. At the time he became actuary, the New York, New Haven & Hartford Railroad had just acquired the Old Colony under lease. Choate was then 65 years of age. After resigning as actuary in 1901, he became president of the Massachusetts Hospital Life Insurance Company.[5]

A continuing trend during this period was the increasing authority of the Committee of Finance. Whether it was a matter of selecting a new director, vice-president, president, or actuary, seeking new powers from the legislature, or selling shares in possession of the company, the Committee of Finance and the actuary normally were appointed to act or to make recommendations. The increasing power of this committee was due in part to the relatively brief periods of service of the actuaries and the fact that they had other interests. It was also due to the general caliber of the committee itself.

In 1892 the board of directors further formalized the Committee of Finance by voting that it should meet regularly once per week and more often if necessary.[6] By 1894 these regular weekly meetings had been increased to two, and the board provided that each member of the Committee of Finance should be paid $2.50 for each meeting attended.[7] At about the same time the board also passed a resolution that members of the annual committee of examination should be paid $20 "in gold" each.[8] The introduction of these fees suggests the increasingly detached and professional way in which the company was being regarded by its officers and directors.

As Cobb's memorialist indicated, the critical problem facing the company during most of the last quarter of the nineteenth century was finding profitable investments. To this end, in November, 1880, the directors appointed Cobb and the Committee of Finance to approach the legislature for an enlargement of the company's investment powers.[9] The resulting grant of authority was roughly equivalent to that possessed by the New England Trust and the Boston Safe Deposit & Trust companies.[10] The company was now authorized to invest in the first mortgage bonds of any railroad which had earned and paid dividends on its stock for two years before the purchase of the bonds, or in the bonds of any railroad incorporated in New England which was unencumbered by mortgage. Such securities were also made acceptable as collateral for loans by the company. The company was further authorized to make loans to any New England corporation, the property of which was unencumbered by mortgage, and to invest in any stock or security eligible for savings banks. In opening these avenues, the new statute was undoubtedly helpful to the company, but investment continued to be a difficult problem. There was also a limitation of authority contained in the new statute, for under it the

Massachusetts Hospital Life, like the New England Trust and the Boston Safe Deposit & Trust companies, was made subject to inspection by the commissioners of savings banks.

A committee from the Massachusetts Hospital Life returned to the legislature late in 1882 to request an increase in the company's authority to hold real estate in the city of Boston. The company had been limited to $100,000 by the Act of 1818. The resulting legislation empowered the company to hold real estate to an amount not exceeding $1,500,000.[11] This permitted the company to write up at once the value of its office building, which had been undervalued for years in order to stay within old legal limits. The company also drew up plans to replace the building, which was more than 50 years old. After purchasing adjacent property from the Old Boston National Bank and from the American Insurance Company, the Massachusetts Hospital Life razed these buildings as well as its own. On the site it built a seven-story office building valued at $700,000. The new structure, later increased to nine stories, was ready for occupancy in October, 1886.[12] It is the company's present home.

Because of declining earnings on the company's fund in a period of low interest rates and intense competition, Cobb recommended to the directors in November, 1881, that the time-hallowed annual charge of ½ of 1 per cent on trust deposits be lowered to ¼ of 1 per cent, so that the charge would conform more closely to that levied by other trust companies.[13] After consideration by a committee composed of George Higginson, George R. Minot, and Charles P. Bowditch, the board voted a reduction to 3/10 of 1 per cent as of the beginning of the year 1882.[14] This rate was maintained until 1905.[15]

The change in rate was the prelude to a number of minor revisions in the deposit contract forms, which had been virtually unaltered since their origin. In the spring of 1882 the actuary and the Committee of Finance in association with the solicitor (Nathaniel Bowditch's youngest son, William) were appointed a committee to make the revisions.

Aside from the adjustment in language required by the new charge, most of the other revisions were concerned with repayment. These latter changes in the contract gave verbal recognition to the facts that a substantial minority of the depositors had permitted interest to accumulate as new capital and that repayment had always been in money, though provision for repayment "in real estate, stocks, notes, bonds, mortgages, or other property belonging to said company, all, any, or either of them, at the pleasure and discretion of the Directors. . ." was retained as an alternative.

Significantly, although the description of the means of figuring interest on the deposits was retained in fine print at the bottom of the contract, the balance of the language was changed. No longer did the contract state that "if repayment were made wholly or in part in money, the Company shall make such reasonable allowance for any increase or decrease in the price of the common property as the Directors shall judge equitable." Instead it stated that once in five years, or oftener if convenient, the directors would make an accurate adjustment and payment of any surplus due depositors, including proportionate payments to the representatives of depositors who had died during the interval since the last adjustment.[16]

It would seem that one purpose of these revisions was to eliminate disputes arising from claims of depositors to an increment in addition to principal at the time of repayment because of capital appreciation in the fund, as had occurred in 1864. At the same time the opportunity of the company to share losses was preserved. The new provision requiring an adjustment and payment of any surplus due depositors at five-year intervals was deleted in 1901. The result of these changes was to reduce the similarity of the company to the modern investment company.

In 1893 the only deposit-in-trust contract to be developed after the company began operation was brought into use. This contract, form "A," took its place alongside the five earlier forms.[17] Its purpose was to permit any among the gradually increasing number of nonprofit religious, charitable, civic, and educational institutions depositing money in the Massachusetts Hospital Life to do so more directly than in trust upon the life of some one of the institution's officers, who might die, resign, or be replaced. Thereafter these institutions could, as formerly, make deposits on the same terms as individuals but in the name of the institution rather than of one of its officers. Sixty-three "A" contract forms were written between 1893 and 1900. The new form was undoubtedly an improvement for this long-established group of depositors.

As the total fund continued to increase, it placed a progressively heavier burden upon the company's administration. This was especially true because of the difficulty with which satisfactory new investments were made. By 1885 deposits were fully 30 per cent larger than they had been a decade previously. At this time Cobb requested and received from the directors an authorization for the Committee of Finance and the actuary "to exercise their discretion in the matter of receiving moneys offered for deposit with this company." [18] It is interesting to note that in this instance there is no record of a discussion of unacceptable sources of deposits, as had occurred in the earlier attempts at limitation. For the next few years the total number of deposits declined slightly, but the total value of the deposits grew rapidly. The question of restricting new deposits arose once more in 1899. The fact that there is again no record of discussion of unacceptable sources of funds underlines the transition here occurring in the spirit of the company.[19] The main impetus toward restriction in these later times seems to have been the desire to protect the rate of return to old depositors, regardless of their status in life. This the company tried to accomplish by putting curbs on new deposits at a time when investment of new money probably could not bring so high a yield as older investments.

In 1888 Cobb made a request for some relief for the actuary.[20] Although there had been no increase in the size of the staff of five since 1838, the business of the office had greatly increased. During that period deposits had more than tripled in value and had increased in number by 20 per cent. As a result of Cobb's request, a new office of assistant to the actuary was written into the bylaws when they were revised in 1889, the first revision since 1839. But the directors had provided that the assistant to the actuary could, at the same time, be secretary.[21] Thus Cobb received some relief through the enlargement of the powers of the secretary, who was given the new title. No new member was added to the staff until 1900, however, when the office of assistant secretary was established. At that time Alfred Litchfield, father of the present vice-president and secretary of the company, became assistant secretary.[22]

During these years the accounting procedures of the company

were revised. The continuing growth of the company in itself probably was one spur, and the annual inspection by the commissioners of savings banks may have been another. But also in the picture was the development of outside professional accountants as an aid to business and the special interest taken by several of the officers and directors, especially Charles P. Bowditch, in the company's accounting problems.

A number of departures from past practice occurred. In 1884, at the suggestion of the actuary, a special mortgage guaranty fund was established on the company's books to absorb losses sustained on mortgages. Thus instead of charging such losses to the interest account, they were charged to a special account established with funds from the interest account and, consequently, were more clearly and steadily in view before officers and directors.[23] This was the first of several such accounts to be established. In 1894, largely through the efforts of Charles P. Bowditch, an annuity suspense account was set up. This account was intended to give clearer recognition to the two separate elements determining profit or loss in the life annuity business. Annuity rates were based in part on an estimated yield of 4 per cent; if the company earned more than 4 per cent on its investments, it enjoyed a "business profit"; if less, it experienced a loss. A second element in the life annuity rate structure was mortality; if the mortality rate among annuitants exceeded the estimate, the company earned a "speculative profit"; if it was less, the company sustained a loss. By establishing the new annuity suspense account and transferring to it the "speculative" profits and losses, the directors hoped to avoid the striking fluctuations which frequently occurred from year to year when the two possible sources of profit were combined. They also hoped to get a clearer awareness of the adequacy of the estimate on yield and of the estimates on life expectancy used in preparing the annuity tables.[24]

More significant was the employment of outside professional accountants. Because of the 1881 amendment to the charter requiring an annual examination by the savings bank commissioners, the committee of examination of the Board of Control, in its audit of the company's records and holdings, had been assisted each year since 1881 by one of the commissioners. Such assistance the successive committees may have found useful. In 1886 they "availed themselves of the labors of an expert accountant," George R. Chapman of Boston.[25] The precedent thus established was thereafter maintained. Beginning in 1887, outside accounting help was also provided the examining committee of the month.[26] With the aid of professional accountant Rodney McLaughlin, the accounting records of the company were revised and simplified in the following year.[27] As a result of these changes, general accounting procedures were improved. More precision was given to auditing the books and possessions of the company than had been possible when such audits were merely adjunctive activities of busy men. Though the old system continued to be maintained along with the new, the burden on the examining officers and directors had been removed. One result was that after 1888 the Board of Control met only once a year. At that time (the second Monday in January) the report of the committee of examination for the prior year was received, and a new committee was appointed to conduct the examination at the end of the next 12-month period.[28]

Funds for investment by the company continued to come predominantly from deposits in trust and in minor but increasing degree from life annuities. No longer was life insurance a significant provider of funds. The last insurance policy of the company expired in 1894, at which time the company was freed from the obligation of making annual reports to the state insurance commissioner.[29]

The funds on deposit with the company at the end of 1880 came from the sources shown in Table 11.[30] Compared with the table for 1857, it is apparent that the business from churches, educational institutions, philanthropic organizations, libraries, and similar bodies had increased, and that the "G" (five-year term) deposit remained the most popular form of contract. These deposits, moreover, were maintaining their stability even in a time of declining earnings. An analysis of the 124 "G" deposits made in the year 1888 indicates that the average "G" deposit remained with the company approximately 16 years. In nearly 25 per cent of these cases interest was left with the company and was permitted to accumulate as new capital.[31]

It is also apparent that, in general, the Massachusetts Hospital Life was continuing to serve the same class, the same families, and the same areas. Perhaps the most noticeable difference is that the size of the average deposit was becoming larger. Thus the trend away from the smaller deposits, which may have been finding their way increasingly to savings banks, continued. The 1,624 trust deposits of all types amounting to $14,488,000 at the end of 1880, averaged about $9,000 in size; the 1,843 deposits of $23,829,000 at the end of 1900 averaged about $12,900.[32]

An analysis of the 124 "G" deposits made in the years 1888 and 1889 shows that 41 (approximately one-third) were made by women and an additional 29 by trustees. Seventeen deposits were made by organizations, including several churches and church organizations, two cemeteries, the Widows Society of Boston, the Sailors' Snug Harbor, Concord Free Public Library, and the Massachusetts Institute of Technology. Of the "G" deposits, 63 (approximately one-half) came from Boston, 20 from Cambridge, and, with a few exceptions, the balance from elsewhere in eastern Massachusetts. Two of the deposits were made by Oliver Wendell Holmes as executor and beneficiary under a will, and two were made by his wife, Fanny Bowditch Holmes, a granddaughter of Nathaniel Bowditch.[33] Henry Adams as co-trustee under a will was another distinguished depositor, and was himself also the beneficiary of a deposit.[34]

TABLE 11

Amounts Held in Trust at the End of 1880

Endowments "EG"	$ 222,804
Deferred annuities "D"	761,250
Strict trust for females for life "SF"	3,750,665
Strict trust for males for life "SM"	1,576,626
Public institutions "G"	1,590,748
Individuals "G"	6,585,736
Total	$14,487,829

Life annuities purchased from the company and in force at the end of the year 1900 (432) had increased fivefold in number since 1877. They were of approximately the same average size as at the earlier date, and they were still purchased by more women than men in the ratio of about four to one.[35] Since the purchase of life annuities was increasing, the company sought to make certain that this aspect of its business continued profitable. In 1881 the company reinstituted a common table of rates for both men and women.[36] Since the table used was the former table of rates for women, the effect of the change was to increase the rates for the smaller number of men who purchased annuities.

In 1893, after consultation with Walter C. Wright, actuary of the New England Mutual Life Insurance Company, the company returned to its former practice of separate tables for men and women. The rates for the higher age levels were also raised.[37] Subsequently, in 1897 Wright was hired as an outside specialist to make a survey of the company's annuity experience. His findings indicated that the average duration of life of the annuitants exceeded the estimates on which the company's annuity rates were predicated. This conclusion was also substantiated by the new annuity suspense account, for in its first five years through 1897 it had shown losses in excess of $32,000.

The Committee of Finance therefore recommended that there be constructed for both men and women new tables which would conform roughly to those recently adopted by several major New York life insurance companies. In addition the company modified its estimate of a 4 per cent yield on the investment of life annuity funds, which had been used in determining the rates since the days of Dr. Bowditch, and substituted a 3½ per cent yield. The result was to raise rates, especially for purchases made by elderly persons.[38] So great had been the decline in mortality expectancy in later life toward the end of the century that the life annuity account frequently fluctuated from profit to loss from year to year and produced only $92,000 in net profits during this whole period. The company again found it necessary to raise rates in 1900.[39]

As was true earlier, no aggressive attempt was made to sell life annuities. Those who purchased annuities took the initiative in making their purchases. As of the end of the year 1900, life annuities were supplying $1,365,000 for investment. This was approximately 5 per cent of the total fund.[40]

Investment Policy

Investment of the Massachusetts Hospital Life fund in the last two decades of the nineteenth century was controlled by a Committee of Finance the members of which were a blending of the old and the new in their investment interests. As those long-time members, Ignatius Sargent, Edward Austin, and J. Ingersoll Bowditch, resigned between 1878 and 1880, a new group moved in. Some of the new group confined themselves largely to New England and its traditional areas for investment, especially in the textile industry, while others were leaders of that middle and later nineteenth-century movement which found new opportunities for investment of Boston capital, especially in the railroads of the Middle West.

Membership of the Committee of Finance from 1878 until the turn of the century is shown in Table 12. To a greater degree than their forebears, various members of this committee held positions of responsibility in other financial institutions. As investors several were reaching into business and geographic areas undreamed of by their predecessors. Yet, while too large and diverse to be called Boston Associates any longer, they had a substantial common core of interest.[41]

TABLE 12

Membership of the Committee of Finance in the Period 1878–1901

YEAR	COMMITTEEMAN	COMMITTEEMAN	COMMITTEEMAN
1878	David R. Whitney	Edward Austin (since 1861)	J. Ingersoll Bowditch (since 1855)
1880	David R. Whitney	Abbott Lawrence, Jr.	J. Ingersoll Bowditch
1881	David R. Whitney	Abbott Lawrence, Jr.	H. H. Hunnewell
1884	T. Jefferson Coolidge	Abbott Lawrence, Jr.	H. H. Hunnewell
1891	T. Jefferson Coolidge	Nathaniel Thayer, Jr.	H. H. Hunnewell
1892	George A. Gardner	Nathaniel Thayer, Jr.	H. H. Hunnewell
1893	George A. Gardner	Nathaniel Thayer, Jr.	Howard Stockton
1901	George A. Gardner (until 1914)	Nathaniel Thayer, Jr.[a]	Howard Stockton

[a] Thayer went off the Committee of Finance in 1901 but returned the following year and remained a member until 1910.

The common interest of the members is most clearly evidenced by their appearance on the boards of various Boston financial institutions. Five of their number in 1890 were a majority of the seven-member board of the Merchants National Bank, at that time the largest of the Boston commercial banks, and another, David R.

Whitney, had been president of the Suffolk National Bank from 1876 to 1882. Two of the group, T. Jefferson Coolidge and Nathaniel Thayer, in 1890 were founder-directors of the Old Colony Trust Company, which soon became the largest Boston trust company.

As had been their predecessors, the members of the Committee of Finance were important figures in the textile field. Among the group were directors (and frequently treasurers and presidents) of a number of the mills of Lowell, Lawrence, Chicopee, Holyoke, and also of several mills in New Hampshire. Probably fittingly, those Committee of Finance members most deeply interested in textiles were T. Jefferson Coolidge, who had married a daughter of William Appleton; Howard Stockton, who had married a granddaughter of Amos Lawrence; Abbott Lawrence, son of Abbott Lawrence; and George A. Gardner, son of John Lowell Gardner. Thus the descendants of the Boston Associates even late in the nineteenth century were continuing their association with the New England textile industry.

Also like their predecessors, but in greater degree, these men invested in railroads, not only in New England but westward. One of the group was a director of the Boston & Providence, leased in 1887 to the Old Colony, and three were directors of the Old Colony, which was leased in 1893 to the New York, New Haven & Hartford, of which Nathaniel Thayer was a director. Two were directors of the Boston & Lowell, which in 1885 was leased to the Boston & Maine. H. H. Hunnewell, in particular, was a Massachusetts Hospital Life director whose railroad interests ran far beyond New England. In association with Nathaniel Thayer (father of the Massachusetts Hospital Life Committee of Finance member), J. Murray Forbes, and others, Hunnewell had been active in the management of several of the Midwestern railroads from almost the mid-century. From 1856 to 1876 he had been vice-president of the Michigan Central, from 1862 to 1871 a director of the Illinois Central, and from 1876 to 1901 chairman of the board of the Kansas City, Ft. Scott & Memphis Railroad, with which Nathaniel Thayer, Jr., was also associated. At one time or another, Hunnewell was a director of some 40 railroads, both in and outside New England. T. Jefferson Coolidge also had active interests in western railroads. Among his positions of responsibility were a directorship of the

Chicago, Burlington & Quincy and the presidency of the Atchison, Topeka & Santa Fe Railroad for a year, 1880–1881.

As in the past, mortgages were the main outlet for the company's fund, through in the stock market boom of the later 1890's, collateral loans and notes were briefly more important. In 1878 approximately 70 per cent of the fund ($15,443,461) was in mortgages. As business revived and outlets for investment were broadened by the amending legislation of 1881, this percentage sharply declined. In 1885 it was 43 per cent. Thereafter the ratio of mortgages to other forms of investment remained fairly constant until the turn of the century. At the end of 1900 this ratio was 41 per cent of a fund amounting to $26,280,000.[42]

Mortgages were the steadiest portion of the company's investments and the most routine in nature. Despite the routine character of these mortgages, the company still retained a careful check upon their issue and sought to make certain that it was troubled with few cases requiring foreclosure. Mortgages were rarely issued for more than two-thirds of the value of the property and were primarily secured by Boston residential real estate. Few mortgages were granted on property outside Boston. They were issued for terms ranging from one to five years, with three years the most common.[43] After the panic of 1884, the company instituted the mortgage guaranty fund and also the policy of annual revaluation of all property under mortgage.[44] So long as property value was maintained and no difficulty was experienced in collecting interest, the company readily renewed mortgages for additional terms. But it is indicative of a more competitive mortgage market during these years that instead of maintaining the same interest rate, as was usual in the past, the company fixed the rate at renewal according to the state of the money market. For most of this period, rates on prime mortgages ran 5 per cent or less, in some cases as low as 4 per cent.

One indication of the times was the fear of an unstable currency. In 1883 Cobb tried to place a clause in new mortgage contracts requiring repayment in gold. With the support of the directors, he endeavored to get agreement of all large Boston financial institutions to such a course, but failed.[45] Beginning in March, 1893, however, gold clauses were inserted in many, if not all, of the company's new mortgages. By that time fear of silver was sufficiently widespread in the Boston community to make such action feasible. In 1896 the company appropriated $5,000 "for the preparation, printing and distribution of papers and documents in favor of sound money." This was one of few expenditures which departed from the run of normal business expense.[46]

Loans on stocks and notes by the Massachusetts Hospital Life had their core, as they had ever since the 1840's, in loans to textile companies and in loans to individuals who, in the main, were prominent Bostonians. To these borrowers a third important group, a number of Boston brokerage firms, was added toward the end of the nineteenth century, as both the volume of corporate securities and of security transactions markedly increased. In 1878 loans on notes and collateral amounted to approximately 13 per cent of the company's total fund. The amount of these loans gradually increased, especially after the company's lending base was broadened by the amendment of 1881. Except for slight decreases immediately following the panics of 1884 and 1893, the increase continued until in 1900 loans on notes and collateral occupied 45 per cent of the total Massachusetts Hospital Life fund.

The textile companies whose notes the Massachusetts Hospital Life had held so regularly, in 1880 were still mainly the old companies of the Boston Associates plus a few more recent mills, such as the Indian Orchard of Springfield, the Naumkeag Steam Mills of Salem, and the Ocean Mills of Newburyport. The amendment of 1881 legally permitted the company for the first time to follow the interests of the Boston group across the state line into New Hampshire and Maine and to help meet the working capital needs of the textile companies of those states. Table 13 suggests the importance of loans to textile companies in 1890.[47]

These loans were just under 25 per cent of the total in number and just under 55 per cent of the total in value in 1890. Several of the textile companies to which loans were made were among the largest in New England. Others with a capital of another $20,000,000 were frequent or occasional borrowers. Together these groups represented more than one-fourth of the textile capital of Massachusetts, New Hampshire, and Maine.[48] The company thus continued to be probably the most important single source of working capital for the New England textile industry. By the end of the nineteenth century, however, the Massachusetts Hospital Life was sharing textile financing with many New England financial institutions, endowed philanthropic, civic, and educational bodies, and private individuals, especially trustees.[49] It is noteworthy that only one of the mills in the newer Fall River-New Bedford area, the Wamsutta Mills, was ever a borrower, and this company borrowed very in-

TABLE 13

Loans to Textile Companies
1890

COMPANY	LOCATION	CAPITAL (000 *omitted*)	NO. OF LOANS	AMT. OF LOANS (000 *omitted*)
Amoskeag Mfg. Co.	Manchester, N.H.	$3000	3	$400
Appleton Co.	Lowell	600	1	50
Arlington Mills	Lawrence	2500	2	100
Arnold Print Works	North Adams	3000	1	50
Assabet Mfg. Co.	Marlboro	1000	1	50
Bates Mfg. Co.	Lewiston, Me.	1000	2	100
Berkeley Co.	Ashton, R.I.	600	1	125
Bigelow Carpet Co.	Clinton	2030	1	50
Boott Cotton Mills	Lowell	1200	3	250
Boston Mfg. Co.	Waltham	800	1	100
Cabot Mfg. Co.	Brunswick, Me.	480	1	50
Cocheco Mfg. Co.	Dover, N.H.	1500	4	250
Edwards Mfg. Co.	Augusta, Me.	1100	1	50
Everett Mills	Lawrence	800	3	125
Fisher Mfg. Co.	Fisherville	500	1	25
Hadley Co.	Holyoke	600	2	125
Hamilton Mfg. Co.	Lowell	1800	1	50
Lawrence Mfg. Co.	Lowell	1500	5	400
Lowell Bleachery	Lowell	400	2	40
Lowell Mfg. Co.	Lowell	2000	1	50
Lyman Mills	Holyoke	1470	2	90
Manchester Mills	Manchester, N.H.	1800	1	50
Massachusetts Cotton Mills	Lowell	1800	3	275
Merrick Thread Co.	Holyoke	750	1	50
Merrimack Mfg. Co.	Lowell	2500	4	250
Nashua Mfg. Co.	Nashua, N.H.	1000	3	300
Naumkeag Steam Mills	Salem	1500	2	150
Otis Co.	Ware	500	1	50
Pacific Mills	Lawrence	2500	6	400
Whittenton Mfg. Co.	Taunton	600	1	100
York Mfg. Co.	Saco, Me.	900	2	150
Total		$41,730	63	$4,305

frequently. Textile company loans in number, value, and general location were approximately the same in 1900 as they had been in 1890.

The loans to textile companies were usually made on notes signed by the treasurer and the selling agent as sureties. Unlike the period before 1873, notes were no longer written for terms of more than one year, nor were old notes extended at the will of the parties beyond the date of maturity. Loans were very frequently renewed by new notes, however, with the interest rate fluctuating from year to year depending on the state of the money market and the credit of the particular company. Until the 1870's it was unusual for a discrimination in rate to be made between companies, but in the more delicate financial markets of the later nineteenth century the stronger textile companies were able to reap the benefit of lower rates. These changes were typical not only of textile loans but of all loans made by the Massachusetts Hospital Life.

Loans to individuals reflected both general business conditions and the volume of securities acceptable as collateral. As the volume of securities increased, especially after 1881, and as business conditions improved, especially after 1896, the number of loans became greater. The borrowers were frequently stockholders, directors, or even members of the Committee of Finance itself. Many, if not most, of the major borrowers were from the old families; for instance, Charles Francis Adams used the credit resources of the Massachusetts Hospital Life freely in repairing his financial position after the disastrous panic of 1893.[50] Fewer were men of fortune, like Frank Jones and Charles A. Sinclair of the Boston & Maine Railroad and other enterprises, who had made their way aggressively forward in a single generation. Some of the loans were as large as $200,000, but loans of about $50,000 or less were more common. Until the 1890's these loans were always made on collateral, which in the case of shares of stock was normally accepted at about two-thirds of market value. Thereafter certain large and well-established borrowers like H. H. Hunnewell or Frederick F. Ayer of the American Woolen Company were granted loans on notes secured only by co-signers.

Table 14 includes the names of all individuals who borrowed from the company 12 or more times in the last quarter of the nineteenth century. From it one may get an idea of who were important bor-

TABLE 14

Major Individual Borrowers: 12 or More Loans
January 1, 1875 to January 1, 1901

BORROWERS	1875–1880	1880–1885	1885–1890	1890–1895	1895–1901
Total loans during period	233	537	552	699	1,165
Total loans this group	8	62	98	115	189
Charles Francis Adams;[a] *capitalist*; investor chiefly in industrials and real estate, especially in Kansas City area; pres., Union Pacific and Kansas City Stockyards Co.			1	7	26 (*181*)
Oakes Ames; *capitalist*; of the famous Ames family, of which F. L. and Oliver Ames were also occasional borrowers; borrowed chiefly on western railroad securities.				6	9 (*10*)
Francis Bartlett;[b] *lawyer*; *trustee*; interested in manufacturing, railroad, and mining enterprises, New England and the West.		1	6	7 (*100*)	
Lyman Belknap; *merchant*; collateral chiefly western railroad securities, especially Chicago, Burlington & Quincy.			6	5 (*20*)	8
J. Ingersoll Bowditch;[c] *insurance company president*; *trustee*; collateral chiefly western railroad securities, especially C. B. & Q., Chicago, Milwaukee & St. Paul.		7	7		
Henry B. Chapin; *broker*, Schirmer, Chapin, & Emmons; collateral chiefly New England railroads, American Bell Telephone Co.		3	7	3 (*58*)	
George B. Chase; friend of George T. Bigelow; dir., Columbian Bank; collateral, securities of several western railroads.		2	6	9 (*130*)	
T. Jefferson Coolidge;[c] *capitalist*; collateral primarily securities of New England textile companies, New England and western railroads.	4	7	4	2 (*100*)	3
F. Gordon Dexter; *trustee*; collateral chiefly western railroads, Union Stockyards & Transit Co.			1	12 (*150*)	14 (*33*)

TABLE 14 *(continued)*

Major Individual Borrowers: 12 or More Loans
January 1, 1875 to January 1, 1901

BORROWERS		1875–1880	1880–1885	1885–1890	1890–1895	1895–1901
	Total loans during period	233	537	552	699	1,165
	Total loans this group	8	62	98	115	189
John L. Gardner;[a] *capitalist*; son of George A. Gardner; borrowed on railroad securities, New England and Far West; textile stocks; Chicago Junction Railways & Union Stockyards.					8	16
H. H. Hunnewell;[c] *capitalist*; collateral New England and western railroad securities.			9 (*33*)	13		4 (*150*)
Walter Hunnewell;[a] *capitalist*; *trustee*; son of H. H. Hunnewell; collateral principally western railroad securities.				4	6 (*110*)	5 (*40*)
Frank Jones; *capitalist*; former pres., Boston & Maine; interested in several "north of Boston" railroads.					2	29
Abbott Lawrence;[c] *capitalist*; son of Abbott Lawrence; collateral chiefly textile and western railroad securities.			5	3	4	
Augustus Lowell;[c] *capitalist*; son of John A. Lowell; collateral impressively New England textile stocks.			10 (*75*)	10	5 (*40*)	2
Charles E. Perkins; *president*, C. B. & Q.; nephew-in-law of R. B. Forbes, an important figure in the history of several western railroads; collateral chiefly C. B. & Q. system securities.				3	6 (*100*)	5 (*100*)
Henry L. Pierce;[a] *sole owner, Walter Baker & Co.*; former mayor of Boston; borrowed chiefly on railroads, New England and West.			1	10	14 (*200*)	
William J. Rotch; New Bedford *capitalist* whose brother was a son-in-law of Abbott Lawrence; borrowed chiefly on western railroad securities.			4	4	8 (*70*)	

TABLE 14 (*continued*)

Major Individual Borrowers: 12 or More Loans
January 1, 1875 to January 1, 1901

BORROWERS	1875–1880	1880–1885	1885–1890	1890–1895	1895–1901
Total loans during period	233	537	552	699	1,165
Total loans this group	8	62	98	115	189
Charles A. Sinclair; *capitalist*; son-in-law of Frank Jones and allied with him in his enterprises, chiefly northern New England railroads.				2	24 (*100*)
E. C. Swift; *eastern manager, Swift & Co.* and brother of G. F. Swift; collateral chiefly Swift & Co., St. Louis National Stockyards securities.					27 (*150*)
Nathaniel Thayer;[a] *banker and railroad capitalist,* New England and the West.	4	8 (*233*)			
Nathaniel Thayer, Jr.;[c] *capitalist*; wide-ranging investments, New England and the West.		5	3	5 (*50*)	2 (*50*)
William F. Weld; of distinguished New England family; collateral primarily western railroad securities.			10	4 (*90*)	
George E. Whiting; *Boston organist, composer*; frequent small borrower, chiefly on New England textile and railroad securities.					25 (*11*)

[a] Stockholder, Massachusetts Hospital Life.
[b] Vice-President, Massachusetts Hospital Life.
[c] Director, Massachusetts Hospital Life.

NOTE: Italicized figures in parentheses beneath the number of loans indicate the total amount of loans in thousands of dollars made to the specified individual during the calendar years 1880, 1890, and 1900.

rowers, the nature of their interests, and when they were most active as borrowers. One can readily note the importance of the Midwest to most of these men. This is especially true of those Midwestern railroads in which Boston capital had been pioneering for more than a generation, first under the guidance of J. Murray Forbes, Nathaniel Thayer, and H. H. Hunnewell, and subsequently under T. Jefferson Coolidge, Charles E. Perkins, and others.

The third group of borrowers, brokerage firms and private banking houses, rapidly came into prominence in the last quarter of the nineteenth century, and especially after 1896. Ever since the founding of Lee Higginson & Company in the early 1850's, that next-door neighbor of the Massachusetts Hospital Life had been an occasional borrower. It became a much more active borrower in the 1890's. Brokerage firms which became occasional to frequent borrowers included Blake Brothers, R. L. Day & Company, J. M. Forbes & Company, Charles Head & Company, Hornblower & Weeks, Jackson & Curtis, E. Rollins Morse & Brother, Parkinson & Burr, F. H. Prince & Company, E. H. Rollins & Sons, and Tucker, Anthony & Company. Loans to these companies tended to be larger than most loans. Though many of them were written for a year, others were written for a term of months, making them the most liquid group of loans in the company's portfolio. Five of the 126 loans made during 1890 were to banking or brokerage houses, for a total of $550,000; a decade later there are 29 of 226 loans clearly recognizable as made to banking or brokerage houses for a total of $2,566,000. Nor was the traffic one way or solely in loans. When the Massachusetts Hospital Life purchased securities, it bought usually through Lee Higginson & Company, with which its relations were so close. From time to time it also bought notes of individuals, business firms, and governmental units from other brokerage firms.

A brief analysis of the company's major collateral holdings in 1900 suggests the gradually changing location of Boston capital after the middle of the nineteenth century, when it had been so heavily, if not dominantly, located in the textile and railroad enterprises of New England.[51] In 1900 collateral holdings of the Massachusetts Hospital Life in the top 10 companies in descending order (based on par value) were the following: Pere Marquette Railroad, Chicago Junction Railways & Union Stockyards, Chicago, Burlington & Quincy Railroad, American Telephone & Telegraph Company, Boston & Maine Railroad, Federal Steel Company, Ogdensburg & Lake Champlain Railroad, Concord & Montreal Railroad, Chicago, Rock Island & Pacific Railroad, and the Union Pacific Railroad. Stocks or bonds, or both, in each of these companies were offered as collateral in at least five instances, and in the case of the Chicago Junction Railways & Union Stockyards 13 times. Eight of the 10 companies were railroads; not one was in the textile industry.

Of the 10, only the Boston & Maine and its lessee, the Concord & Montreal, carried on their activities wholly in New England. The only other company geographically close to New England in the totality of its business was the Ogdensburg & Lake Champlain Railroad, which was controlled by the Rutland Railroad. Of the 10 companies, only the Boston & Maine Railroad and the American Telephone & Telegraph Company had their head offices in Boston.

But in nearly all these companies Boston capital was important. Thus in 1900 one or more current or former members of the Committee of Finance of the Massachusetts Hospital Life sat on the boards of the Pere Marquette Railroad, Chicago Junction Railways & Union Stockyards, Chicago, Burlington & Quincy Railroad, and the Federal Steel Company. The Pere Marquette Railroad had its Boston office, in fact, in the Massachusetts Hospital Life Building. The American Telephone & Telegraph Company, the Boston & Maine Railroad, and the Union Pacific Railroad each had a son of a former member of the Massachusetts Hospital Life Committee of Finance as a director.

The company made least use of its power to own securities as a means of investing its funds. At the end of 1877 approximately 9 per cent of the total fund was invested in securities. In 1880, as a result of the purchase of additional government bonds and of nearly one thousand shares in eight of Boston's national banks, this ratio had increased to 17 per cent. A further increase was made to 22 per cent in 1886, largely as the result of the purchase of western railroad securities. Thereafter the security portfolio of the company declined to approximately 11 per cent in 1900. With interest rates so low in the early 1880's, the bonds purchased were usually at a substantial premium because of a high coupon rate. Such premiums were charged off against the interest account, though at times over a period of two or three years. In most cases the bonds yielded between 4 and 5 per cent and, consequently, were not particularly attractive in comparison with mortgages, notes, and collateral loans.[52]

The influence of H. H. Hunnewell is especially apparent in building up the company's portfolio during these years. When Hunnewell became a member of the Committee of Finance in 1880, the railroad securities owned by the company consisted of 1,267 shares valued at $233,000 in two New England railroads and $157,000 in bonds of five New England railroads. When he retired early in 1891, the company's security portfolio amounted to $3,576,500. All but about $200,000 of this amount was in railroad securities, and all but about $600,000 of the remainder was grouped among four railroad systems with which Hunnewell had been personally connected: the Boston & Maine and Old Colony railroads in New England, and the Chicago, Burlington & Quincy and the Kansas City, Ft. Scott & Memphis railroads in the Middle West. In addition he was also a director (and Nathaniel Thayer, president) of the Chicago & West Michigan, in which the Massachusetts Hospital Life owned $200,000 in 5 per cent bonds. The latter proved the least satisfactory of all these railroad investments, for the Chicago & West Michigan almost foundered in the panic of 1893 before it was merged, late in 1899, into the newly organized Pere Marquette Railroad.[53]

The investment program during those years was sufficient to earn the depositors a consistent 4 per cent from 1879 through 1900. This was a meager record indeed in comparison with the past history of the company, but probably creditable enough in a time of severe downtrend in interest rates and of intense competition. The Provident Institution for Savings paid its depositors as much as 4 per cent in only eight of these years. In three the return was as little as 3 per cent.[54] At the very end of the century there was grave doubt whether the company could maintain even the 4 per cent rate because of the difficulty of finding investments of a sufficiently high yield for new money. When the directors met late in January, 1899, Robert Codman questioned "whether under the present public financial conditions and the increased pressure upon the company to receive deposits it would be best to receive further deposits, or to make any regulation to limit them." This time the company inaugurated a new policy by establishing a discrimination of ½ of 1 per cent in favor of old deposits over deposits made after that date.[55]

Dividends to stockholders were maintained at $10.00 per share until 1883 (plus an extra of $6.00 in 1881). Then, as a result of the reduction in the annual charge to trust depositors, the rate was reduced to $8.00 per year, plus an extra of $6.00 in 1886. By 1890 deposits had grown sufficiently over the preceding decade so that it was possible to restore the $10.00 rate, which was not interrupted until 1899. At that time the rate became again $8.00. Earnings to stockholders were thus reasonably well maintained. During the period 1878–1901 only three of the Boston banks and one trust company surpassed the dividend performance of the Massachusetts Hospital Life.[56]

◆ VI

THE STOCKTON ERA

(1901–1937)

Financial institutions of the nation generally were growing rapidly in the first three decades of the twentieth century. Such was not the case with the Massachusetts Hospital Life. It continued to grow, but not rapidly. Between the end of the years 1900 and 1928 (its peak) the resources of the company increased by only 41 per cent (to $36,877,000) at a time when the resources of many other institutions were multiplying severalfold. The disparity in rate of growth was most marked after 1910. Until 1910 the company ranked among the top eight Boston financial institutions in resources; thereafter, it fell away rapidly in relative size and significance.[1]

Probably the greatest problem for the company was that after about 1870 and increasingly in the twentieth century it was losing its reason for being. During its first half-century the officers and directors took great pride in the community service features of their institution. Because of its size, they could also recognize its value as a source of financing for many of the industrial enterprises of New England. But pride in the unique community service features of the institution gradually lessened as the company became no longer unique — as other trust companies came on the scene and as the mutual savings banks gained by law a steadily increasing maximum for individual deposits. Over the past three-quarters of a century and longer, private trusteeship had also become more firmly rooted.

The decline of the charitable motive within the company was evident in 1905, when the officers and directors very seriously considered trying to break the profit-sharing link with the Massachusetts General Hospital, its largest shareholder and its first reason for being.[2] The act of incorporation had provided that profit-sharing was to endure only so long as it was required of all other Massachusetts life insurance companies. Since the later life insurance companies were mutuals, the profit-sharing provision had been of no value in their cases in supplying additional revenue to the Hospital. Although the profit-sharing requirement had been omitted from the General Insurance Company Law of 1887, it had been inserted in every Massachusetts life insurance company charter until the founding of the Columbian National Life Insurance Company, a stock company, in 1902. When, stimulated by low earnings, the Massachusetts Hospital Life discussed the matter with the Massachusetts General Hospital, the legal representative of the Hospital pointed out that the scope of profit-sharing had been enlarged to include all aspects of the company's business by mutual agreement and an act of the legislature in January, 1824.

The question at issue was never brought to court, but a new agreement was negotiated. Under its terms the Hospital continued to share to the extent of one-third of all profits in excess of 6 per cent paid out annually. But the Hospital agreed to make no claim to share in undistributed profits and also agreed not to oppose the expansion of the capital of the company to $1,000,000 except as it might choose to vote its Massachusetts Hospital Life stock against such a move. As a result of this agreement, the company felt somewhat freer in building up its surplus accounts, though its capital was never increased to $1,000,000. This agreement went into effect in March, 1906, and endured until the negotiation of a new agreement in October, 1948.[3]

As the company's pool of capital declined in relative importance, the company became less significant as a source of financing. Although many leading Boston citizens continued to be associated with the Massachusetts Hospital Life, there were none after the days of H. H. Hunnewell, T. Jefferson Coolidge, and Nathaniel Thayer, Jr., who could match that powerful trio in the range of their interests. The later officers and directors tended to be more "New England minded" – perhaps also an indication of the relative decline in the importance of New England capital nationally. As the company's community service features and financing potentialities declined in significance, the company had less meaning for its officers and directors. What remained solely in full force was the bond of sentiment among members of later generations of those families who had led the company all the way.

Administration and Business Policy

Howard Stockton was leader of the company during most of the years 1901–1937. He was 59 years of age when he succeeded Charles F. Choate as actuary in February, 1901.[4] Younger than his two immediate predecessors, he was a little older than the average of the earlier actuaries at the time of their appointments to the chief office. In period of service, he surpassed all earlier actuaries, for his 31 years in office until his death in April, 1932, were more than twice those of any other actuary. Stockton had been a director of the company since 1891 and a member of the Committee of Finance since 1893. At the time he became actuary the directors revised the rules so that the actuary was made an official member of the Committee of Finance. Because of Stockton's long service, and his vigor despite his age, the power of the actuary in comparison with the Committee of Finance grew markedly during his incumbency. In temperament he had a touch of the autocrat, and he ran the company with a strong hand.

Stockton was probably the most distinguished actuary in the company's history in the scope and importance of his business interests. Through much of his long career, he was a director of the Merchants and Old Boston national banks, of the Old Colony and City trust companies, and of the American Mutual Liability Insurance Company and the Boston Manufacturers Mutual Life Insurance Company. His start had been in textiles. He had served as treasurer of the Cocheco and Salmon Falls manufacturing companies of New Hampshire and of the Merrimack Manufacturing Company of Lowell and the Essex Company of Lawrence. Later he was president of the Nashua and Jackson manufacturing companies of New Hampshire. From 1887 to 1889 Stockton was also president of the American Bell Telephone Company, the key company in the Bell system before its absorption in 1900 by the American Telephone & Telegraph Company. His associations are of more than usual significance because of his period of service as actuary and his great influence upon the company. There were few even among the members of the Committee of Finance who had had so impressive a business career or so wide a range of connections with financial institutions and business organizations. Stockton also found time to serve as trustee and president of the Boston Athenaeum and as a member of the executive committee of the corporation of the Massachusetts Institute of Technology.

As has already been indicated, family is of continuing significance in determining the officers and directors of the Massachusetts Hospital Life. Succeeding Charles F. Choate as president in 1911 was a Lyman (Arthur T.), who was in turn succeeded by a Bowditch (Charles P.). Louis Curtis, son of Thomas B. Curtis, of the mercantile banking firm of Brown Brothers & Company, was president from 1921 to 1931, and George Peabody Gardner from 1931 to 1936. Associated with Curtis on the 14-member centennial Board of President and Directors in 1923 were at least four private trustees. As interesting as any in his family relationships was Augustus P. Loring, who had written a famous guide for private trustees, *A Trustee's Handbook.*[5] Augustus Loring was a grandson of Charles G. Loring; his mother was a Peabody; his wife was a daughter of George A. Gardner; and his son (of the same name and his successor as a Massachusetts Hospital Life director) married a Bowditch.[6]

Acceptance of trust deposits continued to be by far the dominant activity of the company, although its life annuity business grew at a slightly more rapid rate during these years. Because of the low yield to the depositors early in this century, the fee for management of the deposits was reduced from 3/10 to 1/4 of 1 per cent per year in 1905.[7] This fee was a little more than 6 per cent on the 4 per cent then being paid on the old and the 3 3/4 per cent being paid on the new deposits. The discrimination in yield upon deposits placed with the company before and after the dividing line of January, 1899, had been reduced in 1904 from 1/2 to 1/4 of 1 per cent.[8] This discrimination was probably still a psychological and economic deterrent to new depositors and a brake on the growth of the company.

In 1911 the trust deposits of the company fell into the pattern shown in Table 15.[9] Over the preceding 30 years the "G" form of contract, as well as the "D" and "EG" for children, had fallen off somewhat in use. By contrast, use of the strict forms of contract for women and for men had increased, as had also institutional deposits under the more convenient new "A" form. Probably the rather low yield during these years plus the growing number of alternatives for investment made the company somewhat less attractive to shorter term depositors, while individuals depositing substantial sums for a lifetime were more likely to appreciate the record of stability established by the Massachusetts Hospital Life throughout its long history.

By 1929 the average trust deposit was about $17,800 in comparison with $12,900 in 1900. The increase in size had been paralleled by no

TABLE 15

Amounts Held in Trust at the End of 1911

Endowments "EG"	$ 321,297
Deferred annuities "D"	578,782
Strict trust for females for life "SF"	8,280,574
Strict trust for males for life "SM"	3,761,461
Public institutions "A"	3,820,144
Individuals "G"	9,935,940
Total	$26,698,198

such increase in number. The number of deposits had in fact declined from 1,843 to 1,643, indicating that at the peak of prosperity the company was serving a somewhat smaller number of somewhat larger depositors (see Table 16 for amounts on deposit).[10]

TABLE 16

Amounts Held in Trust at the End of 1929

Endowments "EG"	$ 600,543
Deferred annuities "D"	1,278,914
Strict trust for females for life "SF"	9,678,614
Strict trust for males for life "SM"	4,437,767
Public institutions "A"	4,173,899
Individuals "G"	9,071,556
Total	$29,241,293

An analysis of the duration of the 60 "G" deposits made in 1912 and 1913 shows the continuing stability of the company's deposit structure, for even these most volatile of all Massachusetts Hospital Life deposits remained with the company an average of about 14 years.[11] Women continued to predominate as a depositing group (40 of the 60), with wives being more apparent in making deposits than hitherto. Of the remaining 20 deposits, 11 were made by trustees or executors, 2 by guardians, and 7 by men. Only one-fourth of the deposits came from Boston, but practically all other deposits were from the smaller communities ringing Boston. This suggests social change in the movement of the wealthy to the suburbs as transportation improved. The larger number of wives depositing for themselves may also reflect the growing emancipation of women.

An important change in the term of the "G" deposit contract, from a five-year to a three-year term, occurred gradually during the first two decades of this century. Before 1900 rarely, if at all, was a "G" contract written for less than five years. Beginning early in the century, however, a few deposits began to be written for three years and, much less often, for one year. By 1912 approximately three-fourths of the "G" deposits were still written for five years. About one-sixth were for three years, and the balance for one year. During World War I more and more of the "G" deposits were written for three years, and after 1920 virtually all. Since the discrimination in rate between old and new deposits continued to exist until 1920,[12] it appears that the reason for the change was to offer some choice to depositors as to the term of deposit and thus perhaps to offset in some degree the discrimination in rate. But the effect of the change was to make the "G" deposits, still nearly one-third of the total deposits in 1929, potentially more volatile. Where formerly only one-fifth of the "G" deposits had matured annually, one-third of the three-year deposits would so mature.

Terms of all forms of the deposit contracts were further altered from the original pattern of 1823. At the beginning of 1920 the old phrasing "annuities in trust" was dropped in favor of "deposits." At the same time the repayment provision was changed. Thereafter principal and accumulations, if any, were made payable solely in money. The former alternative, providing for repayment at the discretion of the directors in a proportionate and equitable share of the investments of the company, was deleted from the contracts.[13]

In 1926 the company went a step further. At that time the provision for repayment was changed so that the company guaranteed the full amount of the principal sum on all deposits made thereafter, regardless of any losses sustained in the total fund, whether or not these losses were the actual fault of the company.[14] The new deposit contract, however, helped make the condition of the company far more critical in the years immediately ahead. Had the company maintained its earlier pattern for repayment, its stockholders would not have had to bear the losses incurred on deposits during the depression of the 1930's.

The new deposit contract completed the transition, begun in 1883, of changing the company's terms of contract from something quite similar to those of the modern investment company to something very close to the mutual savings bank (except for terms of management, withdrawal, and size of deposit). Thus the company made a further retreat from the modern investment company pattern at the very time that that pattern was first being used impressively on a national scale. Two important investment companies, the Massachusetts Investors Trust and the State Street Investment Corporation date from 1924, and there were many others.[15]

Life annuities as a source of funds increased from a sum equivalent to 6 per cent of total deposits in 1900 to 9 per cent ($2,538,000) in 1929. The total number of annuities meanwhile had increased from 432 to 543. Profits had a tendency to fluctuate because of the relatively small number of annuitants, but after the first years of the century life annuities were consistently profitable until the depth of the depression in the 1930's. A tabulation for the years 1901 through 1930 shows a business profit of $526,690 and a "speculative" profit in the annuity suspense account of $549,055.[16] Revenue from life annuities was thus of substantial importance in building up the surplus accounts and permitting high dividends to stockholders in years which were not always marked by high interest rates to depositors, especially early in the century.

Investment Policy

The Committee of Finance of the Massachusetts Hospital Life during the years 1901–1937 consisted, in addition to the actuary, of the men listed in Table 17. Comparing these men with their counterparts of the late nineteenth century, we see their common core of strength and interest: finance. Contrasting them with their predecessors, however, we find their power limited to New England, though broader than the textile industry. Only George P. Gardner was significant for his representation on boards of corporations located in areas outside New England, but even he not to the extent of H. H. Hunnewell or of Nathaniel Thayer.

Aside from textile companies and certain Boston financial institutions, the only companies in which the members of the group were frequently represented as directors were the American Telephone & Telegraph Company and its predecessor, the American Bell Telephone Company. Among these members of the Committee of Finance

TABLE 17

Membership of the Committee of Finance in the Period 1901–1937

YEAR	COMMITTEEMAN	COMMITTEEMAN	COMMITTEEMAN
1901	George A. Gardner (since 1892)	Charles W. Amory	Charles F. Choate
1902	George A. Gardner	Nathaniel Thayer, Jr.	Charles F. Choate
1910	George A. Gardner	Francis W. Hunnewell	Charles F. Choate
1911	George A. Gardner	Francis W. Hunnewell	Louis Curtis
1914	Theophilus Parsons	Francis W. Hunnewell	Louis Curtis
1915	George P. Gardner	Francis W. Hunnewell	Louis Curtis
1917	George P. Gardner	George Wigglesworth	Louis Curtis
1930	George P. Gardner	Henry S. Howe	Louis Curtis
1931	George P. Gardner	Henry S. Howe	Samuel H. Wolcott
1932	George P. Gardner	Moses Williams	Samuel H. Wolcott
1936	William Dexter	John C. Kiley	Samuel H. Wolcott
1937	William Dexter (until 1940)	John C. Kiley (until 1939)[a]	Samuel H. Wolcott (still serving 1954)

[a] John C. Kiley served again from 1947 to 1952.

were three who had been directors (and Howard Stockton, president) of the American Bell Telephone Company. Two of these Bell Telephone directors became directors of the American Telephone & Telegraph Company, as did also two other Committee of Finance members. In addition, Henry S. Howe was a director of the Western Electric Company. It is interesting that these men were directors at a time when control in the telephone field was being wrested from Boston by New York capital.[17] The transit of control in the telephone company at least suggests that New England capital was no longer of sufficient relative size in the twentieth century to maintain its former position in many major national enterprises.

In this Committee of Finance group there were six directors of the Merchants National Bank, two of the Old Boston, two of the National Union Bank, one of the First National Bank, and one of the National Shawmut Bank. Seven were vice-presidents or trustees of the Provident Institution for Savings, and one was connected with the Suffolk Savings Bank. Six were directors or officers of the Old Colony Trust, four of the Bay State Trust, four of the New England Trust, two of the City Trust, and one of the State Street Trust companies. Two also were members of the private banking firm of Brown Brothers, three were directors of the Boston Manufacturers Mutual Life Insurance Company, and two were directors of the American Mutual Liability Insurance Company. The group also continued the close association of their forebears in the textile companies of Lowell, Lawrence, Holyoke-Chicopee, and New Hampshire.

Legislative limitations on the Hospital Life's investments from 1900 to 1936 remained virtually the same as they had been since 1881. The only amendment sought from the legislature during these years – an act of 1903 – increased the maximum to which the company could acquire real estate in Boston from $1,500,000 to $4,000,000.[18] The main impetus for the amendment seems to have been a desire to help the company protect its investment in its own building by acquiring more property in the immediate area. This legislative action was used only to a limited extent, for the maximum at which the company's real estate was valued on the books of the company in the period 1901 to 1937 – aside from foreclosed property – was $1,641,000 in 1930. The only other expansion of the company's powers of investment occurred when the savings bank commissioners from time to time extended the list of securities legal for purchase by savings banks and trust companies.

Mortgages retained their pre-eminence as the main medium of investment for the fund of the company. From a temporary low of 42 per cent of the total fund ($26,430,000) in 1901, they increased to 47 per cent in 1908, at or near which percentage they remained until after World War I. Thereafter, perhaps because of the intensity of competition for commercial and personal loans in the 1920's, the proportion in mortgages grew to 57 per cent in 1926 and was 55 per cent of the total fund ($36,822,500) at the end of

1929.[19] This latter figure compares with an average of 58 per cent for the mutual savings banks of Massachusetts in 1930.[20] As had been customary throughout the company's history, these mortgages were written for terms of not more than five years and provided for payment of lump sum at maturity.

The extent of investment in mortgages was not out of line for the type of business being conducted, but the manner in which mortgages were selected in this period ultimately proved almost disastrous. Standards were being maintained in the proportion of the money loaned to the value of the property, and in such matters as searching titles. But most of the mortgages were continuing to be located in the same areas from which the company had received mortgages for so long. Because of the people connected with the company, the Massachusetts Hospital Life had frequently held mortgages on some of the city's finest homes on Beacon Street and in adjacent Back Bay. Since the later nineteenth century it had also been investing considerable sums in mortgages on property in the immediate vicinity of the company's building. Its long and successful experience with mortgages in these locations tended to blind the company to such significant facts as the suburbanization of many of Boston's wealthy families and the gradual shift southward of Boston's business and financial district. The result was that the company became vulnerable to the sharp decline in property values in residential or business areas no longer quite first class. The mortgagor's incentive to retain his property was not so great as if the property were truly first quality. According to a survey made in the fall of 1937, 90 per cent of the mortgages still outstanding were located within the limits of old downtown Boston and the Back Bay, and 93 per cent of the foreclosures which had been made had been on properties in those areas.[21]

Loans on notes and collateral were made mainly to the same three groups as in the later nineteenth century – to textile companies, to prominent Bostonians (frequently closely associated with the Massachusetts Hospital Life), and to financial houses.[22] A significant change had occurred in the amount of such lending, however, especially in the 1920's. In 1901, 45 per cent of the total fund of the company was invested in notes which matured annually. By 1914 this ratio had declined to 35 per cent, and at the end of World

War I to 26 per cent. Thereafter the decline continued to a low of 7 per cent in 1927. In the tighter money market just preceding and during the crisis of 1929 this ratio grew briefly to 14 per cent.

The apparent major reason for the decline in this type of investment was the great growth of commercial banks and the broadening of their lending pattern from the one-to-six months loans and discounts of a half century earlier to include many loans running for a year or even longer in some cases. Savings banks were also continuing to grow rapidly. In the face of this intensified competition, the share of the Massachusetts Hospital Life in one-year-term lending declined. A problem thus arose in the 1920's of making certain that the alternative means of investment provided as much liquidity protection as had the old pattern. The problem seems not to have been considered very carefully and, as the company's subsequent history shows, was by no means solved.

Loans to textile companies continued to be made primarily to the group of companies with which the Massachusetts Hospital Life had so long been associated – the New England textile companies to the north and west of Boston. In 1913, 36 different companies in the textile industry borrowed $5,165,000 in 78 loans. This was a little less than half of the 177 loans made during the year and a little less than half of the total amount loaned ($12,054,000). These loans to textile firms were more than three times the amount loaned to all other corporate enterprises, chiefly local utilities. The most important new textile borrower in New England during these years was the Plymouth Cordage Company, with which the Loring family was associated. A number of loans were also made to a few mills in the South. The great majority of these were made to the Lannett Cotton Mills and the West Point Manufacturing Company of West Point, Georgia, outposts of the selling agent firm of Wellington, Sears & Company of Boston.

As late as 1920, 63 loans totaling $4,780,000 were made to 23 different textile companies. This number was almost half of the 127 loans made during the year and more than half the total amount loaned ($8,640,000). Thereafter, as the cotton textile industry of New England passed into crisis in the middle and later 1920's, the number and amount of loans to textile companies also declined.*

* Chief borrowers among the textile companies in number of loans during the

Loans made to individuals reflect the ties to Boston's first families. Like the loans to textile companies, they tended to fall away both in number and amount, especially after 1920. Table 18 shows the 22 individuals who borrowed 14 or more times between January, 1901, and January, 1930. These loans continued to average much less in amount than loans to textile companies. Loans shown on this chart, which were by no means all the loans made to individuals, are a little more than one-sixth of the total number of loans made during the period.

Loans to the third group of borrowers, brokerage firms and private banking houses, varied usually according to the condition of the stock and bond markets. Most important among this category of borrowers was Lee, Higginson & Company, which borrowed a larger total sum during these decades than any other company or individual. Loans to this group amounted to 14 in number and to $1,500,000 in 1913 and to 15 in number and $920,000 in 1920; or to approximately 18 and 24 per cent in number and 29 and 19 per cent in amount of those made to textile companies in the same years. Loans to brokerage houses and banking firms were slightly less than 10 per cent of the total number between 1920 and the end of 1928, but between January 1, 1929, and June 1, 1930, they were slightly more than half (67) of the 125 loans made in that tense time. Eighteen of these loans were made to Lee, Higginson & Company, 14 to Jackson & Curtis, 11 to Curtis & Sanger, 10 to Blake Brothers, and 10 to Pyne, Kendall & Hollister. A sum amounting to $3,050,000 was advanced to brokerage and banking firms in 26 loans in the four months of stock market stress between September 1 and December 31, 1929.

Security ownership remained the least significant of the three major means for the investment of the company's fund until after the end of World War I. In 1901 approximately 10 per cent of the Massachusetts Hospital Life fund was invested in securities. As late

1920's were the Arlington Mills of Lawrence, West Point Manufacturing Company of West Point, Georgia, Ipswich Mills of Ipswich, Lancaster Mills of Clinton, Plymouth Cordage Company of Plymouth, Nashua Manufacturing Company of Nashua, New Hampshire, Merrimack Manufacturing Company of Lowell, Warwick Mills of Centreville, Rhode Island, Pacific Mills of Lawrence, and the American Woolen Company. Each of these companies borrowed at least 12 times, and the Arlington Mills on 32 different occasions.

TABLE 18

Major Individual Borrowers (14 or More Loans)
January 1, 1901 to January 1, 1930

BORROWERS	1901–1905	1905–1910	1910–1915	1915–1920	1920–1925	1925–1930
Total loans during period	847	1,056	1,031	590	396	291
Total loans this group	78	244	178	131	84	30
Grafton S. L. Abbott; *lawyer*; associate of Charles Francis Adams.		14	11 (*74*)	2		
Charles Francis Adams;[a] *capitalist*; investor in real estate and industrial securities, especially in Kansas City area; pres., Kansas City Stockyards Co.	20	36	21 (*91*)	4		
Francis I Amory;[b] *trustee*; pres., Cabot Mfg. Co.	2	5	5 (*75*)	4		
Frederick Ayer; *capitalist*; first pres., American Woolen Co.	4	8	14 (*140*)	1		
George F. Babbitt; *journalist*; editor, Boston *Herald.*	2	6	4 (*50*)	5	5 (*50*)	1
Charles E. Cotting; *real estate trustee.*	3	11	4 (*300*)	9		
J. Murray Forbes;[a] *capitalist*; member of the Forbes family; investor in western railroad securities; Pullman Co., General Electric, and various industrial companies.	7		6 (*105*)	9	1 (*35*)	4 (*35*)
Eugene N. Foss; *manufacturer*; gov. of Mass., 1910–13; treas. and gen. mgr., B. F. Sturtevant Co.		3	4 (*25*)	8	7 (*50*)	
George P. Gardner, Sr.;[bc] *capitalist; trustee*; son of George A. Gardner; pres., Lawrence Mfg. Co.; v.p., Chicago Junction Railways & Union Stockyards; dir., General Electric, A. T. & T., Old Colony Trust Co.		1	8 (*45*)	11	9 (*60*)	3
Stephen Holman	12	38	27 (*250*)			

TABLE 18 (*continued*)

Major Individual Borrowers (14 or More Loans)
January 1, 1901 to January 1, 1930

BORROWERS		1901–1905	1905–1910	1910–1915	1915–1920	1920–1925	1925–1930
	Total loans during period	847	1,056	1,031	590	396	291
	Total loans this group	78	244	178	131	84	30
Charles E. Hubbard; *lawyer*; dir., A. T. & T.		7	15	16 (*50*)	11	12 (*28*)	
Walter Hunnewell;[c] *capitalist*; *trustee*; son of H. H. Hunnewell; investor chiefly in railroads, Midwest and New England.		2	9	9 (*90*)	3		
F. L. Higginson;[c] *capitalist*; son of George Higginson, a founder of Lee, Higginson & Co.; dir., Merchants Natl. Bank (Boston), Calumet & Hecla, Kansas City Stockyards Co.		3	5	5 (*50*)	5	5 (*50*)	20 (*88*)
A. P. Loring, Sr.;[c] *trustee*; grandson of Charles G. Loring; author of *A Trustee's Handbook*; pres., Plymouth Cordage Co., Mass. Cotton Mills.					17	16 (*75*)	20 (*88*)
Jesse P. Lyman; *manufacturer*; pres., American Glue Co.			12	2			
William L. Putnam;[b] *lawyer*; dir., A. T. & T., Walter Baker & Co., Ltd., and several textile companies and financial institutions.			8	7 (*100*)	5	2 (*50*)	
William A. Russell; *engineering and management consultant.*		4	10	2 (*300*)			
Francis Shaw;[a] *capitalist.*		4	8	8 (*25*)	13	6 (*47*)	
E. V. R. Thayer, Sr.;[a] *capitalist*; brother of Nathaniel Thayer, Jr.		2	13				
E. V. R. Thayer, Jr.;[bc] *capitalist*; pres., Merchants Natl. Bank (Boston), Kansas City Stockyards Co.; v.p., Chicago							

TABLE 18 *(continued)*

Major Individual Borrowers (14 or More Loans)
January 1, 1901 to January 1, 1930

BORROWERS	1901–1905	1905–1910	1910–1915	1915–1920	1920–1925	1925–1930
Total loans during period	847	1,056	1,031	590	396	291
Total loans this group	78	244	178	131	84	30
Junction Railways & Union Stockyards; dir., A. T. & T.			4 *(75)*	5	5	
Nathaniel Thayer, III; [c] *capitalist*; v.p., Chicago Junction Railways & Union Stockyards; dir., U. S. Steel, A. T. & T., Kansas City Stockyards, New Haven, and St. Louis & San Francisco railroads, Merchants Natl. Bank.	4	21	3			
William Whitman; *textile manufacturer*; pres., Arlington Mills.			7 *(75)*	11	14 *(150)*	2
William M. Wood; *textile manufacturer*; son-in-law of Frederick Ayer; pres., American Woolen Co.; dir., Merchants Natl. Bank.	2	21	11 *(100)*	8	2 *(40)*	

[a] Stockholder, Massachusetts Hospital Life.
[b] Vice-President, Massachusetts Hospital Life.
[c] Director, Massachusetts Hospital Life.
NOTE: Italicized figures in parentheses beneath the number of loans indicate the total amount of loans in thousands of dollars made to the specified individual during the calendar years 1913, 1920, and 1928.

as 1912 this ratio was no higher, but thereafter the proportion invested in securities grew substantially. At the end of World War I, 23 per cent of the fund was in securities and, at maximum in 1924, 33 per cent. Thereafter the ratio declined to 25 per cent in 1929.

As late as 1913, the security portfolio of the Massachusetts Hospital Life showed the influence of H. H. Hunnewell in the company's holdings in New England and midwestern railroads. To these holdings a substantial quantity of bonds in the utility field had been added, especially those of the American Telephone & Telegraph Company, the New England Telephone & Telegraph Company, and the Boston Elevated Railway. Smaller investments had also been made in the bonds of the Chicago Junction Railways & Union

Stockyards Company, the Metropolitan Coal Company of Boston, and the Aroostook Construction Company of Maine.

During and after World War I the security holdings of the company grew rapidly. Most of the increase was in holdings of United States government bonds, although part was in rails, and part in the public utility, industrial, and banking fields. On January 1, 1929, approximately half (49 per cent) of the portfolio ($10,058,000) was in rails, 29 per cent in United States governments, 10 per cent in public utilities, 8 per cent in industrials, and 4 per cent in stocks of Boston national banks and trust companies. Eighty-four per cent of the portfolio was in bonds or notes, of which 10 per cent were scheduled to mature within two years and 3 per cent more within the next two years. During 1933 an additional 30 per cent of the bonds and notes, principally those of the United States government, would mature. Eighty-four per cent of the portfolio was rated "A" or better by Moody's Investors Service in 1929 and another 12 per cent "B" or better. The remaining 4 per cent was not listed.

Especially in the later 1920's, substantial gains, apart from interest, were made on the security portfolio. In part these gains were from occasional sales of securities at an advance over their purchase price, but they were also due to bonds which were called above par and to bonds, bought years earlier at a discount, which matured and were paid in full. Profits from these sources amounted to $139,000 in 1928 and to $172,000 in 1929.[23] They helped to make the 1920's, from a stockholder's point of view, the most prosperous years in the history of the company.

Dividends to stockholders increased from the $8.00 rate at the turn of the century to $10.00, declared in January, 1913, and to $11.00 in 1920 and 1921. The $12.00 rate established in January, 1922, was maintained plus extras of $4.00 in 1923 and $2.00 in 1925 until January, 1927, when the rate was raised to $14.00 for that and the following year. The rate went to $15.00 in 1929 and 1930, only to lapse back to $12.00 in 1931 and 1932. From 1933 through 1937 it was $6.00 and in 1938, $2.00.

The yield to depositors was hardly so impressive, but after 1908 it never fell below 4 per cent. In 1920 a common rate of 4¾ per cent was established for all depositors, which was increased to 5 per cent in 1921 and to 5¼ per cent in 1924. Thereafter 5 per cent was paid until 1930, when the rate was reduced to 4¾ per cent. Further reductions were made to 4¼ per cent in 1931, to 3¾ per cent in 1932, and to 3 per cent in 1933. This rate was maintained until 1936, when it was reduced to 2½ per cent.

Although the return to the depositors in this more competitive age failed to match that achieved in the early years of the company it was considerably better than that of the last quarter of the nineteenth century. The rates paid until 1930 were also normally from ¼ of 1 per cent to 1 per cent better than those of the Provident Institution for Savings, with its somewhat greater liquidity needs and greater restrictions on investments. From 1931 on, by contrast, yield of the Provident Institution for Savings to its depositors was equal to that of the Massachusetts Hospital Life, and in 1933 greater by ¼ of 1 per cent.[24]

Impact of Depression

When the crisis occurred in the fall of 1929, few financial institutions were in a position to view the situation with greater equanimity than the Massachusetts Hospital Life. The company had met a number of major crises with minimal loss. It had a deposit structure in which slightly more than half of its deposits were payable only on the death of the individual in whose name the trust deposit contract had been drawn. Very few other deposit contracts had been written for a term of less than three years. Nor were there many men possessed of knowledge in economic affairs who were of the opinion that the crisis was more than temporary. Consequently the officers and directors of the Massachusetts Hospital Life were relatively undisturbed. They made considerable sums available to brokerage houses and private banking firms to reap the benefit of temporarily higher interest rates, and they failed to see what might happen to the company if the nation entered a prolonged depression.

As late as the end of the year 1930, actuary Stockton was viewing the situation with relative calm. He considered the Massachusetts Hospital Life in good shape, although the company had had to foreclose on property mortgaged at a value of $685,000 during the year. He estimated the various capital and surplus accounts at $3,804,000, and the value of the company's building and its security portfolio at an additional $964,000 above book value.[25] Despite the sharp decline in security prices in 1931 and the continuing heavy rate of foreclosure on mortgaged property, this basic confidence in the future welfare of the company is reflected in the declaration of $12 dividends in January, 1931, and January, 1932. In November, 1930, earnings of 4¾ per cent were declared for deposits for the year 1930, and in November, 1931, earnings of 4¼ per cent for deposits for the year 1931.

But there were other factors, in addition to the less satisfactory condition of the investments, which were a threat to the company, especially if the depression lengthened. For one of the few times in its history, and in far greater degree than ever before, the company was faced with a net cash outflow. Few new deposits were being received, and a number of old deposits were being withdrawn. Between the end of 1929 and the end of 1932 deposits declined in number by 139 from the 1929 figure of 1,643 and in amount by $2,523,000 from the 1929 total of $29,241,000.[26] Most of this reduction was in "G" and "A" deposits. These were mainly three-year or five-year term deposits and were thus most easily accessible for withdrawal. In addition, that minority of depositors who permitted their interest payments to accumulate as new capital was smaller. Formerly, it had run as high as one-fourth.

Meanwhile the company's position in relation to the common fund continued to grow worse. At the end of 1931 the extent of depreciation in the security portfolio (carried on the books at $13,025,000) was estimated to be at least $2,400,000.[27] This figure grew to even greater size as the prices of securities continued to fall during 1932. Foreclosed property held by the company had increased to $804,000 at the end of 1932 and to $2,066,000 at the end of 1933.[28] A large proportion of the $16,096,000 in mortgages at the end of 1933 – no one could know how much – also seemed to offer slight chance of recapture of principal without some loss.

Although the company could easily persist in paying the full face of all deposit contracts for a number of years from funds derived from the maturing of its investments or their sale in a depressed market, to do so would be a violation of all deposit contracts written before 1926. By the terms of those contracts, losses incurred without the company's being at fault were to be shared equitably in proportion to the total fund between stockholder and depositor interests. Not to share losses equitably would be to favor depositors who could get out early over those who had to wait and to invite legal action on the part of these latter depositors. The situation was further complicated in that upward of $5,000,000 in deposits had been made after the introduction of the "special" deposit contract in 1926. This contract guaranteed the depositor against loss of principal.

Howard Stockton died early in April, 1932, after 31 years as actuary, just as the critical condition of the company was being recognized. He was succeeded by his son-in-law, Alexander Whiteside, a prominent Boston lawyer and, on his mother's side, a member of the Shattuck family.[29] Mr. Whiteside had been vice-president of the National Union Bank of Boston from 1917 to 1920, but his experience in the operation of a company controlling trust funds was limited. He had had no prior connection with the Massachusetts Hospital Life.

During the following years the company addressed itself to meeting its obligations to depositors so that they would suffer minimal loss and to the even more difficult problem of trying to build again a sound future. In moving toward the first of these goals, the company was spurred on by a committee representing large depositors who had reason to be concerned about the future payment of their deposits. Early in 1933 the company ceased taking deposits, of which few were being offered anyway, under the old terms of contract. In time, this suspension became permanent.

Two immediate problems faced the company in the middle 1930's: protecting the common fund from further losses, and determining how existing losses could be shared equitably among depositors and stockholders in conformity with the terms of the deposit contracts.

In attempting to solve the first problem, both the actuary and the Committee of Finance sought the advice of the directors and of outside sources with reference to the purchase and sale of securities.[30] By this time the company was lending hardly any money on notes or new mortgages. In 1935 the company entered into a six-month contract with the Fiduciary Trust Company of Boston, of which one of the Massachusetts Hospital Life directors, Robert H.

Gardiner, was president, to guide its investments. This was done after the aged and distinguished Episcopal Bishop William Lawrence had requested that the company seek outside professional advice in managing its securities.[31] Bishop Lawrence, a grandson of Amos Lawrence, at the time was acting as one of a three-member committee officially representing the interests of the larger depositors. David H. Howie, who handled this assignment for the Fiduciary Trust Company, subsequently became a vice-president of the Massachusetts Hospital Life in 1936 and a director in 1938.

The second problem was extremely involved. As early as June, 1932, the new actuary pointed out that almost half of the deposits ($12,800,000) dated from before 1920 and consequently were payable either in money or in the investments of the company at the will of the directors. Although the actuary urged then and subsequently that a policy be adopted for "payment in kind," no such action was taken until the time of the bank holiday in 1933. But payment in kind involved difficulties of selection and valuation and was little desired by depositors. The policy was therefore suspended after a three-month trial.[32]

An accurate statement of the relative position of stockholder and depositor interests required an adjustment of former accounting practices. The maintenance of securities and mortgages at their old asset values, which could not be realized, offset by a guaranty fund and other reserve accounts, was of little help in showing the actual condition of the company. As Robert H. Gardiner phrased it, the annual statement was "somewhat blind." [33] The judgment of professional experts was especially required to know the market value of the real estate and mortgages held by the company. Consequently, in November, 1935, the Committee of Finance authorized John C. Kiley, Stephen Sleeper, and Edwin D. Brooks, all of whom had had long experience in Boston real estate, to make such an appraisal. At the same time the Committee of Finance appointed a second committee to seek outside accounting aid to make the company's balance sheets more realistic and meaningful.

The work of these two committees resulted in a more accurate picture of the company's financial condition. The committee appointed to appraise mortgages reported that the mortgages, foreclosed properties, and real estate held by the Massachusetts Hospital Life were worth $4,230,000 less than the value at which they were carried on the books. After contemplating the size of this adjustment in the value of the mortgages and the estimated deficiency between book and market value of the securities of the company, the committee appointed to revise the balance sheet abolished the several reserve accounts, which in their dollar amount had become so dubious, and consolidated them in a single reserve.[34]

On the basis of these revaluations, during the spring of 1936, the directors worked out a policy providing for payment of the slightly more than $24,000,000 in deposits as they matured and were demanded. By dividing the claims of the depositors and the stockholders, against the assets at current value, the directors arrived at a figure (approximately 86 per cent) indicating the liquidating value of the claims as a proportion of the total assets as of that moment. Since the "general" (pre-1926) deposit contracts made those depositors co-adventurers with the stockholders sharing proportionately with the stockholders in any losses sustained free from fault of the company, this figure, subject to minor adjustments, provided one basis for the settlement of the claims for the $19,370,000 in general deposits as those deposits matured. There was no question but that the $4,660,000 in "special" deposits had to be paid in full in accordance with the terms of the special deposit contracts. Losses sustained on the special deposits as they matured were assessable solely against the stockholder interest in the assets.

In May, 1936, the directors offered to pay general deposits, currently due and demanded, at 82½ per cent of the face of each deposit. The per cent of the face to be offered as full payment was made subject to adjustment each month as determined from a continuing reappraisal of the company's investments.[35] As required by the contracts written prior to 1920, the directors also offered to pay these older general deposits in a fair cross section of the investments proportionate to the value of each deposit, but this option was rarely requested. Thus a basis was established for the orderly liquidation of the company's obligations to its depositors. The situation remained difficult well into the 1940's, however, because of the continuing unsatisfactory condition of the Massachusetts Hospital Life mortgage portfolio.

The other and long-range problem facing the company in the

middle 1930's was on what basis the Massachusetts Hospital Life should attempt to continue its business. To attempt to attract new depositors to place their funds in a common fund which contained so high a fraction of dubious assets, especially before the revaluation of 1935–1936, was impossible. To continue to use the "special" deposit contract guaranteeing the deposits against loss seemed undesirable, for this contract had been a major contributing factor to the company's serious condition during the depression.

What the board finally sought to do late in 1933 was to return to first principles and to develop the common-fund idea of 1823 into a modern Massachusetts-type trust. On November 1, 1933, a trust indenture was executed providing for the establishment of a new commingled fund to be known as the Hospital Life Trust. It was to issue certificates valued initially at $100 per unit, against which a management fee of 1/4 of 1 per cent would be charged annually. Principal was made payable at the election of the Trustee, the Massachusetts Hospital Life Insurance Company, 60 days after the date or the event upon which each trust matured. An additional charge of 1 per cent was levied at the time of payment of the principal. In the main, the terms of the contract followed as closely as possible the terms of the old contract.[36]

The Hospital Life Trust failed to grow as its sponsors had hoped. For this there were several reasons. For one thing, the terms of the trust looked too much to the company's past rather than to current investment company practice, and, to make matters worse, the indenture was, by its terms, unamendable. Thus an extremely unfortunate rigidity was established in the trust at a time when the whole field of investment company operations was in process of being re-examined and modified under the impact of New Deal reform legislation.

One unfortunate result of its unamendable instrument was that capital gains made by the Hospital Life Trust were taxed in their totality in the hands of the Trust, for no provision had been made for their distribution to the certificate holders, in whose hands the gains would have been taxed at a lower rate. Another unsatisfactory feature was that investments made for the Hospital Life Trust had to be made within the limits of the laws governing Massachusetts Hospital Life investments, while trustees of competing investment trusts were free to operate under the "prudent man" rule. The result was that by the end of 1936 the commingled fund of the Hospital Life Trust amounted to only $485,000.

By this time it had become clear that the Hospital Life Trust could be the answer to the problem of the company's future only if it could be placed on a better competitive footing in relation to other investment trusts.[37] The company's powers of investment were finally broadened in 1938 to equal those of any other investment company, but because of its other disadvantages, the Hospital Life Trust grew slowly. Recently it has even declined in size. At the end of the year 1953 the market value of its assets was $1,862,000.[38]

A second step taken under actuary Whiteside's aegis was to seek aggressively a larger share of life annuity business. For the first time in more than a century the company began to advertise, and for the first time in its history an agent was hired to sell annuities on commission and in conjunction with units of the Hospital Life Trust. Between the end of 1933 and the end of 1936 the value of the life annuity contracts held by the company increased from $2,105,000 to $2,748,000 at an expense for commissions and advertising totaling a little more than $44,000.[39] The campaign to sell life annuities had the further advantage of bringing liquid funds into the company at a time of financial strain. But the return on investments was so low that a business profit on the life annuity account proved hardly possible. Moreover, life annuities had always been only a slender fraction of the company's business. It seemed extremely doubtful whether the life annuity business could ever be built up to sufficient size to justify the company's existence on life annuities alone.

At the annual meeting in February, 1936, there was a major turnover in the officers and directors of the company. At that time George P. Gardner resigned as president, terminating a period of association with the company dating from 1901. He was succeeded as president by Samuel H. Wolcott, who resigned as director. Four other long-time directors also resigned from the 13-member board. A. P. Loring, Jr., succeeded his father as director, and G. Peabody Gardner, son of the retiring president, also became a new director. Of the three other new directors, John S. Lawrence was a great-great-grandson of Amos Lawrence. George L. Batchelder, Jr., had served, along with Bishop Lawrence, as a member of the committee of large depositors, and Edwin D. Brooks had assisted in the difficult appraisal of the company's mortgages.

At the same time the constituency of the Committee of Finance was changed. John C. Kiley, a leading specialist in Boston real estate, who had shared with Edwin D. Brooks and Stephen W. Sleeper in appraising the Massachusetts Hospital Life mortgages in 1935–1936, now became a full-fledged member of the committee. For the previous year he had served as an alternate to Moses Williams. William Dexter, a lawyer and member of the famous private trustee family, was the other new committee member. He was a son of Philip Dexter. Samuel H. Wolcott, like his two immediate predecessors as president, combined his new office with continued membership on the Committee of Finance.[40]

Two of the new directors, A. P. Loring, Jr., and George L. Batchelder, were appointed with Robert H. Gardiner in February, 1936, as a special committee to consider future policies for the company. When the committee was enlarged in September, John S. Lawrence and Bentley W. Warren (a prominent attorney, president of the Boston Symphony Society, and a Massachusetts Hospital Life director) were also made members. During a seven-month period the committee considered a range of alternatives. Among the early alternatives was the possibility of disposing of the company's business to an out-of-state life insurance company which would guarantee that the depositors would be paid. This suggestion was dropped after consultation with a specialist, who believed it highly unlikely that a life insurance company would be willing to negotiate on such terms.[41]

Alexander Whiteside resigned as actuary in February, 1937. During his period in office the company had fashioned a workable policy for sharing losses among general depositors and stockholders when maturing deposits had to be paid. But the other great problem of a future for the company remained unsolved. By the end of 1936 the Massachusetts Hospital Life deposits had declined about 20 per cent from their peak at the end of 1928 ($29,252,975). Unless a better way was discovered to put the company back in business than the Hospital Life Trust then offered, the road ahead seemed to lead toward orderly liquidation and death for an historic and once important New England financial institution.

VII

A RETURN TO FIRST PRINCIPLES (1937–1953)

The story of the Massachusetts Hospital Life in the past 17 years has been that of hard work, skill, and patience, combined with more favorable economic conditions. The company has been revitalized and refashioned along modern investment company lines, while at the same time its flexible forms of trust have been maintained. The result has been an investment company possessing unique characteristics. In this accomplishment new names have been linked with those long associated with the company's activities.

Struggle for Reorganization

Following the considerable shakeup in personnel of the officers and directors, the company gained in February, 1937, a new actuary, Edward H. Osgood.[1] Although Osgood had had no prior connection with the Massachusetts Hospital Life, he had long known of the company through association with various brokerage firms and private banking houses of Boston, especially Lee, Higginson & Company. He had been a member of that firm from 1922 to 1932 and treasurer of Lee Higginson Corporation from 1932 to 1934. In 1933–1934 he had also served as New England manager of the Reconstruction Finance Corporation. Before becoming actuary, Osgood had been Assistant Federal Reserve Agent of the Federal Reserve Bank of Boston.[2]

Osgood thus brought a broad experience in finance and investments to the leadership of the company. He worked diligently for the welfare of the company, but with a rare patience. If a goal he sought could not be achieved at once, he was able to wait or to seek another way. Osgood made use of his distinguished board for guidance and support. He could also fashion a team and a "team spirit" within the office of the company, not always so readily apparent in its past history. Among the older employees, he relied particularly upon Paul T. Litchfield, a staff member since 1911 and secretary since 1937. Not long after he became actuary, Osgood hired a young Harvard Business School graduate and specialist in investment analysis, D. George Sullivan, to make a special study of the condition of the company. Sullivan subsequently became a permanent member of the staff. He served as assistant treasurer from 1939 to 1942, and as treasurer thereafter. When the administrative structure was redesigned in 1949 to eliminate the Board of Control and the nonfunctional vice-presidents, the two new vice-presidents then appointed were Paul T. Litchfield and D. George Sullivan.

Osgood also brought into the employ of the company James M. Stauss, who had been on the Reconstruction Finance Corporation staff and whose work Osgood knew well. Stauss later became assistant secretary and assistant treasurer of the company. In addition he served as president of the Fifty State Street Company, the subsidiary which had been established to market units of the Hospital Life Trust.

At the time Osgood became actuary the crucial problems of where the company should go in the future and how it should get there were still unresolved. As a contribution to the solution of these problems, Osgood presented Sullivan's comprehensive report, with recommendations to the board at its October, 1937, meeting.[3] Not all the recommendations were adopted. The suggestion that the annuity business be continued and aggressively pursued was not followed because of the intense competition in the life annuity field and the low yield on investment of the life annuity account. After a temporary suspension, the sale of life annuities ceased in April, 1941. Nor did it prove possible to sell units of the Hospital Life Trust effectively because of shortcomings in the trust indenture. The management fee on all deposits, including the Hospital Life Trust, was raised from 1/4 to 3/10 of 1 per cent in January, 1938.[4] To raise it further to the 1/2 of 1 per cent recommendation of the report must have seemed unwise to the board at a time when the yield to Massachusetts Hospital Life depositors had just been reduced to 2 per cent.

But the board did agree heartily with the central theme of the report: that the salvation of the company lay in its becoming a modern investment company.[5] The board also resolved to take action on the subordinate and necessary recommendation that the company seek authorization from the legislature for broadened powers of investment so that it could compete on equal terms with other investment companies. As a first step, early in 1938 Bentley Warren was appointed to draft a bill for submission to the legislature.[6] This bill, signed by the Governor at the end of April, gave to the company the right to invest funds "in the same way, to the same extent, and under the same restrictions as an individual trustee in this Commonwealth may invest trust funds or assets." The Massachusetts Hospital Life was also authorized to adopt "one or more forms of declaration of trust containing provisions for the management and conduct of the funds to be held thereunder and for the reciprocal rights and duties of the trustee and beneficiaries. . . ." The act provided that money and securities so received would be held in a common fund "separate and distinct from all other funds and property" held by the company.[7]

This amendment to the charter, which put the company under the "prudent man" rule, was a significant step toward making the Massachusetts Hospital Life a modern investment company. Its effect was to permit the company investment powers equal to any other investment company. In February, 1939, the board defined a new investment policy. It voted that all stocks, both common and preferred, held by the company should not exceed 30 per cent of the total amount of the following: the sum of all cash, the value of all securities at the market, and 75 per cent of the face value of mortgage loans. In September, 1939, this ratio was increased to 40 per cent.[8] The new powers were of substantial benefit in getting assets of "better quality, liquidity, and marketability."

Unfortunately, this act could not be *the* answer in helping the company to turn the corner and begin active operations as a growing, modern investment company. Too many of the company's investments were still of dubious value. They required close attention. At the end of 1939 the company held $8,296,000 in mortgages and $3,997,000 in foreclosed property. This was approximately 53 per cent of the total assets. There was also the possibility that the basis for settlement of the general deposits laid down in 1936 might be challenged. No regulatory agency or court had yet ruled on this program of settlement. While the condition of the company was still uncertain, no forthright action toward becoming a modern investment company was possible. Instead, time and a series of steps culminating in a major effort were required.

A companion activity to seeking new powers for the company during these years was that of modernizing its internal administration. During 1938 and 1939 the bylaws received their first major revision since 1889. Three new offices — treasurer, assistant treasurer, and chairman of the board — were established, and the size of the Committee of Finance was increased to six. Samuel H. Wolcott resigned as president to become chairman of the board, while Osgood took on the titles of president and treasurer in addition to that of actuary. Meanwhile the authority of the Board of Control was reduced. Its power to fix a maximum size for the Massachusetts Hospital Life, a power held since the beginning of the company, was withdrawn, and its audit authority was reduced to an annual examination of the company's fund. The membership of the Board of Control was also made flexible between 6 and 15, depending on the number of vice-presidents.[9]

Legislative action was required for two other changes: to make the Board of Directors flexible in number between 10 and 20, and to change the annual meeting of the stockholders from the third Monday in January to the more convenient first Monday in March. This act, signed in June, 1939, also authorized the company to change the par value of its shares and to increase or reduce its capital, subject to the approval of the Commissioner of Corporations. The way was thus opened for an adjustment in capital, impaired by losses in the depression.[10]

These changes were not sufficient to re-establish the company on a firm footing, but the changes did contribute powerfully to a feeling of faith in the future. In December, 1940, when some New York parties offered to purchase a controlling interest in the Massachusetts Hospital Life, a meeting of stockholders was called. The New Yorkers offered to pay from $30 to $50 per share and to leave the membership of the Board of Directors about as it was. Not a single director or stockholder spoke in favor of the offer. Nor was there any letter from a depositor urging acceptance. On the contrary, several letters were filed in opposition.[11] Later in the month a voting trust was established controlling 3,155 of the 5,000 shares to make certain that control was not wrested from the officers and directors, even though by the rules of the company a shareholder desiring to sell his shares was required to offer them to the company in the first instance. The voting trustees were Samuel H. Wolcott, chairman of the board; George L. Batchelder, Jr., a board member; and Francis C. Gray, of the Fiduciary Trust Company.[12]

During the following years not much of significance was accomplished until toward the end of World War II. The single subsequent piece of legislation passed prior to 1945 was an act of 1943 changing the legal status of the Massachusetts Hospital Life from an institution similar to a savings bank (as suggested in the legislation of 1881) to an institution similar to a trust company. The new law provided that the Commissioner of Banks should have supervision of the company's affairs as if it were "the trust department of a trust company." [13] This change was useful in suggesting that the central spirit of the company was akin to that of a trust company, for funds in trust in a trust institution can vary in the amount of the principal due at the time of repayment.

Meanwhile time and improved economic conditions were working on the side of the company. The company was gradually thawing out its frozen mortgages, disposing of its foreclosed properties, and in general getting a higher quality and much more readily marketable body of assets. At the end of 1945 the mortgage account amounted to $3,590,000 and the foreclosed property account to $1,701,000. This was a reduction of approximately 57 per cent in each of these accounts since the beginning of 1940.[14]

Early in 1944 there began a last great endeavor to reorganize the company and to map out a promising program for its future operations. Three prominent Boston law firms were linked with the company in this effort. Because Bentley W. Warren was a director of the Massachusetts Hospital Life and Alexander Whiteside had been actuary, the firm of Warren, Garfield, Whiteside & Lamson had firsthand personal knowledge of the company. The firm of Rackemann, Sawyer & Brewster was retained to consider tax questions associated with any plan of reorganization. Over-all responsibility in all legal matters was lodged with the firm of Ropes, Gray, Best, Coolidge & Rugg. William H. Best of this latter firm gave unstintingly of his time and effort in helping the Massachusetts Hospital Life to formulate and to implement a satisfactory plan.

The problem of creating a bridge from the company's past to its desired future as a modern investment company was extremely difficult. Central was the fact that the company had four different groups of claimants to its assets. These assets were still not sufficient in 1944 to match the claims of each group in full. If a plan was to be feasible, it had to offer each group a reasonable promise that its position would be bettered through reorganization. The plan itself could be structured only after a most careful consideration of the company's obligations. In devising a plan, therefore, special attention was paid not only to the current legal and economic environment affecting modern investment companies, but also to the company's origins and history.

After months of consideration, early in 1945 a measure was introduced into the legislature providing a general frame for reorganization. This measure became law in May.[15] The law provided that if the Commissioner of Banks considered that the Massachusetts Hospital Life required reorganization, he could approve such a plan as he believed to be "fair and equitable." In such a case the commissioner was empowered to place a fair value upon the assets of the company (apart from the Hospital Life Trust) and to determine the respective rights of the individual special depositors, general depositors, and annuitants to those assets.

The law specified that assent to the plan must also be gained from special depositors, general depositors, and annuitants with claims to at least two-thirds of the principal amount in each of the three categories, and from holders of a majority of the stock outstanding. If any claimant made known his opposition to the plan within a reasonable period of time, the commissioner was ordered to set aside a fair cross section of the assets in favor of the objector. All other claimants would be bound by a favorable vote for the plan, whether they had voted or not. The Hospital Life Trust was specifically exempted from the reorganization.

During the next two and a half years careful attention was given to creating a plan which would meet the test of fairness and equity in the eyes of the respective claimants and of the Commissioner of Banks. The company was also anxious that the plan conserve the values inherent in its long and historic relationship with its depositors and adapt its old procedures to investment company operation as practiced in the mid-twentieth century. After repeated discussion with the Commissioner of Banks and consultation with the Securities & Exchange Commission concerning the establishment of a new fund, on December 29, 1947, the Commissioner of Banks approved the plan of reorganization as submitted and fixed a valuation upon the assets of the company as of August 31, 1947. A month earlier, on November 26, 1947, the Massachusetts Hospital Life had executed the declaration of trust establishing the Massachusetts Life Fund.

The commissioner valued the assets of the company as of August 31 at $14,437,042, less current liabilities and interest at the end of the year amounting to $569,417. Almost half of these assets (48 per cent) were United States government bonds, and 35 per cent were other stocks and bonds. Against the net $13,867,625 the company carried liabilities on its books which were tentatively adjusted by the commissioner as shown in Table 19.

TABLE 19

Adjustments in Liabilities Recommended by the Massachusetts Commissioner of Banks August 31, 1947

LIABILITIES	BEFORE ADJUSTMENT	AFTER ADJUSTMENT
General Deposits	$10,738,676	$ 9,035,555
Special Deposits	3,127,733	3,127,733
Annuity Reserve	1,126,469	1,539,337
Capital and Surplus	1,265,162	165,000
Total	$16,258,040	$13,867,625

General deposits were thus valued at about 84 per cent of their face value, and special deposits at their full value. Under reorganization the stockholders' equity would be sharply reduced. Since the equity was the only protection for the annuitants if the annuity reserve account should prove inadequate, the annuity reserve was revalued upward. This was accomplished by using an actuarial table based on the mortality experience of the mid-1940's (rather than the rates current at the time the annuities were individually purchased) and by using a 2 per cent yield on the investment of the account. Some of the annuity reserve could be recaptured as profit if the mortality experience proved more favorable to the company than mid-1940 rates and if yield on the account amounted to more than 2 per cent. Thus far such has proved to be the case. General and special deposits were made exchangeable into units of the new Massachusetts Life Fund.

After the approval of the Commissioner of Banks, the task remained of getting the assent of claimants representing two-thirds of the amount of the claims in each of the three categories: general deposits, special deposits, and life annuities. Assent also had to be obtained from stockholders holding a majority of the outstanding stock of the company. The campaign began early in March, 1948.[16] This task was made particularly complex by the fact that all individuals with an interest in a deposit had to agree to the plan to make an assent valid for that deposit. Very frequently a number of different parties were involved: e.g., an individual with the right to income from the deposit and one or more remaindermen with right ultimately to the principal.

But the campaign proved less difficult, even with the general depositors, than might be imagined, because of the long close personal relations which had existed between the company and its depositors. By mid-August claimants holding (in value) 71 per cent of the general deposits, 76 per cent of the special deposits, 82 per cent of the annuities, and 81 per cent of the outstanding stock had given their assent in writing. In only three cases, involving a total of approximately $15,000, did depositors by their protests avail themselves of the option of having a separate trust set up from a proportional cross section of the assets of the company. In a series of weekly meetings held between November 1, 1948, and January 3, 1949, the directors resolved the last details of the new program necessary to get the Massachusetts Life Fund under way.[17]

Meanwhile a new profit-sharing agreement was signed with the Massachusetts General Hospital in mid-October, 1948. It provided that the Hospital would be eligible to half the excess above $12,000 paid out as dividends to stockholders in any one year. After revaluation of the capital stock to a par of $20 per share in January, 1949, this meant that profit-sharing would begin when dividends were in excess of 12 per cent. The agreement was subject to termination by the company when the accumulated sum paid to the Hospital under the new plan amounted to $25,000.[18]

In March, 1949, the bylaws were further revised.[19] The Board of Control was eliminated, as was also the historic office of actuary. At the same time the Committee of Finance was redesignated as the Investment Committee in keeping with common investment company practice. In managing the Massachusetts Hospital Life, the Board of President and Directors was specifically authorized to exercise all powers which belonged to the company under its charter and the subsequent amendments. The active part of the business was now principally the Massachusetts Life Fund and, secondarily, the Hospital Life Trust. If circumstances warranted, however, the company stood ready to enter any field of business it was empowered to enter, including life insurance and annuities.

Massachusetts Life Fund

The Massachusetts Life Fund is one of a number of diversified open-end funds. It operates under a declaration of trust which is clearly amendable and which provides for the distribution of capital gains as well as income on the individual certificate. The earnings of the fund are consequently not subject to income tax while in the possession of the company, and the beneficiaries of the fund receive a maximum tax benefit. The main unfortunate characteristics of the trust instrument for the Hospital Life Trust were thus avoided in drafting the declaration of trust for the new fund. Fifty State Street Company, the subsidiary established to market units of the Hospital Life Trust, became also the marketing agent for units of the Massachusetts Life Fund, and in July, 1949, a contract was entered into with the banking firm of Estabrook & Company to push sales aggressively. During 1950 and 1951 Massachusetts Life Fund units were qualified for sale under the laws of the District of Columbia and 19 states, including New York, Illinois, Ohio, and Texas.

The Massachusetts Life Fund is similar to other mutual funds in the amount of the fee charged for management (½ of 1 per cent); in the way all assets of the Fund are invested in a single commingled fund; in the way units are distributed; in the way unit value is computed twice daily; in the presence of a distributing charge which the purchaser must pay for his units in addition to net asset value; and in the option of redemption at the will of the certificate-holder. It is also similar to many of the more recent "balanced funds" in the pattern of its investments.

But in certain other aspects the Massachusetts Life Fund differs from other mutual funds, for it came into being partially grown and with a unique heritage. This heritage, developed through 125 years of successful experience by the Massachusetts Hospital Life in handling trust deposits, is responsible for the distinctive characteristics of the new Fund.

The difficulty in qualifying the new Fund with the Securities & Exchange Commission under the Investment Company Act of 1940 points up the impact of this heritage and the essential difference between the Massachusetts Life Fund and other mutual investment funds. Because of certain earlier abuses in investment company operation, the Investment Company Act of 1940 required that certificate-holders be given broad voting rights in such matters as the choice of directors of a fund, the selection of an auditor, and the approval of general investment policies. But the historic contracts under which the Massachusetts Hospital Life deposits were being exchanged into units of the Massachusetts Life Fund contained no voting rights. They had not resulted merely from an individual's buying a participation in a fund. The Massachusetts Hospital Life deposits were trust obligations, involving frequently more than one party. In many instances two or more persons had an interest in the obligation — one or more as to income, and others as to principal. If votes were given with the units, to whom should the votes be given? To the income recipients? Or to the remaindermen?

Because of this dilemma, the directors of the Massachusetts Hospital Life asked an exemption. This the Securities & Exchange Commission granted. The commission's reasons included not only the difficulty of determining who should vote, but also the fact that the directors of the company are elected annually by the stockholders. The stockholders have an interest parallel to the certificate-holders in the success of the Fund, for management fees continue to be the main source of income to the company. Moreover, unlike any other Massachusetts investment company, under the act passed in 1943 the operations of the company are subject to check in being supervised by the Commissioner of Banks.

Among investment companies two forms of organization have been common. In one of these, individuals serve as trustees of the fund under a declaration of trust, with the participants holding shares or certificates of beneficial interest in the total assets of the fund. In the other, there is a corporate form of structure. Here the company owns the assets outright, and its stockholders are the beneficiaries of the Fund. In each case, if some person wished to put his units or shares in trust, with the income or principal designated for some other party, it would be necessary for him to draw up a separate trust instrument with an outside trustee.

The Massachusetts Hospital Life is different from both these types. The company is distinctive among investment companies in that it has both stockholders and certificate-holders, with the certificate-holders alone being direct beneficiaries of the Fund. In contrast to any other investment company, the Hospital Life is corporate trustee of its own funds. Most significantly and without extra fee, the Massachusetts Hospital Life is also trustee of each separate trust certificate in the Fund. The close personal relations formerly existing between the company and each depositor thus continue to exist with each certificate-holder in the new Fund.

Because of the company's trustee relationship to each separate trust certificate, the wide variability of terms of the old trust deposits endures in the certificates of the Massachusetts Life Fund, old or new. Distribution of earnings on the certificate may be made payable quarterly, semiannually, or annually, or be permitted to accumulate with a minimum of effort, for these facts may be entered upon the face of the certificate. A term of years may be specified for the duration of the certificate. If the certificate-holder chooses, a "spendthrift" clause may be written upon the certificate, declaring the certificate, principal and income, inalienable from the claims of creditors. Or, as is true in so many cases, the claimant to income and the claimant to principal may be two or more persons. In its structure the Massachusetts Life Fund greatly resembles a common trust established by a trust company, in which a number of separate trusts having variable provisions are commingled and invested in a common fund.

From its beginning the Massachusetts Hospital Life invested almost exclusively in fixed income investments. Only rarely did its common stock holdings amount to as much as 5 per cent of its total fund. With the amendment to its charter in 1938, however, the company came under the "prudent man" rule in its investment powers, and as a result broadened appreciably and at once its holdings of high-grade common stocks. By carefully investing a portion of the Fund in equities, the company is attempting to secure a higher current return to the income beneficiaries of Massachusetts Life certificates than investment in fixed income securities alone could provide. By distributing net realized capital gains as new units of the Fund, except where the individual certificate specifies distribution as income, the company is also operating in a way to limit the inroads inflation might otherwise make on the principal sums of the participants in the Fund. This is especially important in cases where the remainderman and income recipient are different persons. As of December 31, 1953, the proportion of common stocks in the Massachusetts Life Fund was approximately 56 per cent of total assets.

Through its Massachusetts Life Fund the company continues to serve a wide range of investors. First and foremost, these include individuals investing for their own benefit or for the benefit of others. As has been true historically, this group includes a large proportion of single women, widows, wives, guardians, and trustees. In addition, a substantial number of charitable, religious, educational, and civic organizations are certificate-holders of the Fund. More recently, the company has reached into a new field of service in becoming the trustee of a few corporate pension, retirement, and profit-sharing plans. Because of the diversified sources from which the moneys of its certificate-holders come and the variety of terms under which the moneys are held, in contrast to most investment companies, the Massachusetts Hospital Life believes that its new Fund should exhibit unusual stability in times of crisis and depression similar to that characteristic of the old fund until the depression following 1929.

By the end of 1953 the Massachusetts Life Fund had been in operation a little more than five years. In this period of time the net value of its assets had increased approximately 40 per cent from the starting fund of $11,573,611 to $16,148,335. This increase had occurred partly because of the sale of new units and partly from capital gains not fully distributed. In the same period the net value per unit (adjusted to the new $25 unit adopted in December, 1951) had increased to $28.61. As of the end of the year 1953 the general depositor who had come into the Massachusetts Life Fund at approximately 84 cents on each dollar of the face of his deposit had units of the Massachusetts Life Fund roughly equivalent in value to the full face of his deposit. In addition, the 2 per cent return which the general depositor had been receiving before 1949 had been more than doubled under the new arrangement. A recapitulation of the past five years is given in Table 20.

TABLE 20

Statistics on the Massachusetts Life Fund
1949–1953

END OF YEAR	NUMBER OF UNITS OUTSTANDING	NET VALUE OF ASSETS	NET VALUE PER UNIT	DISTRIBUTIONS PER UNIT	
				INCOME	REALIZED GAINS
1949	446,610.12	$11,943,849	$26.74	$0.988	$0.125
1950	474,767.36	12,854,615	27.08	1.075	0.3125
1951	507,328.01	14,211,750	28.01	1.125	0.45
1952	540,064.91	15,953,403	29.54	1.10	0.20
1953	564,370.75	16,148,335	28.61	1.06	0.30

The general economic environment was undoubtedly favorable during this period, but the officers and board must also be credited with able leadership. President Osgood stayed at the helm for nearly four years following the reorganization until his death in October, 1952. Henry R. Guild became his successor. A prominent lawyer and trustee, he had served the Massachusetts Hospital Life as a vice-president since 1935 and as a director since 1949. He had also been a member of the Board of Trustees and treasurer of the Massachusetts General Hospital since 1939. Guild continued as president until August, 1953, when he was succeeded by Kennard Woodworth. Before coming to the Massachusetts Hospital Life, Woodworth had been an investment specialist and vice-president of Eaton & Howard, the operator of a large and well-known balanced fund and of a smaller stock fund.

Members of the old families of the Bay State are still easily identified on the board of the company. Samuel H. Wolcott, chairman of the board, is a direct descendant of William Prescott, who played so significant a role in the founding of the company. John S. Lawrence is in the fourth generation from Amos Lawrence, a member of the first Committee of Finance. G. Peabody Gardner is in the fifth generation from Samuel P. Gardner, an original stockholder, and Augustus P. Loring in the fifth generation from Charles G. Loring, actuary. Henry R. Guild numbers among his ancestors Benjamin Guild and Thomas Motley, both of whom were original stockholders. The board as of December, 1953, is as follows:

David Ames
James B. Ames
George L. Batchelder, Jr.
Edwin D. Brooks
Robert H. Gardiner
G. Peabody Gardner
Henry R. Guild
David H. Howie
John S. Lawrence
Paul T. Litchfield
Augustus P. Loring
D. George Sullivan
Samuel H. Wolcott
Henry A. Wood, Jr.
Kennard Woodworth

Of these, Brooks, Howie, Wolcott, Wood, and Woodworth are also members of the Investment Committee.

These men are true to the standards set by their predecessors in continuing to be prominent in the Boston financial and business community. If there is no one among them of quite the stature in the national economy of a Nathan Appleton, Abbott Lawrence, H. H. Hunnewell or T. Jefferson Coolidge, many of them nonetheless are important men in financial and business affairs. Among them is also exhibited a high sense of civic service, especially in a trustee relationship. Almost half of the board are trustees of one or more educational, philanthropic, or civic bodies. The Investment Committee itself includes individuals who are active trustees, officers, or directors of a considerable number of savings banks, trusts, trust companies, investment companies, and educational institutions. As such they have made professional careers in investing funds in a fiduciary capacity.

In the modernization of the Massachusetts Hospital Life the officers and directors have fashioned a new model based on an old and historic pattern. New England has long possessed a reputation in the minds of American investors for the prudent management of funds. In establishing this reputation, on which the Massachusetts mutual investment funds have built so successfully, the Massachusetts Hospital Life had its important part. It is fitting that the company should now be taking a significant place among modern investment companies with its Massachusetts Life Fund.

APPENDIX 1

OFFICERS

OF THE

MASSACHUSETTS HOSPITAL LIFE INSURANCE COMPANY

FROM ITS ORGANIZATION

Presidents

William Phillips [a]	1823–1827
William Prescott [b]	1828–1842
Peter C. Brooks [a]	1843–1848
Nathan Appleton [a]	1849–1861
George W. Lyman [b]	1862–1870
Peter C. Brooks [b]	1871–1878
John L. Gardner [a]	1879–1884
William Minot [b]	1885–1893
Robert Codman [a]	1894–1900
Charles F. Choate [a]	1901–1911
Arthur T. Lyman [a]	1911–1915
Charles P. Bowditch [a]	1915–1921
Louis Curtis [a]	1921–1931
George P. Gardner [b]	1931–1936
Samuel H. Wolcott [b]	1936–1939
Edward H. Osgood [a]	1939–1952
Henry R. Guild [b]	1952–1953
Kennard Woodworth	1953–

Vice-Presidents

George Cabot [a]	1823
Israel Thorndike [a]	1823–1832
Harrison Gray Otis [b]	1823–1832
Peter C. Brooks [c]	1823–1842
Thomas H. Perkins [a]	1823–1848
Charles Jackson [b]	1823–1853
John Phillips [a]	1823
Josiah Quincy [b]	1823–1856

[a] Died in office
[b] Resigned
[c] Resigned to become president
[d] Resigned to become director
[e] Not re-elected
[f] Resigned to become vice-president

Samuel Parkman [a]	1823–1824
Theodore Lyman [b]	1823–1826
John Parker [b]	1823–1839
Joseph Head [a]	1823–1836
Joseph Peabody [b]	1823–1843
William Pratt [b]	1823–1839
David Sears [b]	1823–1869
William Bartlet[b]	1823–1828
Nathaniel Silsbee [b]	1823–1844
Samuel Appleton [b]	1825–1847
John Lowell [a]	1827–1840
Joseph Tilden [d]	1829–1836
Joseph Tilden [a]	1846–1853
Samuel Hubbard [a]	1833–1847
Titus Welles [b]	1833–1844
John Hooper [a]	1837–1854
John Tappan [b]	1837–1870
Ebenezer Francis [b]	1840
William Minot [b]	1840–1864
John R. Adan [a]	1841–1849
George Ticknor [b]	1841–1862
Thomas B. Wales [a]	1843–1853
Leverett Saltonstall [a]	1844–1845
William Appleton [a]	1845–1862
George W. Lyman [c]	1845–1861
Samuel A. Eliot [b]	1848–1857
Robert G. Shaw [a]	1848–1853
Benjamin R. Curtis [b]	1849–1850
Benjamin R. Curtis [b]	1860–1864
Robert Hooper [a]	1850–1868
John C. Gray [b]	1851–1862
William S. Bullard [b]	1854–1883
Thomas Lamb [a]	1854–1887
Thomas Motley [b]	1854–1860
Robert C. Winthrop [b]	1854–1893
Jonathan Phillips [b]	1855–1859
Josiah Bradlee [a]	1857–1859
Nathaniel H. Emmons [a]	1858–1878
Samuel Hooper [b]	1860–1864
Edward Wigglesworth [a]	1861–1876
Samuel W. Swett [a]	1862–1884
John L. Gardner [c]	1863–1878
Sewall Tappan [a]	1863–1879
Israel Whitney [a]	1863–1871
Peter C. Brooks [c]	1865–1870
Henry B. Rogers [a]	1865–1887

J. Huntington Wolcott [a]	1865–1890
Robert M. Mason [a]	1869–1879
David Sears, Jr.[a]	1870–1873
William Minot, Jr.[c]	1871–1884
J. Thomas Stevenson [a]	1871–1876
William W. Tucker [d]	1872–1873
James S. Amory [a]	1874–1884
Martin Brimmer [a]	1874–1895
Lemuel Shaw [a]	1877–1884
Thomas Wigglesworth [b]	1877–1892
Otis Norcross [a]	1879–1882
Nathaniel Thayer [a]	1879–1883
James L. Little [a]	1880–1889
William Perkins [a]	1880–1887
Henry Lee [a]	1883–1898
William D. Pickman [a]	1884–1890
William G. Russell [a]	1884–1896
John Lowell [a]	1885–1897
Francis E. Parker [a]	1885
Charles S. Storrow [b]	1885–1888
Charles S. Sargent [a]	1885–1927
Henry L. Pierce [a]	1886–1896
John L. Bremer [a]	1888–1895
John C. Gray [a]	1888–1915
Ebenezer R. Hoar [a]	1888–1895
Charles F. Choate [d]	1889–1893
Edward W. Hooper [d]	1890–1899
Robert Codman [c]	1891–1893
Charles P. Hemenway [a]	1891–1893
George P. Upham [a]	1893–1901
Charles U. Cotting [a]	1894–1903
William S. Dexter [a]	1894–1908
John C. Ropes [a]	1894–1899
Roger Wolcott [a]	1894–1900
Francis Bartlett [a]	1896–1913
John L. Gardner [a]	1896–1898
Francis W. Hunnewell [d]	1896–1902
George Dexter [d]	1897–1899
Samuel Hoar [a]	1897–1904
Francis C. Lowell [a]	1898–1911
Alexander Agassiz [a]	1899–1910
Joshua M. Sears [a]	1899–1905
Louis Curtis [d]	1900–1901
Charles L. Lovering [a]	1900–1908
George Wigglesworth [d]	1900–1908
George P. Gardner [d]	1901–1915

Franklin Haven [a]	1901–1908
Amory A. Lawrence [a]	1902–1912
Francis I. Amory [a]	1903–1921
Augustus Hemenway [b]	1903–1926
Edmund D. Codman [b]	1904–1916
Dudley L. Pickman [a]	1905–1939
William Lowell Putnam [a]	1908–1924
Harry Burnett [a]	1908–1927
Charles F. Adams, 2nd [d]	1908–1911
Philip Dexter [d]	1908–1910
Horace D. Chapin [d]	1910–1925
Theophilus Parsons [d]	1910–1911
Charles P. Curtis [b]	1911–1935
Eugene V. R. Thayer [d]	1911–1915
Eben S. Draper [a]	1911–1914
Charles F. Choate, Jr. [a]	1912–1927
Henry Parkman [d]	1913–1918
W. Cameron Forbes [e]	1914–1949
George A. Gardner [a]	1915–1916
Horatio A. Lamb [a]	1915–1926
William Skinner [b]	1916–1926
William Amory [d]	1916–1921
Rodolphe L. Agassiz [a]	1916–1933
John Lowell [d]	1918–1922
Arthur Lyman [d]	1921–1926
S. Huntington Wolcott [d]	1921
Ingersoll Bowditch [a]	1921–1938
Robert H. Gardiner [a]	1922–1924
William Caleb Loring [a]	1924–1930
Louis Curtis, Jr. [e]	1924–1949
Thomas Jefferson Coolidge [d]	1925–1931
John Eliot Thayer, Jr. [e]	1926–1949
James Ripley Hooper [a]	1926–1934
Francis Peabody [a]	1926–1938
Joseph A. Skinner [a]	1926–1946
John S. Lawrence [d]	1927–1936
Moses Williams [d]	1927–1931
John T. Burnett [a]	1928–1929
Robert H. Gardiner [d]	1929–1931
Bentley W. Warren [d]	1930–1933
William Dexter [d]	1931–1934
William C. Endicott [a]	1931–1936
George E. Cabot [a]	1931–1946
Richard C. Curtis [b]	1933–1935
J. Reed Morss [b]	1933–1939
Stephen W. Sleeper [e]	1934–1949

Edwin D. Brooks [d]	1935–1936
Henry R. Guild [d]	1935–1949
G. Peabody Gardner, Jr. [d]	1935–1936
Moses Williams, Jr. [e]	1936–1949
David H. Howie [d]	1936–1938
Paul T. Litchfield	1949–
D. George Sullivan	1949–

Directors

William Phillips [c]	1823
William Prescott [c]	1823–1827
Gardner Greene [a]	1823–1832
John Lowell [f]	1823–1826
Ebenezer Francis [b]	1823–1830
Patrick T. Jackson [a]	1823–1847
Samuel Hubbard [f]	1823–1832
William Sturgis [a]	1823–1826
William Sturgis [a]	1838–1863
Thomas Motley [a]	1823–1853
Nathan Appleton [c]	1823–1848
Amos Lawrence [b]	1823–1837
John C. Gray [b]	1823–1832
Theodore Lyman, Jr. [b]	1823–1825
Nathaniel Bowditch [a]	1824–1838
Daniel P. Parker [b]	1826–1842
George Ticknor [b]	1827–1835
John Bryant [b]	1827–1837
Joseph Balch [b]	1828–1834
Thomas Wigglesworth [b]	1831–1836
John Belknap [b]	1833–1843
Henry Codman [b]	1833–1850
George Hallett [b]	1833
John A. Lowell [b]	1834–1878
Ebenezer Chadwick [a]	1835–1854
Benjamin R. Nichols [a]	1836–1848
Joseph Tilden [f]	1837–1845
Abbott Lawrence [a]	1838–1855
J. Ingersoll Bowditch [b]	1839–1880
Ignatius Sargent [b]	1843–1878
William Amory [b]	1844–1877
Francis C. Lowell [a]	1846–1873
George H. Kuhn [b]	1848–1877
Samuel Austin [a]	1849–1858
J. Wiley Edmands [a]	1849–1877
Charles H. Mills [b]	1851–1856

Francis Bacon [a]	1854–1877
Charles G. Loring [a]	1855–1867
George R. Minot [a]	1856–1883
Amos A. Lawrence [b]	1857–1868
Edward Austin [b]	1859–1879
James M. Beebe [a]	1864–1875
George T. Bigelow [a]	1868–1878
Abbott Lawrence [b]	1869–1893
William W. Tucker [b]	1874–1882
George Higginson [b]	1876–1882
Samuel C. Cobb [a]	1878–1891
T. Jefferson Coolidge [a]	1878–1920
Arthur T. Lyman [c]	1878–1911
David R. Whitney [b]	1878–1911
Charles H. Dalton [a]	1879–1908
H. H. Hunnewell [a]	1879–1902
Augustus Lowell [a]	1879–1900
Samuel Johnson [a]	1880–1899
Charles P. Bowditch [c]	1881–1915
George A. Gardner [f]	1883–1915
Jacob C. Rogers [a]	1883–1899
Nathaniel Thayer [a]	1884–1911
Howard Stockton [a]	1891–1932
Charles F. Choate [c]	1893–1900
George Dexter [a]	1899–1910
Edward W. Hooper [a]	1900–1901
A. Lawrence Lowell [b]	1900–1902
Charles W. Amory [a]	1901–1913
Louis Curtis [c]	1901–1921
Francis L. Higginson [a]	1902–1925
Francis W. Hunnewell [a]	1902–1917
George Wigglesworth [a]	1908–1930
Philip Dexter [a]	1910–1934
Charles F. Adams [b]	1911–1953
Theophilus Parsons [a]	1911–1916
Henry S. Howe [a]	1911–1931
Augustus P. Loring [b]	1914–1936
George P. Gardner [c]	1915–1931
Eugene V. R. Thayer [b]	1915–1918
Philip Y. DeNormandie [b]	1916–1938
Walter Hunnewell [a]	1918–1921
Henry Parkman [a]	1918–1924
William Amory [b]	1921–1937
S. Huntington Wolcott [c]	1921–1936
S. Huntington Wolcott	1939–
John Lowell [a]	1922

Robert Grant [a]	1923–1936
Horace D. Chapin [b]	1925–1936
Arthur Lyman [a]	1926–1933
T. Jefferson Coolidge [b]	1931–1934
Moses Williams [b]	1931–1936
Robert H. Gardiner [a]	1931–1944
Alexander Whiteside [b]	1932–1938
Bentley W. Warren [a]	1933–1947
John C. Kiley [b]	1934–1939
William Dexter [b]	1934–1942
Augustus P. Loring, Jr. [a]	1936–1951
G. Peabody Gardner	1936–
John S. Lawrence	1936–
George L. Batchelder, Jr.	1936–
Edwin D. Brooks	1936–
Edward H. Osgood [a]	1937–1952
David H. Howie	1938–
Paul T. Litchfield	1940–
John C. Kiley [a]	1947–1952
Henry R. Guild	1949–
D. George Sullivan	1949–
James Barr Ames	1950–
Robert H. Gardiner	1950–
Henry A. Wood, Jr.	1951–
Augustus P. Loring III	1951–
David Ames	1952–
Kennard Woodworth	1953–

Actuaries

Nathaniel Bowditch [a]	1823–1838
Joseph Tilden [b]	1838–1845
Francis C. Lowell [b]	1845–1854
Charles G. Loring [a]	1854–1867
George T. Bigelow [b]	1867–1877
Samuel C. Cobb [a]	1878–1891
Abbott Lawrence [b]	1891–1893
Charles F. Choate [c]	1893–1901
Howard Stockton [a]	1901–1932
Alexander Whiteside [b]	1932–1937
Edward H. Osgood [b]	1937–1949

Secretaries

Moses L. Hale [b]	1823–1868
Cyrus K. Hale [a]	1868–1874
James C. Braman [b]	1874–1909

James C. Braman (Secretary Emeritus) [a]	1909–1912
Alfred H. Litchfield [a]	1909–1911
Howard H. P. Wright [b]	1911–1937
Paul T. Litchfield	1937–

APPENDIX 2

PROPOSALS

OF THE

MASSACHUSETTS HOSPITAL LIFE INSURANCE COMPANY

TO MAKE INSURANCE ON LIVES,

TO GRANT ANNUITIES ON LIVES AND IN TRUST,

AND ENDOWMENTS FOR CHILDREN.

AUGUST 18, 1823

Object of the Society

The importance and necessity of an Institution, in which property might be secured for the support of aged persons, widows and children, induced a number of gentlemen of Boston and its vicinity to form an Association, with a capital of Five Hundred Thousand Dollars, which was incorporated by the Legislature of Massachusetts, under the name of the Massachusetts Hospital Life Insurance Company, with authority to make insurance on lives and all kinds of contracts in which the casualties of life and interest of money are principally concerned. In virtue of the authority granted by this Act, the Company will enter into various kinds of contracts, so as to accommodate persons in almost every age and situation in life.

Thus, a young man of small property, by an annual appropriation of a part of the proceeds of his labour, may purchase of the Company a deferred annuity producing an important income in old age – or an annuity in reversion, to be paid to his wife or to his children, in case they should survive him – or he may make insurance on his own life, and thus secure to his family or friends the payment of a large sum in case of his death.

An aged person whose income is not sufficient for his maintenance, can exchange his capital for a life annuity, and thus provide for an expenditure, much exceeding the simple interest of his money, without fear of being reduced to poverty if he should live to an extreme old age.

By a life-annuity, a wife can obtain an equivalent for the surrender of her right of dower, or the assignees of a bankrupt's estate can extinguish a claim for dower.

For persons of moderate property and for the rich, the annuities and endowments in trust, afford the means of making provision for widows and children, and securing the capital in a manner which no other Institution has done.

By an endowment in trust for children, property may be placed with the Company to accumulate at compound interest, till they shall attain the age of 21 years, or shall be married, without any trouble to the guardians or friends; and if a part of the income should be required for their support, the Company will pay to them such sums as shall be agreed upon at stated periods, and the surplus will be added to the capital, and commence drawing interest at the beginning of every year; and the business will be transacted by the Company at much less expense than is usual in private trusts, without any of the difficulties arising from the resignation or death of trustees, or the losses which might ensue from their bankruptcy.

It is unnecessary to mention particularly all the variety of forms of annuities, reversionary payments and insurances. The Tables of rates hereafter given, with the explanatory remarks which accompany them, will suffice to show the general nature and uses of such contracts, and for any particular case, information may be obtained by application to the Office. The usual methods of making these contracts with the Company will be perceived by the following regulations.

Rules and Regulations

Every person desirous of making insurance on his own life, or upon the life of any other person, or who wishes to contract for reversionary payments on annuities,* must sign a declaration by himself or agent according to a printed form to be furnished by the Company, setting forth the age, occupation, place of birth, state of health, and other circumstances attending the life or lives insured, or the life upon the failure of which the reversionary payment of the annuity is to commence. The Company may also require a certificate of the health of the person from a physician of established reputation. An application for an annuity on a life must state the age of the party to whom it is granted. Any misrepresentation in these declarations vitiates the contracts.

Policies of insurance and reversionary contracts are void, if the person whose life is insured shall die upon the seas, or upon any of the great lakes, or shall, without the consent of the Company previously obtained, and endorsed upon his Policy, pass beyond the settled limits of the United States, excepting into the settled limits of the British Provinces of the two Canadas, Nova-Scotia or New-Brunswick; or shall, without such previous consent thus endorsed, visit those parts of the United States which lie south of the southern boundaries of the States of Virginia and Kentucky; or shall, without such previous consent thus endorsed, enter into any military or naval service whatsoever (the militia not in actual service excepted); or in case he shall die by his own hands, in, or in consequence of a duel, or by

* The most common case of reversionary payments on annuities, is where a man contracts for an annuity, to be paid to his wife or children after his decease.

the hands of justice, or in the known violation of any law of these States, or of the United States, or of the said Provinces.

A person must have an interest in the life he insures, if it be not his own life.

No Policy takes effect until the first premium shall be paid, and the annual premiums must be paid the day they fall due, otherwise the Policy expires; but it may be revived at any time within fifteen days, the person on whose life the assurance was made being then alive and in good health, by the payment of said premium, together with an additional sum of ten per cent. upon such premium.

All claims will be settled within sixty days after notice and satisfactory proof of the claim shall be made.

Annuities must be demanded by the annuitant in person, or satisfactory proof must be given that the annuitant is still alive.

A charge of one dollar is made for each Policy of a common form; but where a special contract is required, the expense of drafting it must be borne by the assured.

The Company reserves to itself the right of making any alterations, which the particular circumstances of applicants may in their opinion render expedient.

The Office of the Company, No. 70, State Street, Boston, will be open daily, (Sundays excepted) from 9 to 2 o'clock, for the transaction of business; and any letters directed to the Actuary, post paid, will receive immediate attention.

From this table * it appears, that a person aged 31 years, by paying to the Company $1.85 may secure to his heirs one hundred dollars, if he should die within one year. This insurance may be renewed on the following years, gradually increasing the premium; and making a new contract each year — the Company having the right to decline, if they are not satisfied with the risk. To avoid this difficulty, the applicant may make the contract for a longer time, as for example seven years, or for the whole duration of life. Thus by paying annually $1.96, a person who at the time of making the contract is 31 years of age, may secure the payment of $100 to his heirs, if he should die any time within seven years; or, by paying three dollars annually, the insurance may be continued during the life of the party; so that a person of that age by paying annually *sixty* dollars, may secure to his family the sum of two thousand dollars, to be paid in sixty days after his decease.

A person of any occupation or profession who maintains his family by the annual or daily produce of his industry, may by an appropriation of a small part of his earnings to an insurance of this kind, make a comfortable provision for his family at his decease. A creditor, whose prospect of payment depends upon the life of a debtor, may secure his debt, if the debtor die within one year, by paying the usual premium corresponding to his

* See page 180.

age. A husband possessed in right of his wife of an estate, which, at her death, reverts to other parties, may secure to himself and heirs the value of the estate, by making insurance on the life of his wife.

Insurance on Lives

TABLE

Of the rates of insurance of one hundred dollars on a single life

Ages	1 year	7 years	For life	Ages	1 year	7 years	For life
				36	$2.03	$2.18	$3.37
10				37	2.07	2.24	3.45
to	$	$	$	38	2.12	2.30	3.54
14	0.98	1.18	2.07	39	2.15	2.35	3.64
15	0.99	1.25	2.12	40	2.23	2.43	3.74
16	1.06	1.35	2.18	41	2.31	2.50	3.84
17	1.16	1.43	2.24	42	2.39	2.56	3.94
18	1.27	1.51	2.29	43	2.45	2.63	4.05
19	1.37	1.56	2.35	44	2.50	2.71	4.17
20	1.50	1.62	2.39	45	2.56	2.79	4.29
21	1.59	1.66	2.45	46	2.62	2.89	4.41
22	1.61	1.68	2.49	47	2.69	2.99	4.54
23	1.63	1.70	2.54	48	2.76	3.10	4.68
24	1.65	1.73	2.59	49	2.87	3.21	4.83
25	1.68	1.77	2.64	50	3.03	3.34	4.99
26	1.71	1.79	2.70	51	3.15	3.45	5.14
27	1.73	1.83	2.76	52	3.24	3.56	5.30
28	1.77	1.86	2.81	53	3.35	3.68	5.48
29	1.80	1.89	2.87	54	3.46	3.82	5.66
30	1.82	1.92	2.93	55	3.57	3.96	5.85
31	1.85	1.96	3.00	56	3.69	4.11	6.05
32	1.89	1.99	3.06	57	3.83	4.26	6.27
33	1.92	2.02	3.14	58	3.97	4.43	6.50
34	1.95	2.07	3.21	59	4.13	4.62	6.75
35	2.00	2.13	3.29	60	4.29	4.80	7.00

This kind of insurance has increased very much in England during the last forty or fifty years, and the means of support of many thousands of families have been provided, who would otherwise have been destitute. The Equitable Society in London, in the course of twenty years from the year 1800, made insurance on 151,754 single lives, being more than 7500 policies annually executed by that single office.

Thus, a father 40 years of age, having a child 10 years of age, by paying annually $3.25 as long as they shall both live, may secure the payment of one hundred dollars to his child in case it should survive him.

Also, a husband aged 40 years, having a wife aged 30 years, by paying annually $96, may secure to his wife three thousand dollars, in case she should survive him.

TABLE

Of the rates for insuring one hundred dollars to be paid at the decease of A, provided he dies before B

	Ages of Life Insured (A) (husband or father)				
	20 years	30	40	50	60
Age of Expectant (B) (wife or child)			Annual Premium		
10	$2.01	$2.50	$3.25	$4.45	$6.42
20	2.03	2.53	3.29	4.50	6.50
30	1.97	2.44	3.20	4.40	6.39
40	1.91	2.35	3.07	4.23	6.27
50	1.84	2.25	2.90	4.06	6.08
60	1.76	2.13	2.71	3.71	5.63
70	1.68	2.01	2.53	3.38	4.94

Annuities

The Company will grant annuities during the continuance of any given life or lives, and make the payments either quarterly, half-yearly or annually, as shall be agreed upon. The payments may commence immediately, or be deferred for any given time.

There are two methods of making these contracts upon principles which differ essentially from each other. In the one, a moderate rate of interest is allowed upon the capital paid for the annuity, and, at the expiration of the life, the whole of that capital is paid back to the heirs of the annuitant, or to any person legally authorised to receive it. This contract may, for the sake of distinction, be called an Annuity in trust. In the other case, a large interest is allowed during the life of the party, and at his death the capital becomes the property of the Company. A contract of this kind is generally called an Annuity on a life.

Annuity in Trust

The Company will receive any sum of money, or such stocks * as they are authorised to hold, at the prices which may be agreed upon, to be in trust for a given life or lives, to draw interest immediately, or at any time

* The Company may require this payment to be made in stocks, or an allowance to be made to equalize it with the cost of the stocks and other property held by the Company.

which may be agreed upon by the parties; to be invested with the Capital Stock and other property, and managed by the Directors in the way they shall judge most advantageous, having always in view the safety of the Capital rather than the greatness of the income. A regular interest account shall be kept by the Company and adjusted annually, of all the sums received and paid during the year, on account of their Capital Stock, Annuities, Endowments, Insurances, &c. supposing the rate of interest to be six per cent. By comparing the sum that would be received at this rate of interest, with the income actually received that year, the true rate of interest obtained by the Company on all their property will be ascertained, and this rate is to be paid to the annuitants, deducting one half per cent. per annum for the expenses of the Office and the trouble in managing the property; so that if the Company get 5½ per cent. per annum, they will allow 5 per cent. As the annual income cannot be accurately determined till the expiration of the year, the Directors will order the quarterly or other payments of interest to be made so as to pay as nearly as can be estimated the sum that may be due to the party; and once in five years, or oftener if it can be done conveniently, an accurate adjustment and payment of any surplus shall be made. If any annuitant should die during this interval, his heirs are to be paid the interest due at the time of his death, and afterwards his proportion of such surplus, or an arbitrary adjustment may be made of the claim with the consent of the parties. If a premium be paid for bank or other stock (on account of the capital not being liable to reimbursement for a number of years) such premium must be deducted from the interest, in annual portions, so that at the time of the reimbursement of the capital, it may stand charged on the books of the Company at par. On the contrary, if any stock is purchased below its par value, and afterwards reimbursed at par, the profit shall be added to the interest account in such manner and at such times as the Directors may judge equitable. The smallest sum to be received in this kind of trust is five hundred dollars; and for any sum less than two thousand dollars, the payment of interest is to be made annually.

Manner of Paying Back the Capital

Sixty days after proof of the decease of the person in whose favour the annuity may be granted, the capital put in trust shall be paid to the person legally authorized to receive it. This payment is to be made in money, or stocks, or property belonging to the Company, at the pleasure of the Directors, and at the prices charged on the books at the time of the decease of the party, giving what the Directors shall consider an equitable share of those stocks which may be worth more, as well as those which may be worth less, than the charged prices. It being understood that the Company shall not be obliged to transfer a part of every kind of their stocks, but that any one or more may be selected by the Directors, always having it in view to give what they should consider a just proportion of all the property in possession of the Company; and if the payment be made wholly or in part in money, the Company shall make such reasonable allowance for any increase or decrease in the price of the common property as the Directors shall judge equitable.

In this way, a husband may provide for his wife, if she should survive him, to enjoy the income of any property during her life, and the capital to go to his children at her decease; and a parent might in this way leave property in trust for children, where the capital would be safe and the expenses small. Thus, for example, the annual expense of managing two thousand dollars would be only ten dollars, without any expense of Probate

TABLE

Of the rates at which the Company will grant an immediate annuity of one hundred dollars, on a single life, at the ages specified in the Table. The payments to be made annually, commencing one year after making the grant.

AGES	SUM PAID DOWN FOR PURCHASE OF THE ANNUITY	RATE OF INTEREST ALLOWED	AGES	SUM PAID DOWN FOR PURCHASE OF THE ANNUITY	RATE OF INTEREST ALLOWED
20	$1836.30	$5.45	48	$1341.90	$7.45
21	1823.30	.48	49	1315.30	7.60
22	1809.50	.52	50	1286.90	7.77
23	1795.10	.57	51	1256.60	7.96
24	1780.10	.62	52	1225.80	8.16
25	1764.50	.67	53	1194.50	8.37
26	1748.60	.72	54	1162.70	8.60
27	1732.00	.77	55	1130.00	8.85
28	1715.40	.83	56	1096.60	9.12
29	1699.70	.88	57	1062.50	9.41
30	1685.20	.93	58	1028.60	9.72
31	1670.50	.99	59	996.30	10.04
32	1655.20	6.04	60	966.30	10.35
33	1639.00	.10	61	939.80	10.64
34	1621.90	.17	62	913.70	10.94
35	1604.10	.23	63	887.20	11.27
36	1585.60	.31	64	859.30	11.64
37	1566.60	.38	65	830.70	12.04
38	1547.10	.46	66	801.00	12.48
39	1527.20	.55	67	770.00	12.99
40	1507.40	.63	68	738.00	13.55
41	1488.30	.72	69	704.90	14.19
42	1469.40	.81	70	670.90	14.91
43	1450.50	.89	71	635.80	15.73
44	1430.80	.99	72	602.60	16.59
45	1410.40	7.09	73	572.50	17.47
46	1388.90	.20	74	545.80	18.32
47	1366.20	.32	75	523.90	19.09

fees, and other charges which occur in private trusts. To render the annuity more secure to a daughter, it might be made inalienable, and payable only to her separate order, as the income shall become due, according to a form of bond hereto annexed.

The payments may be made quarterly or half-yearly, and up to the time of the death of the party, by making a small addition to the above rates.

From this table * it appears that a person aged 65 years, having a capital of three thousand dollars, can purchase an immediate annuity of three hundred and sixty one dollars, payable annually.

These annuities are generally purchased by persons somewhat advanced in age, and are peculiarly adapted to the situation of one, whose income from the interest of his property is not sufficient for his support, but by the purchase of an annuity, which will absorb his capital; this income may be sufficiently increased to afford him a comfortable maintenance.

Deferred Annuity on a single life

TABLE

Shewing the rates at which an annuity of one hundred dollars can be purchased, the first payment to be made when the party is 50 years old; the purchase money to be either in a single payment, or by annual payments, continued to the time of the first payment of the annuity.

AGES	SINGLE PAYMENT	ANNUAL PAYM'TS	AGES	SINGLE PAYMENT	ANNUAL PAYM'TS	AGES	SINGLE PAYMENT	ANNUAL PAYM'TS
10	$196.62	$10.56	22	$338.65	$21.56	34	$601.05	$53.62
11	205.41	11.16	23	354.68	23.03	35	631.50	58.88
12	214.66	11.80	24	371.48	24.63	36	663.57	64.93
13	224.37	12.49	25	389.10	26.37	37	697.47	71.97
14	234.56	13.23	26	407.65	28.29	38	733.33	80.26
15	245.30	14.02	27	427.10	30.40	39	771.28	90.11
16	256.70	14.87	28	447.66	32.73	40	811.77	102.03
17	268.77	15.78	29	469.65	35.31	41	855.36	116.70
18	281.47	16.76	30	493.29	38.19	42	902.00	135.14
19	294.78	17.82	31	518.26	41.39	43	951.76	158.96
20	308.73	18.97	32	544.54	44.98			
21	323.37	20.21	33	572.12	49.03			

Thus a person of the age of 21 years, by paying in one sum $323.37, at the time of purchase, or by paying annually $20.21, till he attains the age of 50 years, will be entitled to a deferred life annuity of $100, the first payment to be made when he is 50 years of age.

If the first payment of the annuity is deferred to a greater age than 50, a greater annuity can be obtained without any change in the purchase money, according to the rates in the following Table.

* See page 183.

AGE TO WHICH THE ANNUITY IS DEFERRED	ANNUITY PAYABLE AT THE PROPOSED AGE	AGE TO WHICH THE ANNUITY IS DEFERRED	ANNUITY PAYABLE AT THE PROPOSED AGE
	$		$
50	100.00	57	175.92
51	107.76	58	192.47
52	116.34	59	211.18
53	125.84	60	232.37
54	136.37	61	256.42
55	148.09	62	283.69
56	161.21	63	314.73

Thus by making the same payments as in the above example, a person may purchase an annuity of $148.09, to commence at the age of 55; or $232.37, to commence at the age of 60. In these rates, it is supposed that the payments of the annuity are made annually. By a small addition to the purchase money, the payments may be made half-yearly, or quarterly.

From these tables it appears, that a person who depends on his labour, by putting apart about two dollars of his wages per month, from the time he is 21 years of age, till he is 50, may secure an annuity of $118 after that period, or above $200 per annum, if the first payment is deferred till he is 57 years old.

Annuities on two or more lives

The Company will grant annuities upon two or more lives, in all the various forms of which they are susceptible. As for example — on the joint continuance of the lives, (that is, an annuity which is to cease, when any one of the lives fails) – on the longest of the lives — on one life after the death of another, — as for a wife after the death of her husband, or a child after the death of his father. The following Table will serve as a sample of the rates at which this last kind of annuity will be granted.

Thus, a man 30 years of age, having a wife aged 20, by paying at the time of purchase $508.80, or making annual payments of $35.65, as long as they shall both live, may procure an annuity of $100, payable annually to his wife, in case she should survive him.

Endowments

A parent or friend may procure an endowment for a child at the rates given in the following table, which shows the sums the Company will pay to the party for whom the endowment was purchased, if he should attain the age of 21 years, for one hundred dollars purchase money, received at the ages mentioned in the Table. This kind of contract may be called an Endowment on a life.

TABLE

Of the rates at which an annuity of $100 can be purchased for a wife, in case she should survive her husband, the first payment to be made one year after his death; or for a child in case it should survive its father, the first payment to commence one year after his death, and in general for one life, in case it should survive another.

AGES			
LIFE INSURED (HUSBAND OR FATHER)	EXPECTANT (WIFE OR CHILD)	SINGLE PAYMENT	ANNUAL PAYMENT
		$	$
20	20	429.00	28.46
	30	357.70	25.06
	40	288.70	21.89
	50	216.90	18.54
30	20	508.80	35.65
	30	423.00	31.06
	40	338.00	26.63
	50	251.20	22.12
40	20	617.60	46.84
	30	515.80	40.64
	40	410.10	34.25
	50	300.50	27.66
50	20	766.30	65.50
	30	649.50	57.19
	40	521.00	47.96
	50	379.90	37.73
60	20	984.40	103.42
	30	854.10	91.73
	40	705.20	78.17
	50	530.80	62.00
70	20	1224.60	172.07
	30	1084.20	154.67
	40	921.00	134.18
	50	721.50	108.44

Thus for one thousand dollars, paid at the time of the birth of a child, the Company will pay him at the age of 21 years, if then living, three thousand seven hundred and sixty-eight dollars and forty cents. In this way, means might be provided to place a young person in business, if he should attain the age of 21 years. The time of payment might be varied to accom-

AGES	SUM TO BE PAID AT THE AGE OF 21, IF ALIVE	AGES	SUM TO BE PAID AT THE AGE OF 21, IF ALIVE	AGES	SUM TO BE PAID AT THE AGE OF 21, IF ALIVE
	$		$		$
Birth	376.84	5 years	210.53	13 years	144.12
3 months	344.28	6	198.83	14	137.86
6 months	331.46	7	188.83	15	131.83
9 months	318.90	8	179.97	16	125.97
1 year	306.58	9	171.91	17	120.31
2	271.03	10	164.46	18	114.89
3	243.69	11	157.43	19	109.70
4	225.42	12	150.64	20	104.74

modate a parent who should wish to provide a marriage portion for a daughter, in case the marriage should take place before attaining the age of 21 years. In this case, the sum to be paid would be decreased in the same proportion as the sum in the above Table, corresponding to the age at the actual time of payment, is to 100 dollars. Thus if the Company had contracted to pay $125.97, when the party should be 21 years of age, and payment was required at 16, the sum to be paid must be decreased in the ratio of the tabular number, corresponding to 16 years, $125.97 is to $100; consequently the sum to be paid at the age of 16, would be $100.00.

Endowments in Trust

The Company will receive property for endowments in trust for children, to be kept at interest and accumulate till they attain the age of 21 years, or any other age that may be agreed upon, when the whole amount of principal and interest will be paid to them or their heirs; or the Company will pay a part of the income for their support, at stated times, and add the residue to the capital annually. In case of the death of the party for whom the endowment was granted before attaining the proposed age, the property then due shall be paid in sixty days after proof of his death, to his heirs, or to any person legally authorized to receive it. The rate of interest which will be allowed by the Company on these trusts is the same as shall be allowed on annuities in trust, being the interest they shall actually make on their capital stock and other property, estimated in the manner particularly explained in the article on annuities in trust, deducting one half per cent. for the expenses of the Office and the trouble in the management of the property; so that if the Company get 5½ per cent. per annum, they will allow 5 per cent. and, on the last day of every year, the same interest which has been allowed that year upon the annuities in trust, will be added to the capital of the endowment in trust, and this sum will constitute the capital which is to draw interest on the following year. These annual additions to the capital of the endowment, are to be made on the books of the Company without any trouble or interference of the guardian or friends of the party; and when he shall attain the age mentioned in his bond of endowment, the whole sum that has accrued will be paid to him, or to his legal representatives. The payments are to be made in money or stocks or other property of the Company, in the same manner as for an annuity in trust, giving the party his just proportion of the common stock and property of the Company, in the manner that will cause the least trouble to the Company in making the transfer.

The following Table will shew the amount of $100 put in trust for children of different ages, supposing the net rate of interest allowed to be 4½, 5, or 5½ per cent. by which it appears, that if a parent pays to the Company one thousand dollars at the birth of a child, he or his heirs will be entitled to receive, at the age of 21 years,

2520 dollars, if the rate is 4½ per cent.
2786 dollars, if the rate is 5 per cent.
3078 dollars, if the rate is 5½ per cent.

AGE AT PURCHASE	RATE OF INTEREST 4½ P.CT.	5 P.CT.	5½ P.CT.	AGE AT PURCHASE	RATE OF INTEREST 4½ P.CT.	5 P.CT.	5½ P.CT.
	$	$	$		$	$	$
Birth	252.03	278.60	307.83	11	155.30	162.89	170.82
1 year	241.17	265.33	291.78	12	148.61	155.13	161.91
2	230.79	252.69	276.57	13	142.21	147.75	153.47
3	220.85	240.66	262.15	14	136.09	140.71	145.47
4	211.34	229.20	248.48	15	130.23	134.01	137.88
5	202.24	218.29	235.53	16	124.62	127.63	130.70
6	193.53	207.89	223.24	17	119.25	121.55	123.88
7	185.19	197.99	211.61	18	114.12	115.76	117.42
8	177.22	188.56	200.58	19	109.20	110.25	111.30
9	169.59	179.59	190.12	20	104.50	105.00	105.50
10	162.29	171.03	180.21	21	100.00	100.00	100.00

It may not be amiss to remark, that in the preceding proposals the Company have offered as favorable terms to the applicants as they could consistently with the safety of the property intrusted to their care, which object has been kept constantly in view; and of the profits — if any shall be made — a third part is to be given to the Massachusetts Hospital, as a perpetual bounty to that noble institution. The annual return made to the Governor and Council, which, without expressing the particular sums deposited by individuals, will contain a schedule of the amount of the capital stock and all the property in possession of the Company, with the manner of its investment, will always be open to the inspection of any person transacting business with the Company.

* * * * * *

[The balance of the booklet of *Proposals* is not reproduced here. It contains forms of application and contract, the articles of incorporation, bylaws, and the names of the original board of directors.]

APPENDIX 3

Resources and Liabilities of the Massachusetts Hospital Life Insurance Company

1824–1900

(In dollars; cents omitted but added into totals)

DEC. 31	TOTAL RESOURCES	MORTGAGES	NOTES	SECURITIES OWNED	REAL ESTATE	CASH ON HAND OR IN BANKS & ACC. INS.
1824	534,170	451,841	69,200	0	0	13,128
1825	1,622,406	1,051,618	526,704	5,750	0	38,333
1826	2,380,189	1,647,980	638,527	5,750	0	87,930
1827	3,593,563	2,218,472	1,263,373	35,889	0	75,827
1828	4,188,398	2,562,762	1,467,760	0	0	157,875
1829	4,680,856	3,000,302	1,352,904	20,000	0	307,649
1830	5,480,788	2,911,154	2,030,044	149,295	0	390,294
1831	5,679,275	2,724,365	2,534,981	290,879	0	129,048
1832	5,770,245	2,693,848	2,844,636	77,705	2,700	151,355
1833	5,867,369	2,677,254	3,035,640	0	0	154,475
1834	5,974,297	2,875,660	2,950,440	0	0	148,196
1835	6,139,028	3,119,880	2,298,000	583,000	0	138,147
1836	6,170,211	3,416,574	2,621,732	0	0	131,904
1837	6,223,402	3,542,813	2,571,345	0	0	109,242
1838	6,402,776	3,776,978	2,339,900	111,100	55,000	119,798
1839	6,458,938	3,940,848	2,133,537	100,000	55,000	229,552
1840	6,529,094	4,332,328	1,883,258	0	55,000	258,507
1841	6,723,540	4,596,471	1,837,193	50,000	55,000	184,875
1842	6,784,877	4,755,671	1,664,182	50,000	55,000	260,023
1843	7,143,760	4,633,562	886,950	1,247,250	55,000	320,998
1844	7,501,440	4,263,683	311,100	2,520,952	55,000	350,705
1845	7,585,024	4,487,896	533,900	2,223,015	55,000	285,213
1846	7,703,286	4,614,016	566,130	2,264,315	55,000	203,823
1847	7,911,588	4,528,542	1,386,230	1,698,510	55,000	243,305
1848	7,756,307	4,398,677	1,542,500	1,474,019	55,000	286,111
1849	7,590,121	4,308,193	2,456,170	495,202	55,000	275,555
1850	7,483,743	4,057,148	2,867,070	370,020	55,000	134,504
1851	7,584,628	3,926,804	3,058,270	448,520	55,000	96,033
1852	7,712,102	3,866,440	3,207,170	505,520	55,000	77,972

DEC. 31	TOTAL RESOURCES	MORTGAGES	NOTES	SECURITIES OWNED	REAL ESTATE	CASH ON HAND OR IN BANKS & ACC. INS.
1853	7,799,953	3,616,906	3,540,670	480,520	85,000	76,857
1854	8,047,876	3,538,022	3,879,770	471,880	90,000	68,203
1855	8,018,669	3,497,482	3,927,770	471,880	90,000	31,536
1856	7,977,778	3,535,710	3,752,270	571,880	90,000	27,918
1857	8,204,026	3,654,330	3,778,370	545,880	90,000	135,446
1858	8,553,416	4,639,267	2,999,965	549,525	90,000	274,658
1859	8,881,126	5,204,625	2,542,300	874,600	90,000	169,599
1860	9,050,876	5,466,938	2,526,684	763,900	90,000	203,353
1861	9,328,174	5,516,073	2,581,084	967,495	90,000	173,520
1862	9,781,966	4,982,548	789,170	3,411,337	90,000	508,910
1863	10,040,056	4,009,823	529,070	5,403,937	90,000	7,225
1864	10,292,629	3,526,282	1,260,570	5,404,087	90,000	11,688
1865	10,576,705	3,315,122	1,535,520	5,610,837	90,000	25,225
1866	10,522,188	3,071,281	1,514,570	5,663,712	90,000	182,624
1867	10,596,833	3,054,364	1,664,270	5,738,712	90,000	49,486
1868	10,931,783	3,630,906	1,498,293	5,698,712	90,000	13,870
1869	11,401,098	4,531,214	1,842,170	4,925,875	90,000	11,839
1870	11,680,730	5,025,214	1,721,170	4,548,875	90,000	295,471
1871	12,314,826	5,848,464	2,643,470	3,134,709	90,000	598,182
1872	12,912,130	6,842,029	3,127,770	2,658,109	90,000	194,220
1873	12,794,997	7,801,429	2,906,320	1,920,809	90,000	76,437
1874	13,467,094	8,107,566	3,294,572	1,901,375	90,000	73,581
1875	14,473,828	9,288,963	3,062,670	1,657,375	90,000	374,819
1876	15,122,322	10,253,955	3,245,800	1,524,500	90,000	8,066
1877	15,295,672	10,737,350	2,642,750	1,469,500	90,000	356,072
1878	15,443,461	10,831,358	2,043,670	1,962,697	90,000	515,734
1879	15,590,399	10,240,395	3,251,100	1,929,854	90,000	79,050
1880	15,727,113	9,413,336	3,150,000	2,645,997	90,000	427,779
1881	15,968,559	8,415,637	4,817,700	2,373,497	90,000	271,723
1882	16,723,433	8,449,762	5,683,500	2,320,497	90,000	179,673
1883	17,519,920	8,158,178	6,207,400	2,417,500	240,000	496,841
1884	17,953,044	8,165,878	6,412,000	2,690,500	377,689	306,976
1885	18,813,018	7,896,018	5,998,000	3,874,700	546,166	498,133
1886	19,081,704	8,294,388	5,221,850	4,270,900	741,050	553,515
1887	19,813,116	8,309,013	6,263,166	4,268,900	700,000	272,036
1888	20,260,667	8,332,488	6,608,650	4,138,655	660,000	520,873
1889	21,146,410	8,912,506	7,431,700	3,845,900	650,000	306,304
1890	21,931,659	9,282,143	7,939,100	3,621,900	600,000	488,515
1891	22,008,147	9,295,238	8,014,500	3,421,900	600,000	676,508
1892	22,516,325	9,302,080	8,572,100	3,421,900	600,000	620,245
1893	22,662,417	9,832,955	8,202,972	3,409,500	600,000	616,988

DEC. 31	TOTAL RESOURCES	MORTGAGES	NOTES	SECURITIES OWNED	REAL ESTATE	CASH ON HAND OR IN BANKS & ACC. INS.
1894	22,369,478	9,788,001	7,932,940	3,044,800	600,000	1,003,737
1895	22,797,168	9,920,565	8,689,670	3,014,100	600,000	572,832
1896	23,249,533	10,344,976	8,455,870	2,981,000	600,000	867,686
1897	24,498,851	11,073,449	8,585,670	2,930,250	600,000	1,309,481
1898	25,720,155	10,953,440	10,223,800	2,805,647	600,000	1,137,267
1899	25,589,431	10,767,441	10,826,639	2,692,881	600,000	702,468
1900	26,280,333	10,686,341	11,903,539	2,845,124	600,000	245,327

DEC. 31	TOTAL LIABILITIES	TRUST DEPOSITS	INSURANCE	ANNUITIES	CAPITAL & SURPLUS	RESERVED INTEREST ETC.
1824	534,170	370,677	1,708	14,872	102,613	44,298
1825	1,622,406	1,084,094	1,839	21,126	515,346	....
1826	2,380,189	1,802,122	1,806	26,272	549,988	....
1827	3,593,563	3,006,117	2,968	32,965	548,762	2,749
1828	4,188,398	3,596,202	3,608	37,912	550,675	....
1829	4,680,856	4,087,524	4,524	46,518	542,289	
1830	5,480,788	4,865,254	4,469	63,284	547,779	
1831	5,679,275	5,054,493	5,284	64,749	554,748	
1832	5,770,245	5,139,519	5,585	61,695	563,445	
1833	5,867,369	5,218,303	7,017	70,709	571,339	
1834	5,974,297	5,319,931	7,729	65,153	581,484	
1835	6,139,028	5,472,788	8,818	69,940	587,481	
1836	6,170,211	5,484,829	9,153	77,528	598,700	
1837	6,223,402	5,524,137	9,964	81,409	607,890	
1838	6,402,776	5,690,462	10,936	78,439	622,937	
1839	6,458,938	5,724,994	11,243	83,692	639,008	
1840	6,529,094	5,850,034	12,359	72,689	594,010	
1841	6,723,540	6,036,149	12,747	67,407	607,235	
1842	6,784,877	6,090,393	11,600	61,106	621,777	
1843	7,143,760	6,429,185	12,454	66,084	636,035	
1844	7,501,440	6,764,379	11,846	76,947	648,267	
1845	7,585,024	6,885,710	14,959	82,395	601,959	
1846	7,703,286	6,986,303	14,401	95,592	606,989	
1847	7,911,588	7,180,896	15,612	93,761	621,317	
1848	7,756,307	7,021,722	16,337	87,559	630,688	
1849	7,590,121	6,846,785	16,763	87,365	639,207	....

DEC. 31	TOTAL LIABILITIES	TRUST DEPOSITS	INSURANCE	ANNUITIES	CAPITAL & SURPLUS	RESERVED INTEREST ETC.
1850	7,483,743	6,775,152	15,926	90,911	601,753	
1851	7,584,628	6,865,704	17,291	93,588	608,044	....
1852	7,712,102	6,975,840	16,894	87,202	617,165	15,000
1853	7,799,953	7,071,064	17,194	84,317	627,378	....
1854	8,047,876	7,312,105	18,130	79,173	638,466	
1855	8,018,669	7,318,573	24,784	76,747	598,563	
1856	7,977,778	7,269,429	18,600	78,537	611,211	
1857	8,204,026	7,485,325	19,499	72,769	626,432	....
1858	8,553,416	7,814,753	21,206	79,305	636,358	1,793
1859	8,881,126	8,136,056	19,333	74,395	651,342	
1860	9,050,876	8,338,226	16,037	69,308	627,304	
1861	9,328,174	8,602,554	11,603	67,115	646,900	....
1862	9,781,966	9,031,446	12,417	70,436	656,658	11,008
1863	10,040,056	9,192,313	12,904	91,705	672,570	70,562
1864	10,292,629	9,138,430	13,565	120,704	683,738	336,190
1865	10,576,705	9,615,125	14,353	130,676	638,678	177,871
1866	10,522,188	9,620,152	14,642	136,827	627,142	123,422
1867	10,596,833	9,754,194	15,178	125,535	615,879	86,044
1868	10,931,783	10,137,603	9,572	122,546	612,774	49,287
1869	11,401,098	10,462,014	9,987	131,177	616,143	181,775
1870	11,680,730	10,725,697	10,134	200,889	616,671	127,338
1871	12,314,826	11,357,074	10,937	190,312	621,070	135,431
1872	12,912,130	11,943,511	11,673	187,079	628,674	141,190
1873	12,794,997	11,768,801	11,082	191,578	631,856	191,678
1874	13,467,094	12,489,508	7,754	187,476	642,954	139,400
1875	14,473,828	13,476,810	6,105	215,961	666,529	108,420
1876	15,122,322	14,235,953	6,140	218,250	653,578	8,399
1877	15,295,672	14,403,066	6,228	218,957	667,419	....
1878	15,443,461	14,455,739	6,570	253,717	693,942	33,491
1879	15,590,399	14,468,196	7,057	331,602	692,376	91,167
1880	15,727,113	14,487,828	7,012	364,997	720,783	146,490
1881	15,968,559	14,717,391	8,174	433,614	672,043	137,335
1882	16,723,433	15,403,514	8,619	496,411	651,066	163,821
1883	17,519,920	16,141,749	8,395	493,701	656,030	220,043
1884	17,953,044	16,492,716	6,313	520,303	671,560	262,149
1885	18,813,018	17,401,747	6,572	496,268	699,348	209,081
1886	19,081,704	17,711,262	3,414	497,099	669,800	200,127
1887	19,813,116	18,287,767	3,779	571,715	650,617	299,236
1888	20,260,667	18,750,613	4,050	584,265	638,050	283,688
1889	21,146,410	19,629,380	4,190	603,883	665,691	243,265
1890	21,931,659	20,411,574	2,289	613,110	669,599	235,085

DEC. 31	TOTAL LIABILITIES	TRUST DEPOSITS	INSURANCE	ANNUITIES	CAPITAL & SURPLUS	RESERVED INTEREST ETC.
1891	22,008,147	20,320,889	2,484	716,191	633,953	334,628
1892	22,516,325	20,714,785	2,657	735,106	661,652	402,123
1893	22,662,417	20,776,449	...	742,996	668,046	474,925
1894	22,369,478	20,420,778		850,786	668,957	428,956
1895	22,797,168	20,790,931		909,352	672,560	424,324
1896	23,249,533	21,203,090		942,298	676,107	428,036
1897	24,498,851	22,289,358		1,095,797	682,732	430,962
1898	25,720,155	23,460,007		1,166,726	691,812	401,608
1899	25,589,431	23,174,210		1,329,498	683,832	401,890
1900	26,280,333	23,828,812	...	1,365,019	684,790	401,710

NOTES AND REFERENCES

Chapter I. Significance of the Massachusetts Hospital Life Insurance Company

1. Gras, N. S. B., *The Massachusetts-First National Bank of Boston, 1784–1934* (Cambridge, 1937), pp. 17–30.

2. Whitney, David R., *The Suffolk Bank* (Cambridge, 1878). The Suffolk system is described in almost every textbook in American economic history. The bank was merged with the Second National Bank of Boston in October, 1903. (*Commercial and Financial Chronicle,* LXXVII [October 3, 1903], 802; [November 14, 1903], 1847.)

3. *One Hundred Years of Savings Bank Service* (rev. ed.; Boston, 1930), a booklet published by the Provident Institution for Savings. See also Keyes, Emerson W., *A History of Savings Banks in the United States from Their Inception in 1816 Down to 1874* (New York, 1876), I, 39–43; Stone, Edwin A., *A Century of Banking* (Boston, 1894), pp. 38–42; Bennett, Frank P., Jr., *The Story of Mutual Savings Banks* (Boston, 1924), pp. 15–22.

It is hardly astonishing that some members of the board of directors of any one of these institutions were also members of the boards of one or more of the others. This relationship is particularly apparent between the Massachusetts Hospital Life and the Provident Institution for Savings and scarcely less so with the Suffolk Bank. The first president of the Massachusetts Hospital Life was also president of the Massachusetts Bank and the Provident Institution for Savings. At the same time Ebenezer Francis, one of the key figures in bringing the Massachusetts Hospital Life into being, was president of the Suffolk Bank.

4. On the company's life insurance activities, see Stalson, J. Owen, *Marketing Life Insurance: Its History in America* (Cambridge, 1942), pp. 70–81.

The first life insurance company in the United States was the Pennsylvania Company for Insurance on Lives & Granting Annuities. It was incorporated on March 10, 1812.

5. On the emergence of institutions which engaged in the "indirect putting out of capital" and their significance, see Gras, N. S. B., *Business and Capitalism: An Introduction to Business History* (New York, 1939), pp. 85–88, 220–223.

6. The first scholar to note the importance of the Massachusetts Hospital Life Insurance Company in the development of trust institutions in any detail was Smith, James G., *The Development of Trust Companies in the United States* (New York, 1928), pp. 238–246. His recognition has resulted in frequent mention of the Massachusetts Hospital Life Insurance Company

as the "first" trust company to operate in the United States and, in fact, in the world. See, for example, Riddle, N. Gilbert, *The Investment Policy of Trust Institutions* (Chicago, 1934), p. 3; Stephenson, Gilbert T., *Trust Business in Common Law Countries* (New York, 1940), pp. 538, 542–543; Marsh, David R., *Corporate Trustees* (London, 1952), p. 34. As in the case of most "firsts," definition counts for a great deal. Thus it is also noted that the Farmers' Fire Insurance & Loan Company, incorporated in New York in 1822, was the first company to have trust powers specifically granted in its charter (Smith, *op. cit.*, p. 246), and the New York Life Insurance & Trust Company, incorporated in 1830, was the first to use "trust" in its name (Smith, *op. cit.*, p. 257). The first trust company organized with the primary object of acting as executor and trustee was the United States Trust Company, incorporated in New York in 1853 (Marsh, *op. cit.*, p. 35). Studies of trust companies made earlier than that of Smith – for example, Perine, Edward T. B., *The Story of the Trust Companies* (New York, 1916); Herrick, Clay, *Trust Companies: Their Organization, Growth and Management* (2d ed.; New York, 1915); and Cator, George, *Trust Companies in the United States* (Baltimore, 1902) – make no mention of the Massachusetts Hospital Life.

Smith has also noted the Massachusetts Hospital Life as a first forerunner of the modern investment company, *op. cit.*, pp. 244–245, as has the Securities & Exchange Commission in its searching investigations of investment companies in the later 1930's. See S. E. C. Report: *Investment Trusts and Investment Companies,* 75th Cong., 3d Sess., H. Doc. 707 (1939), p. 42; S. E. C. Report: *Investment Trusts and Investment Companies,* 76th Cong., 2d Sess., H. Doc. 476 (1940), p. 6.

7. There is irony in a letter written by the director of McLean Hospital (the mental institution of the Massachusetts General Hospital) to the archivist of the Massachusetts General Hospital asikng for a "brief history relative to the Massachusetts Hospital Life Insurance Company, how it was formed, what benefits the Hospital was to derive, and whether it is still in existence." (Letter, Dr. W. Franklin Wood to Helen Boyer, December 8, 1941, MGH Archives.) Thus a high official of long service in the Massachusetts General Hospital was barely aware of an institution which had been called into being, in part, to serve his own and which had been an important source of income to the Hospital for more than a century.

8. For one of the few who mention the Massachusetts Hospital Life, see Shlakman, Vera, *Economic History of a Factory Town: A Study of Chicopee, Massachusetts* (Northampton, 1935), p. 45. She notes, in passing, a single loan by the Massachusetts Hospital Life to a Chicopee mill and the near identity of the boards of directors of the two institutions without noting the constancy and magnitude of the loans of the company to the Chicopee mills. In his study of the marketing of life insurance, Stalson (*op. cit.*, p. 70) pauses to mention the desirability of "serious study" of what he calls a "unique institution" and its "metamorphosis from a company organized partly for charitable purposes into a 'savings institution

for the rich and middle classes' and then into a modern financial institution with powers possessed by no other corporate trustee in the country. . . ."

9. On the historical origins of trusteeship, see especially Smith, *op. cit.*, pp. 211–226, and Marsh, *op. cit.*, pp. 1–22. The earliest trusts in English jurisprudence relate to land and its use. They developed out of the bases for feudal landholding and the restrictions on the transmission of land to the next generation.

10. Opportunities for professional trusteeship increased as a larger number of substantial fortunes were accumulated and as the wise investment of capital required greater skill because of the increasing variety of types of investment available for capital. Smith suggests the growth of fortunes in Massachusetts by noting that the aggregate value of houses and lands increased from $84,000,000 in 1799 to $144,000,000 in 1814. This increase of slightly better than 70% may be compared with a population increase of 23% in Massachusetts during a period in which the price level did not change materially. He also cites 235 estates in excess of $10,000 which were filed for probate in Massachusetts during the years 1829–1831. Thirty-six of these ranged in size from $50,000 to more than $500,000. (Smith, *op. cit.*, 231–232.)

11. Compiled from Wiesenburger, Arthur, *Investment Companies: 1951 Edition* (New York, 1951).

Chapter II. Founding of the Massachusetts Hospital Life

1. On the history of the Massachusetts General Hospital, see Bowditch, Nathaniel I., *A History of the Massachusetts General Hospital* (2d ed.; Boston, 1872), and Washburn, Frederic A., *The Massachusetts General Hospital: Its Development, 1900–1935* (Boston, 1939).

2. Minutes of the Trustees of the Massachusetts General Hospital, January 16, 1814, MGH Archives; also *Laws Relating to Massachusetts General Hospital, 1810–1920* (Boston, n.d.), pp. 5–6.

3. Minutes of the Trustees of the Massachusetts General Hospital, March 6, 1814.

4. Jack, A. Fingland, *An Introduction to the History of Life Assurance* (London, 1912), pp. 170–173, 233; Crobaugh, Clyde J., *Annuities and Their Use* (Boston, 1933), pp. 12, 16–18.

5. Maseres, Francis, *The Principal of the Doctrine of Life Annuities; Explained in a Familiar Manner so as to be Intelligible to Persons not Acquainted with the Doctrine of Chance . . .* (London, 1783), pp. 34–40.

6. Minutes of the Trustees of the Massachusetts General Hospital, March 10, 1816.

7. *Ibid.*, March 9, 1817.

8. *Ibid.*, February 1, 1818.

9. Report of the Committee to the Trustees (written by John Lowell), February 15, 1818, MGH Archives.

10. *Laws of Massachusetts, 1818,* chap. 180, sec. 7.
11. *Ibid.,* chap. 180.
12. Minutes of the Trustees of the Massachusetts General Hospital, January 7, 1823.
13. *Ibid.,* January 10, 1823.
14. Stockholders' Record Book, Massachusetts Hospital Life Insurance Company, January 10, 1823.
15. *Ibid.,* January 21, 28, 1823.
16. On Ebenezer Francis, see Mason, R. M., *A Sketch of the Life of the Late Ebenezer Francis of Boston* (New York, 1859) and Forbes, Allan, *Ebenezer Francis, 1775–1858* (Boston, 1946). Mason was a son-in-law, and Forbes is a lineal descendant.
17. Forbes, Abner, *The Rich Men of Massachusetts* (Boston, 1852), p. 29. See also Wilson, T. L. V., *The Aristocracy of Boston* (Boston, 1848), p. 16.
18. Ticknor, George, *Life of William H. Prescott* (Boston, 1863), pp. 525–531; also Young, Alexander, *A Discourse Occasioned by the Death of William Prescott* (Boston, 1844).
19. Greenslet, Ferris, *The Lowells and Their Seven Worlds* (Boston, 1946), pp. 163–189.
20. Stockholders' Record Book, January 28, 1823.
21. *Ibid.,* February 3, 1823.
22. Minutes of the Trustees of the Massachusetts General Hospital, January 21, 1823.
23. Stockholders' Record Book, February 3, 1823.
24. *Ibid.,* February 18, 1823.
25. Compiled from the Minutes of the Board of Directors.
26. Minutes of the Board of Directors, February 7, 1845.
27. Stockholders' Record Book.
28. *Ibid.,* January 16, 1826.
29. Minutes of the Board of Control, February 24, 1949, and Stockholders' Record Book, March 7, 1949.
30. Original Bylaws, Provident Institution for Savings Corporation Records, December 16, 1816. (In the possession of the Provident Institution for Savings.)
31. Stockholders' Record Book, February 11, 1823.
32. *Ibid.*
33. *Ibid.,* February 18, 1823.
34. *Ibid.,* March 3, March 10, March 17, April 8, 1823.
35. Bowditch, Nathaniel I., *Memoir of Nathaniel Bowditch* (2d ed.; Boston, 1840), p. 84.
36. Bowditch, Harold, "Nathaniel Bowditch," *The American Neptune,* V (April, 1945), p. 108; Loring, A. P., Jr., *Nathaniel Bowditch, 1773–1838* (Princeton, 1950), pp. 17–18.
37. Provident Institution for Savings Trustees' Records, November 10, 1818.

38. Provident Institution for Savings Corporation Records, December 26, 1821.

39. Minutes of the Board of Directors, June 5, 1823.

40. *Laws of Massachusetts, 1823,* chap. 34.

41. William Bowditch resigned as solicitor, April 13, 1896. (Minutes of the Board of Directors.)

42. *Ibid.*, August 18, September 2, 1823.

43. Stockholders' Record Book, September 1, October 6, 1823.

44. Minutes of the Trustees of the Massachusetts General Hospital, November 23, December 1, 1823; *Laws of Massachusetts, 1824,* chap. 51.

45. Thus at approximately the time when the first installment of $10,000 was due on the Hospital's 500 shares of stock, the Hospital authorized its treasurer to mortgage its property to the Massachusetts Hospital Life to the extent of $30,000. (Minutes of the Board of Trustees of the Massachusetts General Hospital, September 7, 1823.) Two weeks later it added another $5,000 to the mortgage.

46. Compiled from the records of the company.

47. The Jacksonian "west" in Massachusetts was pre-eminently Berkshire County, that hilly county farthest west in the state. This county, in which the Massachusetts Hospital Life had numerous mortgages in its early years, was the source of several debtor-inspired attacks on the company in the later 1820's. See, for example, letters of Nathaniel Bowditch to Elijah Alvord, the mortgage agent for Berkshire County, June 26, June 30, 1826, May 6, 1829; the friendly attitude expressed toward the company because of its Massachusetts General Hospital connection in the adverse report of the House Committee on Finance on a bill to tax the company, in *Miscellaneous Papers, Massachusetts Legislature, 1829,* H. Rept. No. 5 (January 22, 1829); and the comments of Charles G. Loring to Robert H. Ives in a letter dated February 7, 1867, quoted in this chapter.

48. Letter, Charles G. Loring to Robert H. Ives, February 7, 1867.

Chapter III. The Bowditch Era (1823–1838)

1. Hilliard, George (ed.), *Life, Letters, and Journals of George Ticknor* (Cambridge, 1880), I, 319; Berry, Robert E., *Yankee Stargazer: The Life of Nathaniel Bowditch* (New York, 1941), p. 202.

2. On the life of Bowditch, see Bowditch, Nathaniel I., *Memoir of Nathaniel Bowditch*; Berry, *op. cit.*; and Loring, A. P., Jr., *Nathaniel Bowditch, 1773–1838.*

3. Morison, Samuel E., *Maritime History of Massachusetts* (Boston, 1921), pp. 115–116.

4. Bowditch, *op. cit.*, p. 110.

5. Loring, *op. cit.*, p. 20.

6. Bowditch, *op. cit.*, p. 85.

7. Report to the Board of Control, January 4, 1833, Minutes of the Board of Control. On December 26, 1834, John Lowell wrote to Samuel

Appleton in connection with the report of the Committee of Examination for that year:

> My dear friend,
>
> I send you a report of our Committee in which, I have no doubt, you will cordially concur, from your own careful examination of what fell to your charge, and also in the general but brief remarks I have made on the *institution* itself, of the value of which, your own great experience and kind feelings will lead you to approve. I consider it the best institution on earth, and I am proud that it is the *first* of the *sort* in the whole world.
>
> It is in *truth* so. There is no institution either in Europe or America, of this character. It is *eminently* the *Savings bank of the wealthy.*
>
> After signing it, please to pass it, *with this note,* to your neighbor, D. P. Parker, Esq., and ask him to send it to Mr. H. Codman.
>
> Mr. Bowditch will forward it to Mr. Peabody.
>
> Very truly yours,
> (Signed) JOHN LOWELL
>
> N.B. I wish it may be signed this evening, as it will be wanted next week and will be sent to Salem for Mr. Peabody's signature. [This letter is also quoted in Smith, *op. cit.*, pp. 245–246.]

For still additional evidence of the esteem in which Committees of Examination held the company and Dr. Bowditch, see Report for 1825 in Stockholders' Record Book, January 16, 1826; Report for 1829 in Minutes of the Board of Control, January 11, 1830; and Report for 1833, in Minutes of the Board of Control, January 10, 1834.

8. Minutes of the Board of Directors, January 15, 1827.

9. *Ibid.*, January 19, 1829.

10. Bowditch, *op. cit.*, p. 83. The records of this company are still preserved in the vault of the Massachusetts Hospital Life Insurance Company.

11. Ware, Caroline, *Early New England Textile Manufacture* (Boston, 1931), p. 153; *The Massachusetts Register and United States Calendar for 1829* (Boston, 1829), p. 188.

12. Minutes of the Board of Directors, November 7, 1832.

13. *Proposals of the Massachusetts Hospital Life Insurance Company To Make Insurance on Lives, to Grant Annuities on Lives and in Trust, and Endowments for Children* (Boston, 1823, 1839, and subsequent editions).

14. Minutes of the Board of Control, January 26, 1825.

15. Report, Bowditch to the Board of Control, January 9, 1826, Minutes of the Board of Control.

16. Report, Bowditch to the Board of Control, December 21, 1830, Minutes of the Board of Control; Monthly Schedule, December 31, 1830.

17. Monthly Schedule, December 31, 1837.

18. *Report of the Bank Commissioners, Massachusetts Senate Report No. 5* (Boston, 1839), p. 45.

19. *Abstract Exhibiting the Condition of the Banks in Massachusetts on the Second Saturday of February, 1838, prepared by the Secretary of the Commonwealth* (Boston, 1838). In 1836 there were 28 savings banks in Massachusetts with total resources of $4,375,000. (*Annual Report of the Commissioner of Savings Banks, 1866* [Boston, 1867], p. 81.)

20. Bowditch, *op. cit.*, pp. 91, 138–139; letter, N. I. Bowditch to the Board of Directors, Massachusetts Hospital Life Insurance Company, Minutes of the Board, March 19, 1838.

21. Minutes of the Board of Directors, March 7, 1838.

22. Minutes of the Board of Control, March 19, 1838.

23. Entry of March 16, 1838, Diary of William Appleton, Baker Library, Harvard University.

24. Stalson, *Marketing Life Insurance,* pp. 40–41.

25. *Ibid.*, pp. 49–50.

26. There are in the Massachusetts Hospital Life vault today five volumes which belonged to Dr. Bowditch: *Tables Shewing the Values in a Single Present Payment of an Annuity of One Pound, Payable Quarterly, for the Lives of Persons of All Ages from 15 to 73; Such Annuity to Commence at Any Age Not Younger than 35 Nor Older than 75* (London, 1773); Maseres, *The Principles of the Doctrine of Life Annuities*; Baily, Francis, *The Doctrine of Interest and Annuities Analytically Investigated and Explained, Together with Several Useful Tables Connected with the Subject* (London, 1808); Baily, Francis, *The Doctrine of Life Annuities and Assurances Analytically Investigated and Explained, Together with Several Useful Tables Connected with the Subject: and a Variety of Practical Rules for the Illustration of the Same* (London, 1810); Morgan, William, *The Principles and Doctrine of Assurances, Annuities on Lives, and Contingent Reversions, Stated and Explained* (London, 1821). The author of the last volume had been actuary to the Society for Equitable Assurances on Lives and Survivorships for close to half a century.

27. Letters, Bowditch to Thomas F. Smiley, actuary of the Pennsylvania Company, March 2, 1829; to John Roberts, Jr., actuary of the Pennsylvania Company, February 27, 1832.

28. *Proposals of the Massachusetts Hospital Life Insurance Company,* pp. 3–12, 18–24, 40–47.

29. Letters, Packard to Bowditch, August 5, September 1, 1825.

30. Letter, Phillips to Bowditch, March 17, 1826.

31. Letter, E. Littell to Bowditch, December 27, 1827.

32. Letter, Bowditch to E. Littell, December 31, 1827.

33. This figure is based on a memo prepared by Dr. Bowditch on losses or gains, insurance and annuities, 1823–1834, in "Miscellaneous Papers" folder, and subsequent ledger entries.

34. Letter, Bowditch to William C. Jarvis, March 20, 1825; Report, Bowditch to the Board of Control, January 8, 1827, Minutes of the Board of Control; Minutes of the Board of Directors, August 3, 1829.

35. Register of Life Annuities.

36. Minutes of the Board of Directors, November 7, 1832; letter, Francis C. Lowell, actuary of the Massachusetts Hospital Life Insurance Company, to Samual Lord, September 3, 1847.

37. Daniel Webster took a $5,000 one-year policy on his life in 1823, and a second one-year policy of the same amount in 1830. The following year John Connell, of Philadelphia, wrote Bowditch (December 12, 1831) requesting a $5,000 policy on his life payable to Daniel Webster. By the Treaty of 1831 citizens with claims against France arising from damages to American commerce during the wars following the French Revolution were to be paid, and this request was intended to insure Webster of payment for his work in behalf of various claimants, should Connell die before the funds due from France under the treaty were received.

38. Stalson, *op. cit.*, Appendix 5, contains a policy-by-policy analysis of the first 264 policies issued from September, 1823, through December, 1831.

39. Minutes of the Board of Control, January, 1841.

40. Report of the Committee of Examination to the Board of Control, January, 1837, Minutes of the Board of Control.

41. Letter, F. C. Lowell to Nathaniel I. Bowditch, May 3, 1847.

42. Minutes of the Board of Directors, November 12, 1823; Register of "D" deposits.

43. Letter, Bowditch to Judah Hays, August 4, 1824. In another letter he viewed the company in a slightly different perspective when he identified it as "a species of Savings Bank, having in charge the property of the Widow and the orphan. . . ." (Letter to Abijah Bigelow, March 4, 1824.)

44. The original terms of contract are to be found printed in the *Proposals*, pp. 47–51, and explanatory literature on pages 4–5, 13–17, and 25–28.

45. This statement is based on an examination of approximately 600 "G" deposits made during the years 1828–1830.

46. Trustees' Records, Provident Institution for Savings, February 4, 1817. This bylaw was dropped in the 1842 revision of the bylaws in favor of payment in specie or Boston bills, the same as required for deposits.

47. S. E. C. Report: *Investment Trusts and Investment Companies*, 75th Cong., 3d Sess., H. Doc. 707 (1939), p. 42; S. E. C. Report: *Investment Trusts and Investment Companies*, 76th Cong., 2d Sess., H. Doc. 476 (1940), p. 6.

48. See pages 78–80.

49. Letter, Bowditch to William Silsbee, August 7, 1826; to Charles Morris, March 8, 1836.

50. Letter, Charles G. Loring to Edward E. Pratt, May 5, 1864.

51. Table on Trusts, as of December 31, 1828, in "Miscellaneous Papers."

52. Letter, Bowditch to Judah Hays, January 4, 1830; Bowditch, *op. cit.*, p. 90.

53. Report of the Committee of Examination to Board of Control, December 31, 1838, Minutes of the Board of Control.

54. Letter, Bowditch to Dr. Robert Hare (Philadelphia), April 29, 1831; Bowditch, *op. cit.*, p. 90.

55. Monthly Statements Book, December 31, 1830.

56. "G" deposits, numbers 575, 588, and 715.

57. Letter, D. George Sullivan, vice-president, Massachusetts Hospital Life Insurance Company, to L. O. Hooper, June 21, 1949.

58. Letters, Board of Directors of City Trusts, City of Philadelphia, to G. T. White, August 27, 1953; G. Curtis Pritchard, Secretary, Board of Directors of City Trusts, City of Philadelphia, to G. T. White, February 12, 1954.

59. *Proposals,* p. 14.

60. Register of mortgages in "Monthly Balances" book, 1823.

61. In the cases of the Union, Boston, and State banks, chartered in 1792, 1803, and 1811, respectively, the Commonwealth had imposed requirements that a portion of their capitals be invested in farm mortgages. The proportion was 1/5 and 1/8, respectively, for the Union and Boston banks, to each of which the Commonwealth had contributed a substantial fraction of the capital, and 1/10 in the case of the State Bank. Stone, Edwin A., *A Century of Boston Banking,* pp. 9–12.

62. Register of mortgages in "Monthly Balances" book, 1824.

63. *The Massachusetts Register and United States Calendar for 1829* (Boston, 1829); Thompson, Francis M., *History of Greenfield* (Greenfield, 1904), II, 808; Clark, Solomon, *Antiquities, Historicals, and Graduates of Northampton* (Northampton, 1882), p. 96; Lincoln, William, *History of Worcester, Massachusetts* (Worcester, 1862), pp. 202, 273, 366.

64. Letter, Bowditch to William Bard, September 15, 1830.

65. Letter, Bowditch to Abijah Bigelow, March 4, 1824; Report, Bowditch to Board of Control, Minutes of Board of Control, December 26, 1837. There are literally hundreds of letters, incoming and outgoing, bearing upon the taking of mortgages by the company and revealing policy in regard to them. The letters cited in this and the following footnotes show policy, but are only a few of many which might be cited.

66. Letter, Bowditch to Alvord, March 2, 1824.

67. Letter, Bowditch to Strong, December 17, 1833.

68. Letters, Bowditch to Newton, July 28, 1827, to Alvord, May 8, 1829.

69. Letter, Bowditch to Joseph G. Kendall, March 25, 1824.

70. Letters, Bowditch to Alvord, February 19, 1824, to Strong, April 24, 1824.

71. Letter, Moses L. Hale to Strong, November 6, 1835.

72. Letter, Bowditch to James Bogg, August 9, 1830.

73. Letter, Bowditch to Jonathan Allen, August 10, 1826.

74. Letter, Bowditch to Anna Sweetland, March 17, 1830. If bank notes were received by the Suffolk Bank at a discount, the mortgagor was billed for the difference.

75. Letter, Newton to Bowditch, May 17, 1824.

76. Letter, Packard to Bowditch, February 8, 1826.

77. Letters, Bowditch to Alvord, January 14, 1826; to Newton, April 8, 1829.

78. Letter, Bowditch to Alvord, February 19, 1824.

79. Letter, Bowditch to Newton, August 1, 1827.

80. Letter, Bowditch to Alvord, March 8, 1824.

81. Letter, Bowditch to Alvord, April 4, 1825.

82. Letter, Bowditch to Newton, December 3, 1829.

83. Letter, Bowditch to Strong, September 21, 1829.

84. Letter, Bowditch to Strong, February 23, 1833.

85. Letter, Bowditch to Alvord, May 6, 1829.

86. Letter, Bowditch to Strong, July 14, 1834.

87. Letter, Bowditch to Strong, January 26, 1836.

88. Letter, Bowditch to Alvord, June 6, 1836.

89. Data compiled from the "Receiver's Book."

90. Letters, Joseph Tilden to Alvord, May 12, July 20, August 7, 1840.

91. This and much of the subsequent data for the next few pages was compiled from the "Loan Books" of the company.

92. *Laws of Massachusetts, 1834,* chap. 203; Gras, *The Massachusetts-First National Bank of Boston,* pp. 95, 97.

93. This apt term was first used by Shlakman, *Economic History of a Factory Town,* p. 31, and ably demonstrated by data compiled in her Table I, pp. 39–42, and Appendix A, pp. 243–247.

94. The date of the loan to the Boston Manufacturing Company was February 11, 1826. It was paid on February 24, 1829.

95. The four loans, each of $50,000, were made between August 14, 1827, and January 29, 1828. They were paid between January 1, 1829, and April 12, 1830.

96. Bagnall, William R., "Sketches of Manufacturing Establishments in New York City and of Textile Establishments in the Eastern States." This huge manuscript of 2,662 pages is a rich source of information on the textile industry of New England. A copy is in Baker Library, Harvard University.

97. Between 1821 and 1830 the company accepted stock of the following textile companies as collateral: Hamilton Manufacturing Company, Merrimack Manufacturing Company, Boston Manufacturing Company, Amesbury Flannel Company, Stratford Manufacturing Company, Eliot Manufacturing Company, all of Massachusetts, and the Cocheco Manufacturing Company, Nashua Manufacturing Company, Great Falls Manufacturing Company, and Dover Manufacturing Company, of New Hampshire. Stock of other companies accepted as collateral and seemingly at variance with the terms of the Massachusetts Hospital Life charter include the Boston & Roxbury Mill Dam, Locks & Canals, Bristol & Norfolk Turnpike, the Railway in Boston, and the Boylston Market.

98. *Laws of Massachusetts, 1839,* chap. 35.

99. Report, Bowditch to Board of Control, December 26, 1837, Minutes of the Board of Control.

100. Letters, Moses L. Hale to Abraham and Jacob Wendell, December 29, 1828, and January 14, 1829.

101. Letters, William Appleton to Bowditch, March 24, 1831; Bowditch to Appleton, March 26, 1831.

102. Monthly Statements Book.

103. Catterall, R. C. H., *The Second Bank of the United States* (Chicago, 1903), pp. 370–371.

104. A summary of these transactions was given to the Board of Directors, March 2, 1836. A statistical summary is to be found, in the handwriting of Dr. Bowditch, on the inside back cover of the Loan Book for that year. The correspondence between Bowditch and Appleton covering the purchases and sales has also survived.

105. Minutes of the Board of Directors, January 18, 1840.

106. Report of the Committee of Examination to the Board of Control, January, 1837, Minutes of the Board of Control.

107. Report of the Committee of Examination to the Board of Control, January 9, 1838, Minutes of the Board of Control.

108. Report, Bowditch to the Board of Control, December 26, 1837, Minutes of the Board of Control.

109. Martin, Joseph G., *One Hundred Years' History of the Boston Stock Market, 1798 to 1898* (Boston, 1898), pp. 20–21.

110. Smith, *The Development of Trust Companies in the United States*, pp. 278–280. On page 326 he also lists 12 more life insurance and trust companies – 3 in the South, 4 in Pennsylvania, and 5 in New York – which were founded between 1850 and1875.

111. *Legislative Documents of the Senate and Assembly of New York*, 53d Sess., 1830, Vol. II, Doc. 84. (Letter of Senator Lloyd is dated September 7, 1829.) See also Smith, *op. cit.*, pp. 251–258; Stalson, *op. cit.*, pp. 82–83.

112. *Laws of New York, 1830*, chap. 75.

113. Minutes of the Board of Trustees, New York Life Insurance & Trust Company, April, 1830. (In the possession of the Bank of New York.)

114. Letter, Bard to Bowditch, September 10, 1830.

115. Nevins, Allan, *History of the Bank of New York and Trust Company* (New York, 1934), p. 51.

116. Minutes of the Board of Trustees, New York Life Insurance & Trust Company, October 5, 1830, February 7, 1832.

117. *Ibid.*, May 2, 1833.

118. Finance Committee Minutes, New York Life Insurance & Trust Company, January 11, 1841.

119. Minutes of the Board of Trustees, New York Life Insurance & Trust Company.

120. *Documents of the Assembly of New York, 1833*, Vol. III, No. 209; Nevins, *op. cit.*, p. 51; *Documents of the Senate of New York, 1856*, Vol. III, No. 10. Income to the depositor varied between 3 per cent and 5 per cent, depending on the duration of the deposit. In 1833 deposits made for a year or more were receiving 4½ or 5 per cent.

121. Minutes of the Board of Trustees, New York Life Insurance & Trust Company, April 3, 1832.

122. *Documents of the Senate of New York, 1839,* Vol. II, No. 70.

123. Minutes of the Board of Trustees, New York Life Insurance & Trust Company, January 5, 1843.

124. Minutes of the Board of Trustees, New York Life Insurance & Trust Company.

125. *Girard Trust Company: A Century of Financial Activity, 1836–1936* (Philadelphia, 1936). On pages 17–18 the Massachusetts Hospital Life Insurance & Trust Company is mentioned as the oldest prototype for the Girard company.

126. Letter, Moses L. Hale to M. T. Williams, President, Ohio Life Insurance & Trust Company, March 14, 1835.

127. Stalson, *op. cit.,* p. 60.

128. The last life insurance and trust company to separate its life insurance and trust activities was the Provident Life & Trust Company, founded in Philadelphia in 1865. In 1922 a new corporation, the Provident Trust Company, was established to take care of the trust business, while the life insurance business was retained by the old company, now called the Provident Mutual Life Insurance Company. (Stephenson, G. L., *Trust Business in Common Law Countries* [New York, 1940], p. 543.)

129. Until very recently the Rhode Island Hospital Trust considered itself unique in origin in its profit-sharing relationship to a hospital and in much of its early pattern of operations. (Letter, H. H. Kelley, vice-president, Rhode Island Hospital Trust Company, to G. T. White, August 4, 1952.) It has published two booklets on its early history in this belief: *South Main Street Days of the Rhode Island Hospital Trust Company* (Providence, 1950); and *How This Company Got Its Name* (Providence, 1950).

130. 9 Pick. 460. The Massachusetts General Hospital first achieved a relatively sound financial base as a result of provisions in the will of John McLean, a prominent Boston merchant who died in October, 1823. In addition to being made residuary legatee for the whole estate, the Massachusetts General Hospital was also designated to share equally with Harvard College in $50,000 which was set aside to provide income for the widow, Ann McLean, during her lifetime. The trustees, Jonathan and Francis Amory, segregated $50,000 in textile, insurance, and bank stocks from the estate to constitute this fund. At the time of the death of Mrs. McLean, these stocks were worth considerably less than $50,000, which prompted the suit against the surviving trustee. The trustees had also placed $40,259 in two "G" form trusts (#623 and #761), in the name of Mrs. McLean, with the Massachusetts Hospital Life Insurance Company. In addition to providing an income of 5 per cent or better during these years, there was no deterioration in the principal thus invested.

131. Stevenson, Alec B., *Shares in Mutual Investment Funds* (Nashville,

1946), pp. 23–29; Holbrook, Donald, *The Boston Trustee* (Boston, 1937), pp. 34–35.

132. Quoted in Stevenson, *op. cit.*, pp. 103–104.

133. Quoted in the booklet, *How the Massachusetts Life Fund Provides a Special Program for Each Investor* (Boston, 1952), p. 17, distributed with the Prospectus, and featured on the inside front cover of each quarterly, semiannual, and annual report.

Chapter IV. In the Mold of the Founders (1838–1878)

1. Stockholders' Record Book, January 17, 1870.

2. At the birth of each grandchild, John Amory Lowell established an endowment trust with the Massachusetts Hospital Life which would amount to about $10,000 at age 21, so that no grandchild of his would ever "suffer want." (Quoted in Greenslet, *The Lowells*, p. 316.)

3. A full list of stockholders, their places of residence, and the number of shares each held, is included in the Minutes of the Board of Directors, May 4, 1865.

4. Letter, Lowell to Thomas C. Lord, October 7, 1847.

5. Bowditch, N. I., *Memoir of Nathaniel Bowditch*, p. 102. Other data on Tilden have been gathered principally from Linzee, John W., *The History of Peter Parker and Sarah Ruggles of Roxbury, Massachusetts* (Boston, 1913), pp. 74–79; Shlakman, *Economic History of a Factory Town*, pp. 39–42 and Appendix A; and Bagnall, "Sketches of Manufacturing Establishments," p. 2109.

6. Minutes of the Board of Directors, March 26, 1838.

7. Stockholders' Record Book, January 21, 1839.

8. Minutes of the Board of Directors, July 5, 1838.

9. A committee consisting of Tilden, Samuel Hubbard, the company's first solicitor, and Nathan Appleton, of the Committee of Finance, was appointed on February 12, 1839, to seek this change. Minutes of the Board of Directors.

10. *Ibid.*, February 22, 1845.

11. Data on Lowell have been derived principally from the works of Greenslet, Shlakman, and Bagnall previously cited.

12. Minutes of the Board of Directors, June 4, 1851. Bowditch was president of the company's next-door neighbor, the American Insurance Company, and was also an important private trustee. He was the eldest son of Dr. Nathaniel Bowditch.

13. On Loring, see Parsons, Theophilus, "Memoir of Charles Greely Loring," *Proceedings of the Massachusetts Historical Society*, XI (April, 1870), 263–291; and Davis, William T., *Professional and Industrial History of Suffolk County* (Boston, 1894), pp. 443–445.

14. Minutes of the Board of Control, October 12, 1867.

15. Chase, George B., *Memoir of George Tyler Bigelow* (Boston, 1890), p. 36.

16. The main sources of data for the following brief sketches of the members of the Committee of Finance and the presidents of the company during this period have been the works of Shlakman and Bagnall; the *Dictionary of American Biography*; the *Boston Directory* (various years); Kirkland, E. C., *Men, Cities and Transportation: A Study in New England History* (2 vols.; Cambridge, 1948); Crawford, Mary C., *Famous Families of Massachusetts* (2 vols.; Boston, 1930); and Winsor, Justin (ed.), *The Memorial History of Boston* (4 vols.; Boston, 1881).

17. See also Winthrop, Robert C., "Memoir of Honorable Nathan Appleton," *Proceedings of the Massachusetts Historical Society,* V (October, 1861).

18. See also, Hill, Hamilton A., *Memoir of Abbott Lawrence* (Boston, 1864).

19. Also Sargent, Emma W., and Sargent, Charles S., *Epes Sargent of Gloucester and His Descendants* (Boston, 1923), pp. 150–151.

20. There is a long sketch of this father-in-law of Charles Francis Adams I in the *New England Historical and Genealogical Register,* VIII (October, 1854) and IX (January, 1855).

21. *Abstracts of the Returns from the Banks and from the Institutions for Savings* (Boston, 1864), p. 80; *Report of the Comptroller of the Currency* (Washington, 1878), p. 135.

22. *Annual Report of the Commisioner of Savings Banks, 1866* (Boston, 1867), p. 81; *One Hundred Years of Savings Bank Service* (rev. ed.; Boston, 1930), p. 25. The latter is a booklet publication of the Provident Institution for Savings.

23. Stone, *A Century of Banking,* pp. 33–36; advertisement in the *Boston Directory,* 1872.

24. Advertisements in the *Boston Directory,* 1876.

25. *The New England Trust Company: Act of Incorporation, By-laws, and Regulations* (Boston, 1889); *Charter and By-laws of the Boston Safe Deposit and Trust Company* (Boston, 1879). The terms of contract and pattern of operations for the New England Trust Company are given as of the time it began operations in 1871. The Boston Safe Deposit & Trust Company, originally organized in 1867 as a safe deposit company, was authorized to engage in a trust business by an amendment to its charter in July, 1874.

26. Article 7 of the bylaws of the New England Trust Company; article 8 of the bylaws of the Boston Safe Deposit & Trust Company.

27. Minutes of the Board of Control.

28. Letter, Loring to William Minot, June 1, 1863.

29. Letter, Loring to Mrs. Abby Salisbury (of Connecticut), February 13, 1860.

30. Letter, Tilden to Dr. Oliver Hubbard, March 28, 1845.

31. Letter, Loring to William Parsons, March 15, 1866. See also letter, Loring to William D. Sohier, January 6, 1858; Report, Loring to the Board of Control, December 27, 1858, Minutes of the Board of Control.

32. Report of Committee to Board of Control, January 10, 1859, Minutes of the Board of Control. These data may also be presented after the pattern used elsewhere in this volume:

Endowments	"EG"	$190,000
Deferred Annuities	"D"	
Strict Female	"SF"	1,901,000
Strict Male	"SM"	1,550,000
Public Institutions		582,000
Individuals	"G"	4,330,000
	Total	$8,553,000

33. Minutes of the Board of Control, January 17, 1859.
34. Letters, Loring to George Peabody, April 22, June 1, 1866.
35. Letter, Loring to Wiliam D. Sohier, January 13, 1864.
36. Minutes of the Board of Directors, May 3, 1865.
37. Minutes of the Board of Directors, June 7, 1865.
38. But its maintenance was to create a controversy (stimulated by a descendant of William D. Sohier) in the middle 1920's, when nearly one-third of the company's funds was invested in securities. As a result of this controversy, the company paid an increment proportionate to the increase in value of the common fund on contracts written prior to 1883 and presented for payment between 1927 and 1930. In no case was this increase very large. During these same years a small supplement to principal was also paid on contracts presented for payment which had been written between 1883 and 1900. These payments were made as a proportionate share of the reserved interest account in recognition of the fact that the computation and payment at five-year intervals of any surplus due depositors prescribed by these contracts had not been fulfilled. (Registers of "G," "SM," and "SF" deposits.)
39. Minutes of the Board of Directors, March 3, 1875.
40. Register of "G" deposits.
41. "G" deposit, # 3190.
42. "SF" deposit register.
43. "SM" deposit register, March 21, 1846.
44. On the emergence of the mutuals, see Stalson, *Marketing Life Insurance*, pp. 112–214.
45. *Laws of Massachusetts, 1846*, chap. 109, sec. 9.
46. Letter, Willard Phillips, president, and Charles P. Curtis, and William W. Stone, directors, New England Mutual Life Insurance Company, to William Appleton and John A. Lowell, trustees of the Massachusetts General Hospital, July 25, 1845, Massachusetts General Hospital Archives. The representatives of the New England Mutual argued that the profit-sharing provision with the Hospital in their company's charter could apply only to payments made to the owners of the "guaranty fund" subscribed prior to the launching of the company, and not to any reserve fund

developed out of premium income to meet future claims of policyholders against the company. To interpret the profit-sharing provision as applying to the reserve fund would destroy this company and would result in draining the funds of Massachusetts citizens into the coffers of mutual companies chartered outside Massachusetts. It could also result in action by the legislature, freeing mutual companies from any obligation to the Hospital and perhaps upsetting the arrangement, so profitable to the Hospital, between the Hospital and the Massachusetts Hospital Life Insurance Company.

By chapter 82, *Laws of Massachusetts, 1846,* the obligation of the mutual companies to the Hospital was defined as profit-sharing to the extent of one-third the excess of any dividend beyond 6 per cent paid to the owners of the guaranty fund. Since dividends of more than 6 per cent were not paid and the guaranty fund was soon paid off, this meant that the Hospital received no income from the first of the Massachusetts mutual companies, nor much, if anything, from any mutual company chartered subsequently.

47. *Exposition of the Objects of the New England Mutual Life Insurance Company* (Boston, 1844); *Proposals of the Massachusetts Hospital Life Insurance Company to Make Insurance on Lives,* etc. (Boston, 1839). For rates of the Mutual Life Insurance Company of New York, see Stalson, *op. cit.,* p. 131.

48. Stalson, *op. cit.,* p. 81; Hudnut, James M., *Semi-Centennial History of the New York Life Insurance Company* (New York, 1895), p. 11.

49. Stalson, *op. cit.,* p. 286.

50. Wright, Philip Green, and Wright, Elizabeth Q., *Elizur Wright: the Father of Life Insurance* (Chicago, 1937), pp. 149, 202.

51. Minutes of the Board of Directors, November 5, 1845.

52. *Ibid.,* January 15, 1855.

53. Letter, Tilden to Gratz, December 7, 1844; Hudnut, *op. cit.,* p. 8.

54. By the end of 1844 the New England Mutual Life Insurance Company had agents in 20 different places, chiefly in New England. (Stalson, *op. cit.,* p. 158.)

55. Minutes of the Board of Control.

56. Register of Life Annuities.

57. Minutes of the Board of Directors, November 5, 1845.

58. Compiled from the Massachusetts Hospital Life Insurance Company ledgers.

59. The New England Mutual Life Insurance Company first surpassed the Massachusetts Hospital Life in resources in 1874. Resources of the New England Mutual Life Insurance Company at the end of the year 1874 were $13,542,000 in comparison with $13,467,000 for the Massachusetts Hospital Life, though for most of the following years until the middle of the 1880's the resources of the Massachusetts Hospital Life were greater than those of the New England Mutual. (*Twentieth Annual Report of the Insurance Commissioner of the Commonwealth of Massachusetts* [Boston, 1875], Part II, p. 16.) The Provident Institution for Savings, which had resources of $13,450,000 at the end of 1875, first surpassed the Massachusetts Hospital

Life in 1877 and by 1880 was larger by approximately $5,800,000. (*One Hundred Years of Savings Bank Service* [Boston, 1930], p. 25.) The largest commercial bank at the end of this period was the Merchants National Bank of Boston, which in October, 1878, reported resources of $10,581,000. (*Report of the Comptroller of the Currency, 1878* [Washington, 1878], p. 135.)

60. Minutes of the Board of Control, January, 1844.

61. Data compiled from the Receiver's Book.

62. Minutes of the Board of Directors, April 1, 1840.

63. Letter, Tilden to Alvord, May 12, 1840.

64. Report of the Committee of Examination to Board of Control, Minutes of the Board of Control, January, 1858; letter, Loring to Thomas Twining, April 17, 1865.

65. Letters, Tilden to Franklin Ripley, September 16, 1840, January 7, October 1, 1841; Tilden to Lewis Strong, January 3, 1842.

66. Data compiled from the Receiver's Book.

67. Letter, Loring to William Rice, Register of Deeds, Springfield, Massachusetts, August 19, 1858; Minutes of the Board of Directors, December 8, 1858; Report of Loring to the Board of Control, December 27, 1858, Minutes of the Board of Control.

68. Martin, *Boston Stock Market*, pp. 52, 110.

69. Letters, Abbott Lawrence to John Campbell, Treasurer of the United States, September 24, 1838; to Levi Woodbury, Secretary of the Treasury, February 26, 1839.

70. Bayley, Rafael A., *National Loans of the United States from July 4, 1776 to June 30, 1880* (Washington, 1882), pp. 68–70.

71. Ledger accounts, Massachusetts Hospital Life Insurance Company.

72. *Ibid.*

73. Handlin, Oscar, and Handlin, Mary Flug, *Commonwealth: A Study of the Role of Government in the American Economy* (New York, 1947), pp. 227–228.

74. *Proposals*, p. 15.

75. Ledger accounts.

76. Loan Book.

77. The best sources on the development of the Massachusetts textile industry during this period are the works of Bagnall, Ware, and Shlakman, previously cited, and Green, Constance M., *Holyoke, Massachusetts: a Case History of the Industrial Revolution in America* (New Haven, 1939).

78. Loan Book.

79. *Ibid.*

80. Wright, Carroll D., *A Compendium of the Census of Massachusetts, 1875* (Boston, 1877).

81. Among the Notes Payable, Notes and Bills Payable, Semi-Annual Accounts ledgers, etc., examined were those of the Lawrence, Hamilton, Tremont, and Suffolk companies of Lowell, the Dwight Manufacturing Company of Chicopee, and the Boston Manufacturing Company of Wal-

tham. (See also Ware, *Early New England Textile Manufacture*, pp. 122, 182.)

82. *Annual Report of the Commisisoner of Savings Banks*, 1866 (Boston, 1867), p. 81.

83. Compiled from the Loan Books.

84. Compiled from the Loan Books, other records of the company, and various sources of biographical information.

85. These letters were written to the respective treasurers on December 18 and 19, 1855.

86. Martin, *op. cit.*, pp. 162–163.

87. Letter, Loring to E. R. Mudge and Company, August 12, 1858; Report, Loring to Board of Control, December 26, 1859, December 22, 1862, Minutes of the Board of Control.

88. Report, Loring to Board of Control, December 27, 1858, Minutes of the Board of Control.

89. The Committee for 1857 consisted of George Ticknor, John Tappan, Robert Hooper, William Amory, and Ignatius Sargent.

90. Ayer, J. C., *Some of the Uses and Abuses in the Management of Our Manufacturing Corporations* (Lowell, 1863), p. 16.

91. These data on security ownership are carried in the Loan Books.

92. Fite, Emerson D., *Social and Industrial Conditions During the Civil War* (New York, 1930), pp. 86–88. The rapid increase in the value of inventories of finished goods in a period of low production further reduced the credit needs of the cotton textile companies.

93. It was for $100,000 in 6 per cent notes. Letter, Loring to Salmon P. Chase, Secretary of the Treasury, April 19, 1861.

94. Ledger accounts.

95. Report, Loring to Board of Control, December 26, 1864, Minutes of the Board of Control.

96. Based on Dewey, Davis R., *Financial History of the United States* (New York, 1903), p. 376. The figure of approximately one million dollars has been arrived at by multiplying the average premium for gold in each year by the interest received in gold during that year. It has not proved possible to get a more exact figure from the company's accounting records.

97. Ledger accounts.

98. Loan Book.

99. Wright, *A Compendium of the Census of Massachusetts, 1875.*

100. Notes and Bills Payable Ledger, Dwight Manufacturing Company; Notes Payable Ledger, Hamilton Manufacturing Company, both in Baker Library, Harvard University. In 1871 the largest single loan to each of these companies was a one-year loan of $100,000 from the Massachusetts Hospital Life. In addition, the Dwight company borrowed a total of $90,000 in one-year loans from three savings banks. The Hamilton company borrowed a total of $250,000 in one-year loans from four savings banks; $112,500 in three-to-six month loans from three commercial banks; $50,000 for seven

months from the Boston and Maine Railroad; and $10,000 for a year from James Parker.

101. Reports of the Committee of Examination, December 30, 1876, December 26, 1878, Minutes of the Board of Control.

102. Minutes of the Board of Directors, November 13, 1877, November 6, 1878.

103. According to Frederick H. Curtiss, in 1880 Boston had 54 national banks with a combined capital of $63,000,000. By 1889 their number had grown to 62 and their total capital to $76,000,000. At the latter date New York City had only 45 national banks, with a capital of $48,350,000. Frederick H. Curtiss was chairman of the Board of the Federal Reserve Bank of Boston from 1914 to 1940. (*Fifty Years of Boston* [Boston, 1930], pp. 230–232.)

104. Loan Book.

CHAPTER V. A SLIGHT TRANSITION (1878–1901)

1. *21st Annual Report of the Board of Commissioners of Savings Banks, 1900* (Boston, 1901), Part I, pp. 49, 490; *Report of the Comptroller of the Currency,* 1901 (Washington, 1901), II, 481; *46th Annual Report of the Insurance Commissioner of the Commonwealth of Massachusetts* (Boston, 1901), Part II.

2. Bugbee, James B., "Memoir of Honorable Samuel Crocker Cobb," *Proceedings of the Massachusetts Historical Society,* 2d series, VII (February, 1892).

3. Advertisement, *Boston Directory,* 1888.

4. Green, Samuel A., *Memoir of Abbott Lawrence* (Boston, 1908).

5. *Who's Who in America* (Chicago, 1911). A younger brother was Joseph H. Choate, distinguished lawyer and diplomat.

6. Minutes, December 14, 1892.

7. *Ibid.,* June 13, 1894.

8. *Ibid.,* November 8, 1893.

9. *Ibid.,* November 15, 1880.

10. *Laws of Massachusetts, 1881,* chap. 82. On the investment powers of the New England Trust Company, see section 6 of its charter (*Laws of Massachusetts, 1869,* chap. 182). The provision governing the Boston Safe Deposit & Trust Company (*Laws of Massachusetts, 1874,* chap. 373, sec. 4) is almost identical.

11. In the case of both of these amendments, the committee making representations to the legislature consisted of the actuary and the Committee of Finance. Minutes, November 8, 1882; *Laws of Massachusetts, 1882,* chap. 60.

12. The first meeting of the board in the new building (which was equipped with electric lights and its own power plant) took place on October 6, 1886.

13. Minutes, November 9, 1881.

14. *Ibid.*, December 7, 1881.
15. *Ibid.*, November 14, 1905.
16. The new forms were approved by the board on February 7, 1883.
17. The first "A" form was executed for funds received in the name of Mt. Auburn Cemetery in December, 1893.
18. Minutes, April 8, 1885.
19. *Ibid.*, January 26, 1899.
20. *Ibid.*, November 11, 1888.
21. *Ibid.*, December 12, 1888.
22. *Ibid.*, February 14, 1900.
23. *Ibid.*, December 3, 1884.
24. *Ibid.*, February 8, 1894.
25. Report of the Committee of Examination to the Board of Control, December, 1886, Minutes of the Board of Control.
26. In the period since 1823 the Examining Committee of the Month had been altered to one director rotating monthly.
27. Minutes of the Board of Directors, February 8, 1888. A new daybook, journal, and ledger series dates from this time.
28. Stockholders' Record Book, January 21, 1889.
29. *Laws of Massachusetts, 1894*, chap. 28.
30. From a compilation of the Actuary, "Miscellaneous Papers," 1881.
31. Register of "G" deposits.
32. Minutes of the Board of Control.
33. Register of "G" deposits, #5331, #5388, #5389, and #5420.
34. *Ibid.*, #5295 and #5300. Both of his grandfathers, John Quincy Adams and Peter C. Brooks, had been stockholders and depositors, with Peter C. Brooks being also a founder and later president.
35. Register of Life Annuities.
36. Minutes of the Board, April 4, 1881.
37. *Ibid.*, November 10, 1893.
38. *Ibid.*, December 8, 1897.
39. *Ibid.*, February 14, 1900.
40. Minutes of the Board of Control.
41. The following data on the financial and business connections of these men have been compiled chiefly from the *Dictionary of American Biography*; *National Cyclopedia of American Biography*; *Boston Directory* (various years); *Who's Who in New England* (1909 edition); *Who's Who in Finance* (1911 edition); *The Manual of Statistics: The Stock Exchange Hand-Book for Investors and Operators, 1890* (New York, 1890); *The Manual of Statistics: Stock Exchange Hand-Book, 1900* (New York, 1900); Lamb, James H., *Textile Industries of the United States* (2 vols.; Boston, 1916), and Kirkland, E. C., *Men, Cities and Transportation*.
42. Minutes of the Board of Directors.
43. Receiver's Book.
44. Minutes of the Board of Directors, December 3, 1884.
45. *Ibid.*, April 4, May 2, 1883.

46. *Ibid.*, July 9, 1896. Another more minor instance was a contribution of $100 for a fund sponsored by the Associated Banks of Boston to be invested for the widow and child of J. L. Heywood, Acting Cashier of the First National Bank of Northfield, Minnesota. Heywood had been killed while successfully resisting a raid on his bank by Jesse James and his gang. (Minutes, November 8, 1876.)

47. Compiled from the Loan Books; *Dockham's Textile Register* (1897); and a publication on New England textile companies dated March 1, 1900, by Frank Seabury and Brother, Stock and Note Brokers of Boston. Their office was located at 50 State Street in the Massachusetts Hospital Life building.

48. Bureau of the Census, *Report on Manufacturing Industries in the United States at the Eleventh Census, 1890* (Washington, 1895), Part I, pp. 177, 329.

49. See, for example, the Notes Payable ledger of the Hamilton Manufacturing Company for 1890 in Baker Library, Harvard University.

50. Charles Francis Adams was a brother of Henry Adams and uncle of Charles Francis Adams, who until his resignation in 1953 was honorary chairman of the Massachusetts Hospital Life Board. He records in his *Autobiography* (Boston, 1916), pp. 199–200, the extent of his financial disaster in the panic of 1893 and the labors to which he was put, during the years immediately following, to repair his financial position.

51. The following data were compiled from the Loan Book and the *Manual of Statistics: Stock Exchange Hand-Book, 1900* (New York, 1900).

52. Minutes of the Board of Directors and pertinent ledger accounts.

53. Loan Book.

54. Letter, Bernice Parks, Assistant Treasurer, Provident Institution for Savings, to G. T. White, June 23, 1952.

55. Minutes, January 26, 1899.

56. Martin, *One Hundred Years of the Boston Stock Market*, pp. 104–105.

Chapter VI. The Stockton Era (1901–1937)

1. The institutions larger in resources in 1910 were: National Shawmut Bank ($84,302,000); First National Bank ($70,527,000); Second National Bank ($28,506,000); Old Colony Trust Company ($76,673,000); Provident Institution for Savings ($51,501,000); Boston Five Cent Savings Bank ($43,184,000); John Hancock Mutual Life Insurance Company ($72,104,-000); and New England Mutual Life Insurance Company ($54,445,000). *Report of the Comptroller of the Currency, 1910* (Washington, 1911); *Annual Report of the Bank Commissioner, 1910* (Boston 1911); *56th Annual Report of the Insurance Commissioner of the Commonwealth of Massachusetts* (Boston, 1911), Part II.

2. Minutes of the Board of Directors, March 13, 1905.

3. *Ibid.*, November 9, December 6, 1905; March 2, 1906.

4. *Ibid.*, February 1, 1901. In addition to company records, biographical data here and elsewhere in this chapter have been derived chiefly from *Who's Who in New England* (1909, 1916, and 1938 editions); *Who's Who in America*; *Who's Who in Finance* (New York, 1911); *Who's Who in Finance and Banking* (New York, 1922); *Who's Who in Finance, Banking, and Insurance* (New York, 1925, 1931); *Boston Directory*; Lamb, *Textile Industries of the United States*; and various family histories.

5. (Boston, 1898). This book had gone through five revisions to 1940. The fifth revision was made by Mayo Shattuck, a major current Boston trustee.

6. When A. P. Loring, Jr., died in the fall of 1951, his son, A. P. Loring III, was elected a director of the company. Like his father and grandfather, A. P. Loring III is a Boston trustee.

7. Minutes of the Board of Directors, November 14, 1905.

8. *Ibid.*, January 7, 1904.

9. Trial Balance Book.

10. *Ibid.*

11. Register of "G" deposits.

12. Minutes of the Board of Directors, December 11, 1919.

13. *Ibid.*

14. *Ibid.*, April 13, 1926. "As the return from the investments of the Company had for a number of years proved to be satisfactory, and as it seemed improbable that the value of investments would depreciate to any great extent in the foreseeable future, the management came to the conclusion that the reservation in the General Deposit forms of the right to charge losses against principal was a dead letter upon which the Company would never have to rely and that since it was unnecessary, it could well be eliminated." (Quoted from the long report filed by Neil Leonard [in 1948] who was appointed by the supreme judicial court for Suffolk County to investigate the effect of the plan of reorganization proposed for the Massachusetts Hospital Life upon the deposits of minors, others incompetent to manage their own affairs, and claimants who could not be ascertained.)

15. Fowler, John F., *American Investment Trusts* (New York, 1928), pp. 4–19 and Appendix A; Grayson, Theodore J., *Investment Trusts, Their Origin, Development and Operation* (New York, 1928), pp. 138–160 and Appendix B.

16. Massachusetts Hospital Life Insurance Company Journals.

17. Gras, *Business and Capitalism*, p. 277.

18. *Laws of Massachusetts, 1903,* chap. 92.

19. "Annual and Monthly Statements" Book.

20. Federal Reserve Bank of Boston, *Monthly Review,* XXX, No. 10 (October, 1948), p. 4.

21. Mortgage Record Book, and Survey made by D. George Sullivan, July, 1937.

22. The following data have been compiled chiefly from the Loan Books,

reports in the Minutes of the Board of Directors, and the books of Annual and Monthly Statements.

23. Minutes of the Board of Control, January 14, 1929, January 13, 1930.

24. Letter, Bernice Parks, Assistant Treasurer, Provident Institution for Savings, to G. T. White, June 23, 1952.

25. Minutes of the Board of Control, January 12, 1931.

26. *Ibid.*

27. Minutes of the Board of Directors, January 7, 1932.

28. Annual and Monthly Statements.

29. Minutes of the Board of Directors, April 12, 1932.

30. *Ibid.*, February 8, 1932, August 11, 1932.

31. *Ibid.*, February 14, 1935.

32. *Ibid.*, June 9, August 11, 1932, March 9, June 8, 1933.

33. *Ibid.*, November 14, 1935.

34. *Ibid.*, March 12, 1936.

35. *Ibid.*, May 14, 1936; Minutes of the Board of Control, January 7, 1937.

36. The Committee of Finance was authorized to establish the new fund by resolution of the Board of Directors, June 8, 1933. (Minutes of the Board.)

37. Reports prepared by D. George Sullivan for presentation to the Board of Directors, October 12, 1937 and March 23, 1948.

38. Hospital Life Trust *Annual Report,* December 31, 1953.

39. Minutes of the Board of Control.

40. Stockholders' Record Book; Minutes of the Board of Directors, February 5, 1936.

41. Minutes of the Board of Directors, March 12 and 26, 1936.

Chapter VII. A Return to First Principals (1937–1953)

Materials for this chapter have been derived in great measure from conversations with officials of the company, especially D. George Sullivan and Paul T. Litchfield, vice-president and treasurer and vice-president and secretary, respectively. In addition to unpublished records of the company, and current published matter, such as annual reports, the prospectus for the sale of units of the Massachusetts Life Fund and accompanying sales literature have also been used.

1. Minutes of the Board of Directors, February 1, 1937.

2. *Who's Who in Massachusetts* (Boston, 1940).

3. The date of the report is October 12.

4. Minutes of the Board of Directors, December 9, 1937, January 6, 1938.

5. Of what he hoped the Massachusetts Hospital Life might become, Sullivan had written: "There is a definite field in the United States for sound investment trusts, particularly those which give thought to the selection of securities based not only on diversification of industries, but also,

and most important, on diversification as to types of securities, a trust having in its portfolio mortgages, long and short term bonds, and preferred and common stocks, the emphasis on each group shifting as the economic situation demanded. . . . It is almost inevitable that such a trust would appeal. Stock-mindedness, so prevalent for the last ten years, will some time give way to sound principles of investment. In addition, this plan does exactly what the investment counselor does today and goes further in that no investment counselor is equipped to advise and service mortgage investments. Such a trust would appeal to business men, conservative investors, and trustees, especially if it was managed by men of the character of the present directors of the Massachusetts Hospital Life Insurance Company."

6. Minutes of the Board of Directors, January 6, 1938.

7. *Laws of Massachusetts, 1938,* chap. 248.

8. Minutes of the Board of Directors, February 9, September 14, 1939.

9. *Ibid.,* January 6, 1938; Minutes of the Board of Control, February 17, 1938, February 16, 1939; Minutes of the Board of Directors, March 9, 1939.

10. *Laws of Massachusetts, 1939,* chap. 337.

11. Minutes of the Board of Directors, December 12, 1940.

12. The date of the execution of the voting trust was December 27, 1940.

13. *Laws of Massachusetts, 1943,* chap. 143.

14. Ledger accounts.

15. *Laws of Massachusetts, 1945,* chap. 327.

16. *Plan for Reorganization of Massachusetts Hospital Life Insurance Company.* The plan was printed and, with accompanying documents including a copy of the Massachusetts Life Fund Declaration of Trust, was circulated among all persons who had claims to the assets of the company.

17. Minutes of the Board of Directors.

18. *Ibid.,* October 14, 1948.

19. Stockholders' Record Book, March 7, 1949.

INDEX

Bei Fragen zur Produktsicherheit wenden Sie sich bitte an:
If you have any questions regarding product safety,
please contact:

Walter de Gruyter GmbH
Genthiner Straße 13
10785 Berlin
productsafety@degruyterbrill.com